STAR WARS

THE VISUAL ENCYCLOPEDIA

™

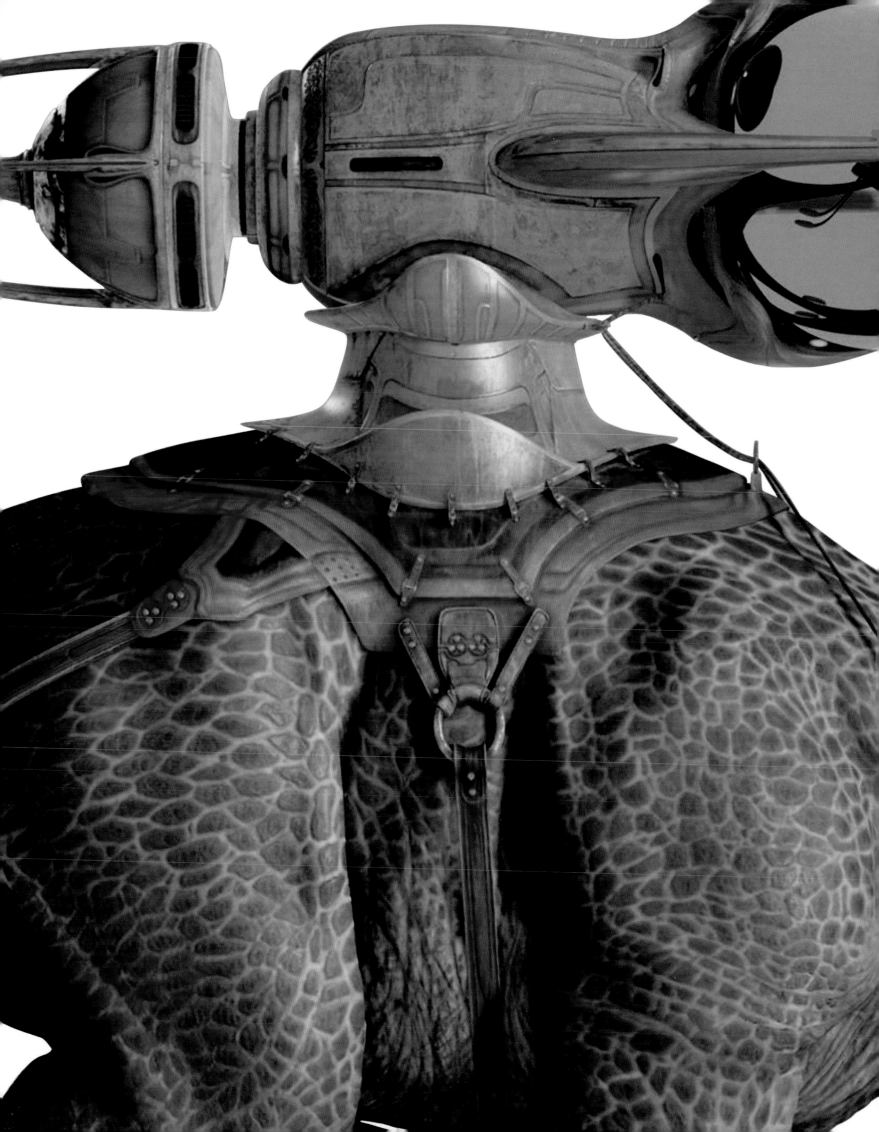

STAR WARS

THE VISUAL ENCYCLOPEDIA

WRITTEN BY TRICIA BARR, ADAM BRAY AND COLE HORTON

CONTENTS

FOREWORD

DENNIS MUREN, SENIOR CREATIVE
DIRECTOR, INDUSTRIAL LIGHT & MAGIC

I've often said that my favourite films to work on are helmed by directors with strong visions – they know what they're chasing, they know the emotions they want to evoke and they have designs in mind that will help them achieve these goals. George Lucas knew what he wanted *Star Wars* to be, he knew how he wanted it to feel and he had the carefully selected details in place to execute that vision.

Part of the beauty of *Star Wars* is that it is at once familiar and brand new, and that is no accident. While you've likely never travelled through space, you've probably played a board game with friends that ended with someone getting a bit grumpy. It's that shade of the familiar – the kind that brought to life the memorable dejarik, or "holochess", scene in Episode IV – which makes countless shots in these films personal for us all. Yes, the *Star Wars* universe is massive, but it's these purposefully designed objects, based in our reality, that also make it more intimate; we love the spectacle, and we can relate to it, too.

This book is a celebration of those details that exist in the service of storytelling. In this title you'll see firsthand the thousands of objects that are inspired by our world, but are uniquely *Star Wars*. They're not a copy of reality as we know it, but reminiscent of it, thoughtfully selected and designed to fulfil a specific purpose and evoke a certain feeling. You'll see costumes and creatures and droids, as well as food and weapons and musical instruments. All of these pieces together fill out the *Star Wars* universe visually and emotionally, helping generations of moviegoers feel they are a part of this story from "a galaxy far, far away".

DENNIS MUREN WORKING ON *STAR WARS: EPISODE VI RETURN OF THE JEDI*

GEOGRAPHY

The galaxy has been explored and travelled for untold millennia. Despite all the heavy traffic, there are still many mysteries – even in its most populated corners. The Core and Mid Rim are the domain of the Republic, later replaced by the Empire. The Outer Rim, Wild Space and Unknown Regions have reputations for lawlessness. The development of civilisations in all of these regions is not only influenced by physical geography, but also by urban geography and architecture, as inhabitants seek to put their own stamp on the worlds in which they live.

DATHOMIR

MAP OF THE GALAXY

Estimates suggest that there are over four hundred billion stars and more than 3.2 million habitable systems in the known galaxy. Not every system has been explored or charted; who knows what is waiting to be discovered!

KEY TO PLANETS

The galaxy is divided into different regions with the Core at its centre, and Wild Space on its outer fringes. On the map, the beginning of each charted region is represented by a coloured line. Planets are numbered in a clockwise direction within their regions.

CORE PLANETS
1 Coruscant
2 Alderaan
3 Hosnian Prime

COLONIES PLANETS
4 Devaron

INNER RIM PLANETS
5 Onderon
6 Jakku

EXPANSION REGION PLANETS
7 Kiros
8 Umbara

MID RIM PLANETS
9 Ord Mantell
10 Balnab
11 Patitite Pattuna
12 Aleen
13 Ringo Vinda
14 Trandosha and Kashyyyk
15 Ruusan
16 Toydaria
17 Naboo
18 Takodana

OUTER RIM AND WILD SPACE PLANETS
19 Carlac
20 Dathomir
21 Mandalore
22 Yavin

23 Maridun
24 Stygeon Prime
25 Zygerria
26 Vanqor and Florrum
27 Kadavo *(Wild Space)*
28 Felucia
29 Lola Sayu
30 Raxus Prime
31 Saleucami
32 Iego
33 Mon Cala
34 Lothal
35 Garel
36 Ibaar
37 Kessel
38 Nal Hutta
39 Teth *(Wild Space)*
40 Rishi
41 Rodia
42 Tatooine and Geonosis
43 Ryloth
44 Christophsis
45 Orto Plutonia
46 D'Qar
47 Lira San *(Wild Space)*
48 Sullust
49 Utapau
50 Dagobah
51 Mustafar
52 Bespin and Hoth
53 Vassek
54 Endor

UNKNOWN REGIONS
55 Starkiller Base

WILD SPACE

UNKNOWN REGIONS

55

6

18

WILD SPACE

54

53

52

OUTER RIM

25 27

26 30

33

28 34 35

22 23 29 32

20 24

21 13 31 36

19

12 37

9 11

10 7

INNER RIM

5 14

8

1 2 15

16 38

CORE 39

OUTER RIM

3

WILD SPACE

EXPANSION REGION

4

COLONIES

MID RIM

40

41 42

44

17 43

46

48

45

BESPIN

SIZE MATTERS NOT
Planets come in various sizes and all sorts of
compositions, but many sustain life. Bespin is a gas
giant, and its residents extract valuable tibanna
gas from its atmosphere. Planets the size of Dagobah
and Naboo often support an abundance of life.
While Hoth and Mustafar are smaller than other
planets and have extreme climates, their residents
have adapted to their challenging surroundings.
Across the galaxy, life adapts to survive.

OUTER RIM

DAGOBAH

NABOO

50

HOTH

49

MUSTAFAR

51

47

DIAMETER:
118,000 KM
(73,322 MILES)

DIAMETER:
14,410 KM
(8,954 MILES)

DIAMETER:
12,120 KM
(7,531 MILES)

DIAMETER:
7,200 KM
(4,474 MILES)

DIAMETER:
4,200 KM
(2,610 MILES)

INNER PLANETS

The course of galactic history has been heavily influenced by the societies and advances on the inner planets. Six regions comprise this area: the Deep Core, the Core, the Colonies, the Inner Rim, the Expansion Region and the Mid Rim.

DEVARON

CORE AND COLONIES PLANETS

The Core and the Colonies form rings around the dense, thinly inhabited Deep Core at the galaxy's centre. Important trade lanes make their planets hubs for fashion, education, finance and technology. The Core has been the seat of galactic power for millennia. Though it has never been proven, some believe Coruscant to be the birthplace of the human species.

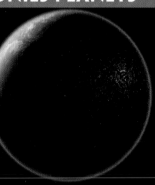
HOSNIAN PRIME

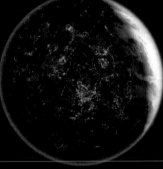
CORUSCANT

ALDERAAN

DOOMED PLANET
Grand Moff Tarkin threatens to use the Death Star on Princess Leia's homeworld of Alderaan if she doesn't confess the rebel base's location. Leia gives Tarkin a location, Dantooine – but Tarkin cruelly destroys Alderaan anyway, to prove the superweapon's powers.

MID RIM PLANETS

A tranquil region until it was torn apart by the Clone Wars, the Mid Rim is brimming with varied galactic worlds that boast successful governments and thriving economies. Their distance from the Core also often gives these worlds less fame or notoriety than planets closer to the galactic centre.

PATITITE PATTUNA

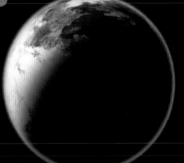
KASHYYYK

RUUSAN

Abundant forests

Surface dotted with small lakes

TAKODANA

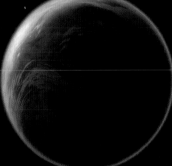
TRANDOSHA

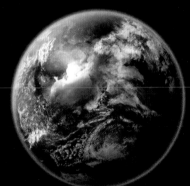
ORD MANTELL

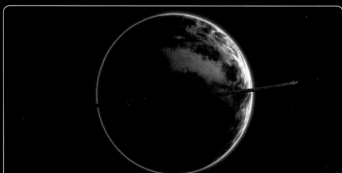
RINGO VINDA

INNER RIM PLANETS

The Inner Rim was colonised by explorers moving out from the Core and Colonies planets. It holds strategic value both for the Separatist group during the Clone Wars, and also for the Galactic Empire.

ONDERON

JAKKU

EXPANSION REGION PLANETS

Because of their location between the Inner Rim and Mid Rim, the planets of the Expansion Region serve as battlegrounds during the Clone Wars. The planet of Umbara is known for its unique, advanced weaponry.

KIROS

UMBARA

Monsoon

Mats of algae

ALEEN

NABOO

Toydarian city

TOYDARIA

BALNAB

OUTER RIM PLANETS

During the time of the Empire, Grand Moff Tarkin oversees the Outer Rim, but the planets are not fully under the Empire's control. Many are ruled by unsavoury criminal organisations like the Hutt families, Black Sun, the Pyke Syndicate and Zygerrian slavers.

COLD CLIMATE

Remote, frozen worlds like Hoth are a great place to hide a rebel base, and blizzard conditions on Stygeon Prime make it the perfect location for a prison. Escaped prisoners won't survive outside the walls, unless they have a tibidee waiting to fly them to safety!

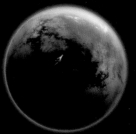

STYGEON PRIME

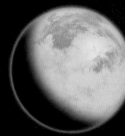

CARLAC

TEMPERATE CLIMATE

VERDANT

These worlds' climates are comfortable, despite challenging ecosystems and dangerous predators. Refugees, like the Lurmen of Maridun, flee there to make peaceful new lives away from watchful eyes. Dathomirians are also reclusive – hiding their dark secrets.

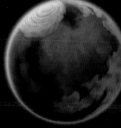

MARIDUN

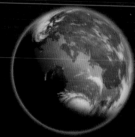

DATHOMIR

MIXED

Lothal is a varied world of rolling grasslands, strange rock formations, snow-covered mountains and gentle seas. It also boasts valuable resources needed by Sienar Fleet Systems factories, where the Empire manufactures TIE fighters.

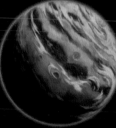

SALEUCAMI

HOT CLIMATE

HUMID

These steamy worlds are a hotbed of life. Important locations like Ryloth, Nal Hutta and Rodia are homes to influential species. Ryloth and Kessel are key planets for the spice trade and use slave labour to produce their goods. The Hutts on Nal Hutta deal in both slaves and spices.

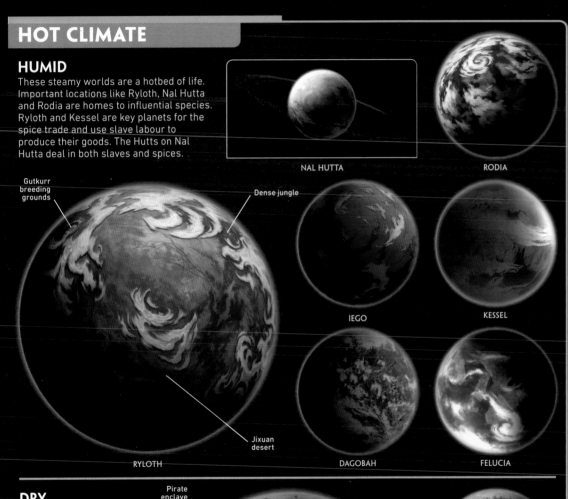

NAL HUTTA

RODIA

Gutkurr breeding grounds

Dense jungle

IEGO

KESSEL

Jixuan desert

RYLOTH

DAGOBAH

FELUCIA

DRY

Seemingly barren planets can hide surprising secrets. Tatooine is home to the legendary Anakin and Luke Skywalker. Geonosis harbours the manufacture of the Separatist droid army, and Hondo Ohnaka's pirates hide on Florrum.

Pirate enclave

TATOOINE

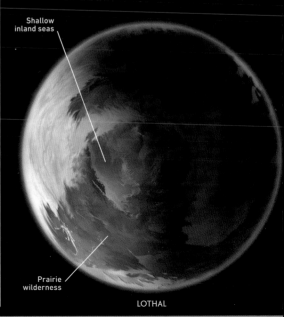

Shallow inland seas

Prairie wilderness

LOTHAL

GEONOSIS

Sulphur geysers

FLORRUM

Barren rocky desert

MANDALORE

EXTREME CLIMATE

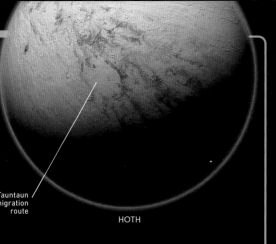

Tauntaun migration route

HOTH

GASEOUS
Cloud City hovers above the gas planet Bespin, where costly tibanna gas is processed for sale off-world. Even though there is no habitable land or water on Bespin, there are still life-forms floating and flying in the sky.

BESPIN

CRYSTALLINE
A dramatic landscape of naturally occurring turquoise crystal spires makes Christophsis a beauty to behold. It is also the site of several key conflicts during the Clone Wars, where Republic forces faced off against the Separatists.

Chaleydonia

CHRISTOPHSIS

DESERT
Deserts need not be hot – just dry – as is the case on Garel. The planet is located near Lothal, and there is much trade and travel between the two. Lothal's rebel cell even relocates there, until the Empire lays siege.

SCARIF

D'QAR

RAXUS

YAVIN 4

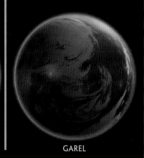

GAREL

VOLCANIC
Molten worlds may seem impractical bases for operations – but lava isn't always bad. Sullust is the centre of an industrial empire. Mustafar hosts facilities for Separatists, Imperials, Sith and Black Sun. An infamous prison known as the Citadel is located on Lola Sayu.

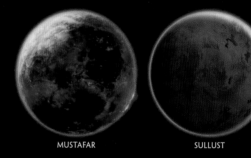

MUSTAFAR

SULLUST

AQUATIC
The peoples of aquatic worlds have been vastly important in the politics, science, art and warfare of the galaxy. Oceanic planet Mon Cala has birthed two influential species: the Quarren and the Mon Calamari.

MON CALA

ROCKY
Rocky worlds can be dangerous places. Vanqor is home to ferocious gundark creatures. A lethal skirmish takes place between arms dealers and the Jedi on Utapau when a giant kyber crystal is found here.

Swirling silica-dust storms

VANQOR

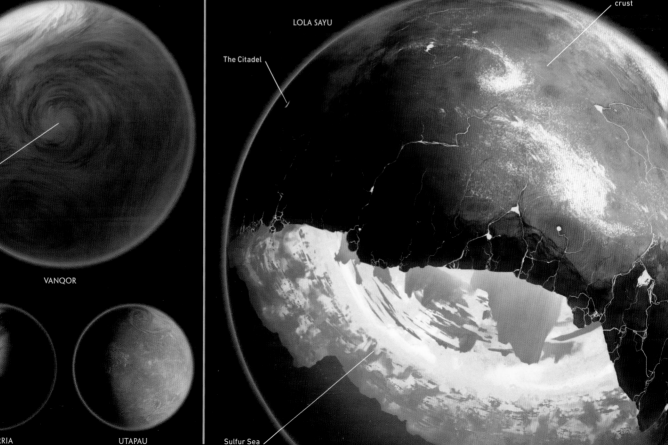

LOLA SAYU

The Citadel

Brittle volcanic crust

Sulfur Sea

IBAAR

ZYGERRIA

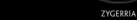

UTAPAU

WILD SPACE AND UNKNOWN REGIONS PLANETS

Though the galaxy has been explored for thousands of years, the areas farthest from the Core still hold many secrets. The Unknown Regions is a patch of space shrouded in mystery to the west of the Outer Core, while the scattered star clusters of Wild Space remain unmapped.

WILD SPACE

Wild Space is a lawless region of dangerous worlds. Kadavo is an ugly, barren planet used by Zygerrians to process slaves. Teth is a jungle planet, once colonised by B'omarr monks. Their empty monasteries later fell under the control of corrupt Hutts. The planet Lira San was once the homeworld of the Lasat species.

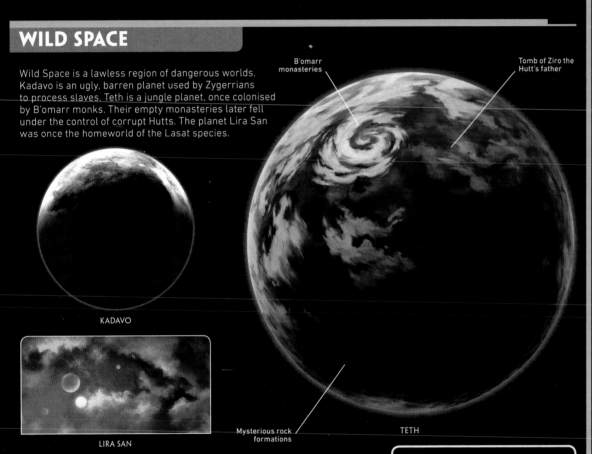

B'omarr monasteries

Tomb of Ziro the Hutt's father

KADAVO

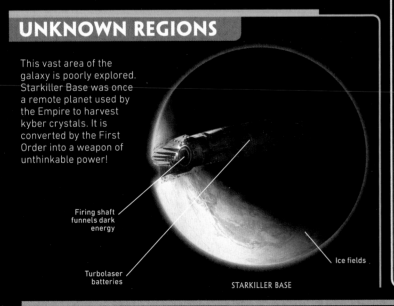

LIRA SAN

Mysterious rock formations

TETH

UNKNOWN REGIONS

This vast area of the galaxy is poorly explored. Starkiller Base was once a remote planet used by the Empire to harvest kyber crystals. It is converted by the First Order into a weapon of unthinkable power!

Firing shaft funnels dark energy

Turbolaser batteries

Ice fields

STARKILLER BASE

DANGER IN WILD SPACE

There is a reason why this region is called Wild Space. The only guarantee on these worlds is that deadly peril awaits!

○ **MORTIS**
On this mysterious forested planet, a family of powerful beings struggle among themselves to overthrow – or maintain – the balance in the Force.

○ **THUNE**
Siblings Lina and Milo Graf fall into a trap set by Imperial Captain Korda, while searching for their missing parents on the planet Thune.

○ **INDOUMODO**
On the jungle planet Indoumodo, assassins capture venomous arthropod creatures called kouhuns, to add to their lethal arsenal.

STARS

Each star represents a system that could potentially contain sentient life, or have valuable resources to compete over. Chains of important star systems form runs, which are vital navigational routes for trade and transit, and may cross through multiple sectors.

STARFIELDS

MOONS

Moons are equally likely to support life as the planets that they orbit. Rishi, Endor and Rugosa, among others, have all been major sites of conflict between warring enemies. The natives of Pantora have great influence in galactic culture and politics.

ZANBAR

VERUNA (ORBITS NABOO)

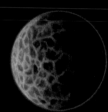

RISHI MOON (ORBITS RISHI)

ALETHEA (ORBITS ALEEN)

ENDOR MOON (ORBITS ENDOR)

RUGOSA

MOONS OF SALEUCAMI

Saleucami means "oasis". It is a planet both arid and swampy, located within Suolriep – a sector full of barren planets. The planet is orbited by three moons of greenish hue, coloured by the crystalline dust in their atmospheres.

CATHER

VICTORI

JOS

OTHER CELESTIAL BODIES

Planets are not the only significant locations in space: moons and large asteroids are also strategic bases, and homes. Stars and nebulae can be dangerous to navigate too closely, but they are important reference points when plotting travel through the galaxy.

SUNS

Without suns, most worlds would be lifeless and frozen. A sun's size and distance will affect many of the features of the planets that orbit it. Some systems boast multiple suns at their centre, but binary star systems like Tatooine have two.

CORUSCANT PRIME (CORUSCANT'S SUN)

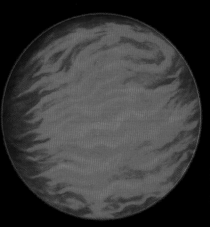
ANZA (THE ABREGADO SYSTEM'S SUN)

TATOO I AND TATOO II (TATOOINE'S SUNS)

TAKODANA'S SUN

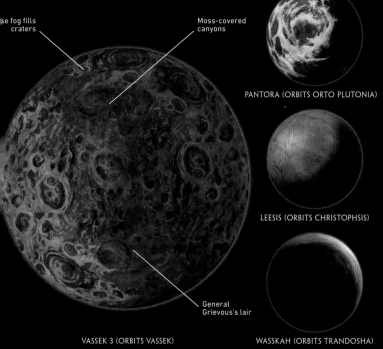

se fog fills craters

Moss-covered canyons

PANTORA (ORBITS ORTO PLUTONIA)

LEESIS (ORBITS CHRISTOPHSIS)

General Grievous's lair

VASSEK 3 (ORBITS VASSEK)

WASSKAH (ORBITS TRANDOSHA)

ASTEROIDS

Asteroids can support life, especially if they have thin atmospheres. Mynocks and fyrnocks thrive on asteroids, where rocks and minerals are the foundation for many food chains. Asteroids like PM-1203 (Fort Anaxes) are also used as bases by the rebels and other forces.

ANAXES ASTEROID RING

ESCAPING THE EMPIRE

In an effort to evade a pursuing Imperial Star Destroyer, Han Solo flies the *Millennium Falcon* through the Hoth Asteroid Belt – a highly dangerous manoeuvre. To hide from TIE fighters, he pilots the *Falcon* into an asteroid cavern, only to discover it is in fact the gullet of a giant space slug!

TRIO OF ASTEROIDS

ONE THOUSAND MOONS

The planet Iego has 1,000 moons, each as mysterious as the planet itself. The largest, Millius Prime, is home to a race of beautiful, luminous beings known as Angels. They are driven from the moon by the Separatists, who also set up a laser grid over Iego that destroys the starships of any inhabitants trying to escape.

CLEPRESDAN   FLITRUDE

WINLION   RAWNDE

COBARB   UNCOVALOR   MILLIUS PRIME

NEBULAE

Nebulae hide many mysteries. Yoda travels to a nebula at the centre of the galaxy to learn more of the secrets of the Force. Zeb Orrelios finds a refuge for the remaining Lasats on Lira San, hidden beyond a treacherous nebula formed by an imploding star cluster.

YODA TRAVELLING INTO A NEBULA

PHYSICAL GEOGRAPHY

Environmental conditions on any planet or moon depend on many factors, such as how close they are to the sun, or what their atmospheres are made of. Some are covered in plant life, but even rocky deserts, windswept plains, rugged mountains and lava fields may support strange alien life and fascinating cultures.

LUSH VEGETATION

GRASSLANDS

Grasslands are perfect habitats for grazing animals, such as shaaks, gualamas and guarlaras on Naboo. Carnivorous felines like Naboo's tusk-cats, or Lothal's Loth-cats and sabercats use the grass as cover when hunting herbivores. Grasses also provide homes for insects, Loth-rats and other small animals.

NABOO GRASSLANDS

LOTHAL PRAIRIE

OCEANS AND ISLANDS

From the surface, Scarif is a tropical paradise, with volcanic island chains featuring verdant jungles and sandy beaches rising from ocean waters. The lush jungles are plentiful with areca nut palm trees but also hide an Imperial base housing armed forces constructing the Empire's first Death Star weapon.

SCARIF BEACH

SWAMPS AND MARSHES

Wetlands can be dangerous places. On Dagobah, gnarltrees are home to flying bogwings. Their roots hide ferocious dragonsnakes and scrange. Rodian swamps are home to giant kwazel maw predators. Naboo's swamps are gateways to seas which harbour legendary beasts.

DAGOBAH BOG

RODIA SWAMP

NABOO MARSHES

FORESTS

Woodlands include the snow-covered forests of Starkiller Base, timberlands of Takodana and the jungles of Teth. Great trees on Kashyyyk and Endor support entire villages. However, not all forests are made up of trees. Felucia is covered in fungus, and Rugosa with coral.

TETH JUNGLE

KASHYYYK FOREST

FELUCIA JUNGLE

RUGOSA CORAL FOREST

TAKODANA FOREST

ENDOR PRIMEVAL FOREST

STARKILLER BASE FOREST

EXTREME GEOLOGY

ICE PLAINS

Strong winds and constant snow make ice plains difficult places to survive, yet wampas and tauntauns live on Hoth, and Orto Plutonia is home to Talz tribes and narglatch. All these worlds, including Starkiller Base, have also been outposts for human soldiers, too.

HOTH ICE PLAINS

ORTO PLUTONIA ICE PLAINS

STARKILLER BASE ICE PLAINS

ROCKY LANDSCAPES

Stones are the foundations and roofs of countless worlds. Hive spires rise in the distance of Geonosis's barren red landscape. Ahch-To's rugged island cliffs are covered in mosses, grasses and ferns. Deep sinkholes on Utapau support great subterranean cities. On Scipio and Alderaan, mountains are covered in snow.

GEONOSIS LANDSCAPE

SCIPIO MOUNTAINS

AHCH-TO

UTAPAU SINKHOLE

ALDERAAN MOUNTAINS

DESERTS

Desert worlds abound across the galaxy, from the barren flats of Seelos and Abafar, to the rolling sand dunes of Tatooine and Jakku, and the rocky dustbowls of Florrum, Ryloth and Jedha. Despite the absence of water, people still make their homes there.

TATOOINE DUNE SEA

LAVA FIELDS

Active volcanic zones are dangerous environments, with rivers of hot lava, toxic gases and unpredictable eruptions. Yet life persists even there. On Mustafar, locals mine precious minerals in the lava flows. Meanwhile, the famous SoroSuub factories on Sullust manufacture starships.

SEELOS SALT FLATS

JAKKU DESERT

FLORRUM ACID FLATS

RYLOTH DESERT

MUSTAFAR LAVA FIELDS

URBAN GEOGRAPHY

Sentient beings build unique villages and cities based on local environmental conditions, available resources and their cultural values. Cities may be centres of industry, such as those on Lothal or Bespin; centres of art and culture, like Theed on Naboo; or centres of politics and government, like the capital world of Coruscant.

GRIMY UNDERWORLD

The Coruscant underlevels are a haven for criminal gangs, pirates and bounty hunters. Nonetheless, they also harbour war refugees and poor immigrants just trying to make a pitiful living. These lower levels of the city are devoid of sunlight, polluted and infested with pests and dangerous escaped pets. The lowest depths are rumoured to hide ancient secrets.

CITIES

LAND-BASED

Solid foundations allow cities to take a variety of forms. Some are modern hubs, like Lothal's Capital City, or Crystal City on Christophsis. Some are mostly underground, like the hives of Geonosis or Utapau's Pau City. Yet others, like Kashyyyk's tree cities and Coruscant's skyscrapers, climb high above the surface.

CAPITAL CITY, LOTHAL

SENATE DISTRICT, CORUSCANT

THEED, NABOO

LESSU, RYLOTH

KACHIRHO, KASHYYYK

STALGASIN HIVE COLONY, GEONOSIS

NIJEDHA, JEDHA

MOS EISLEY, TATOOINE

CRYSTAL CITY, CHRISTOPHSIS

CLIFFHOLD, IEGO

PAU CITY, UTAPAU

WATER-BASED

Aquatic species like the Mon Calamari and Quarren prefer to build cities underwater. The Gungan capital city of Otoh Gunga lies deep under Lake Paonga, hidden from the human concerns of the Naboo, who live above. Some species, like the Kaminoans, construct stilt-cities above the water's surface.

OTOH GUNGA, NABOO

IN-DEPTH ANALYSIS

The "bubble" buildings that make up Otoh Gunga are powerful hydrostatic membranes, which keep water out, but allow Gungans to pass through. These bubbles, which support around one million Gungan residents, are anchored on huge stone pillars on the lake floor. The city's designs are inspired by aquatic plants and fish, fish eggs and air bubbles.

Hydrostatic field

Hydrostatic field generators

OTOH GUNGA BUILDINGS

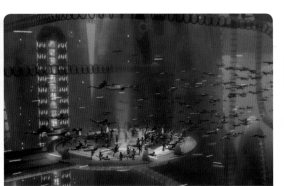

MON CALA CITY, MON CALA

TIPOCA CITY, KAMINO

AIR-BASED

Tackling gravity by building in the sky can be challenging – but it also enhances security and gives access to new resources. The Royal City of Toydaria is perched on a mountain peak. Cloud City mines tibanna gas above the gas planet Bespin. On Cato Neimoidia, cities are suspended between natural stone pillars.

ROYAL CITY, TOYDARIA

CLOUD CITY, BESPIN

BRIDGE CITIES, CATO NEIMOIDIA

VILLAGES

Villagers build homes and communities with local natural materials. Lurmen immigrants make their homes in giant seed pods on Maridun. A religious sect occupies the wattle and daub huts of Tuanul village on Jakku. On Endor, Ewoks build their homes in giant evergreen trees.

TUANUL VILLAGE, JAKKU

LURMEN SEED VILLAGE, MARIDUN

BRIGHT TREE VILLAGE, ENDOR

INDUSTRIES

Industries harvest valuable resources from the galaxy's many environments. On arid worlds like Jakku and Tatooine, moisture vaporators extract precious water from the atmosphere. The ruling parties on Kessel use slaves to mine spice. On Mustafar, the locals refine rare metals from rivers of molten rock.

MOISTURE FARM, TATOOINE

SPICE MINES, KESSEL

LAVA MINES, MUSTAFAR

ARCHITECTURE

Architecture reflects the balance between artistic form and functional need. A palace is much more than just a defensive structure; it's also a building that embodies the galactic culture of its owner. A home shelters its inhabitants, but also mirrors its occupants' sense of grandeur – or practicality.

THREE VERTIGO-INDUCING DESIGNS

Sometimes building design can result in views that leave the occupant breathless if they dare look down!

1 PAU CITY, UTAPAU
Pau City is built into a massive sinkhole, with structures made of animal skeletons jutting from cliff walls.

2 KASHYYYK
Wookiees create entire cities – from treehouses to gathering places – in the wroshyr trees of their homeworld.

3 THE CITADEL
Sitting atop a precarious cliff on the planet Lola Sayu, the Citadel prison is an almost impenetrable fortress.

PUBLIC BUILDINGS

ENTERTAINMENT AND LEISURE

Galactic citizens often gather to dine and be entertained. Eateries range from quaint diners favoured by locals, to raucous cantinas on remote planets. Entertainment venues match the style of events that they hold, from elaborate opera houses to dusty, vast podrace arenas.

MOS EISLEY CANTINA, TATOOINE

PETRANAKI ARENA, GEONOSIS

MOS ESPA GRAND ARENA, TATOOINE

MAZ KANATA'S CASTLE, TAKODANA

DEXTER'S DINER, COCO TOWN, CORUSCANT

OUTLANDER GAMBLING CLUB, CORUSCANT

GALAXIES OPERA HOUSE, CORUSCANT

SACRED BUILDINGS

Temples and monasteries are solemn places. Religious individuals aspire to a higher purpose – and likewise the architecture of their buildings rises upward, reflecting these aspirations. Old and powerful religious orders have erected grand edifices, like the Jedi Temple on Coruscant.

JEDI TEMPLE, LOTHAL

B'OMARR MONASTERY, TETH

GOVERNMENT

Governments need large facilities to house all their members. The ornate Separatist Parliament headquarters lie at the heart of the capital city, Raxulon, and soar above the urban landscape. Coruscant's mighty Senate Building is easily spotted with its iconic domed shape.

SENATE BUILDING, CORUSCANT

JEDI LIBRARY, CORUSCANT

JEDI TEMPLE, CORUSCANT

SITH TEMPLE, MALACHOR

SEPARATIST PARLIAMENT BUILDING, RAXUS SECUNDUS

IMPERIAL COMMAND CENTER, LOTHAL

PRIVATE BUILDINGS

PALACES

Palaces are the residences of the powerful. Some, such as the elegant Royal Palace of Alderaan, capture the opulence of royalty. Other palaces, like Jabba the Hutt's fortress on Tatooine, have a defensive design that focuses primarily on protection from attack.

ROYAL PALACE, ALDERAAN

ROYAL PALACE, THEED, NABOO

JABBA'S PALACE, TATOOINE

COUNT DOOKU'S PALACE, SERENNO

SENATORIAL PALACE, RODIA

HOMES

Homes are designed to fit the lifestyle of their occupants. Tuskens and Lurmen erect dwellings using natural materials. The homesteads of moisture farmers are partially buried in the ground, keeping the residence cool and protected from wind and heat. Expensive city land requires the shared occupancy of tall skyscrapers.

PADMÉ AMIDALA'S FAMILY HOME, LAKE COUNTRY, NABOO

PADMÉ AMIDALA'S APARTMENT BUILDING, CORUSCANT

HOMESTEAD, TATOOINE

TUSKEN RAIDER URTYA TENT, TATOOINE

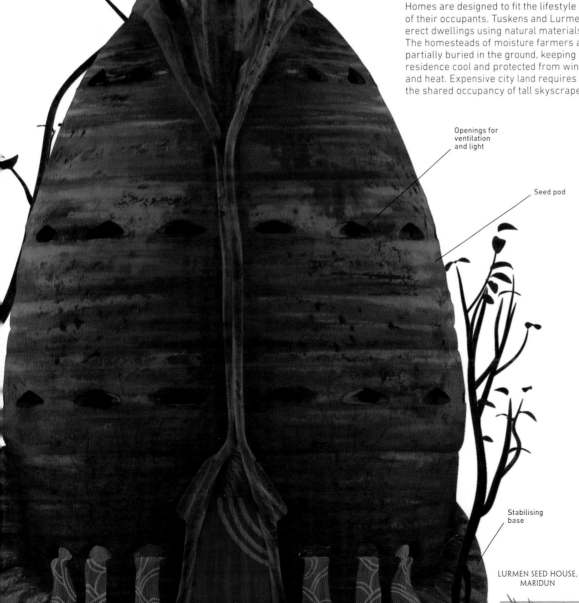

Future seeds

Openings for ventilation and light

Seed pod

Stabilising base

LURMEN SEED HOUSE, MARIDUN

NATURE

Civilisations and empires have come and gone, but many species – including both plants and animals – have migrated between worlds, sectors and entire regions, creating a diverse galaxy full of life. Even seemingly inhospitable habitats make the perfect home for some sort of life-form. Sentient beings may drive galactic history, but non-sentient beasts still have great influence – from giant space slugs that swallow starships whole, to Geonosian brain worms with the potential to control a whole society.

RATHTAR

AQUATIC CREATURES

Aquatic creatures live below the surface of the galaxy's oceans, swamps, lakes and rivers. All have developed different biological features to survive in underwater habitats. Some may be small and peaceful, but others are terrifying predators!

Luminescent skin lures prey

COLO CLAW FISH (FROM NABOO)

OCEAN

On planets with large bodies of water such as Naboo, Kamino and Mon Cala, the oceans hold an abundance of sea life. Most aquatic creatures spend their entire lives underwater and some live a full lifetime without ever seeing the surface.

SANDO AQUA MONSTER (FROM NABOO)

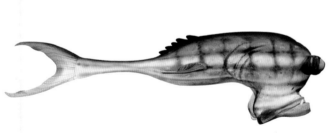

Baleen for filtering krill from seawater

Wingtips propel aiwha in air and below water

AIWHA (FROM KAMINO)

LEE ROMAY CLAM (FROM MON CALA)

SEE

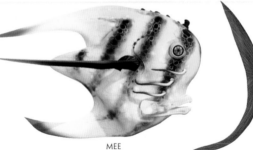

MEE

RAY

MILLENNIUM FALCON (FOR SCALE)

COLO CLAW FISH

GUNGAN BONGO SUBMARINE
(FOR SCALE)

IN-DEPTH ANALYSIS

The food chain in Naboo's oceans is a complex network of predators and prey. The sando aqua monster is a super-sized predator, large enough to dwarf the *Millennium Falcon* starship, and to chomp on the massive colo claw fish. The colo, in turn, preys on creatures like the opee sea killer. The opee lures all kinds of smaller fish into its jaws.

OPEE SEA KILLER

SANDO AQUA MONSTER

SCALE 1CM = 10M

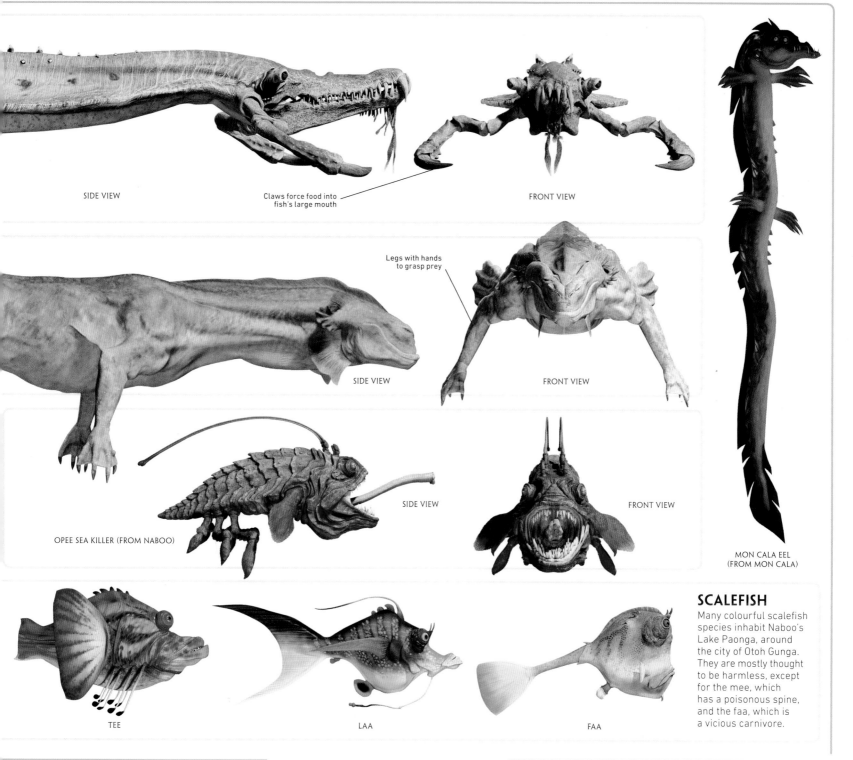

SIDE VIEW

Claws force food into
fish's large mouth

FRONT VIEW

Legs with hands
to grasp prey

SIDE VIEW

FRONT VIEW

OPEE SEA KILLER (FROM NABOO)

SIDE VIEW

FRONT VIEW

MON CALA EEL
(FROM MON CALA)

TEE

LAA

FAA

SCALEFISH

Many colourful scalefish
species inhabit Naboo's
Lake Paonga, around
the city of Otoh Gunga.
They are mostly thought
to be harmless, except
for the mee, which
has a poisonous spine,
and the faa, which is
a vicious carnivore.

SWAMP

Lurking at the bottom of the
swamps of Rodia, the kwazel
maw is large enough to swallow
a humanoid whole. Their skin
is highlighted with glowing
luminescent markings and
is thick enough to resist
blaster bolts, and even
small missiles.

Eyelids close when
sleeping underwater

Mouth opens to roar and
consume prey whole

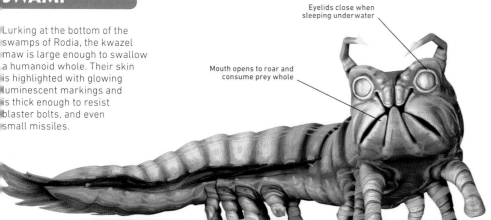

KWAZEL MAW (FROM RODIA)

FRESHWATER

Nos monsters inhabit the lakes, caves and
underground rivers in the sinkholes of Utapau.
Large front fins help the creature paddle through
its home waters and stomp on any prey unlucky
enough to wander into its hunting grounds.

Large eyes help to
see underwater

Swings tail as a weapon

NOS MONSTER (FROM UTAPAU)

AERIAL CREATURES

From a tiny beetle to a massive brezak, aerial creatures take to the skies under the power of their own wings. But don't let their graceful flight fool you. Some of these beasts are weapons of war!

BIRDS

In stark contrast to the ragged, mangy steelpecker, beautiful birds like the kiros or convor are elegant, regal creatures. The sneaky convorees defend themselves by working in pairs to pick up their predators and drop them from the treetops!

KIROS BIRD
(FROM KIROS)

CONVOR
(FROM VARIOUS
LOCATIONS)

MAMMAVIAN

One of many predators native to the planet Iego, xandu patrol the rocky spires that dot the planet. This six-eyed terror fiercely defends its territory and can hunt and carry prey as large as a human.

XANDU (FROM IEGO)

SILICON-BASED

Giant flying creatures known as tibidees inhabit planets like Stygeon Prime and Oosalon. They fly gracefully through the air using large, flat wings and internal gas bags. Some communication frequencies sound similar to the tibidees' mating call, and so attract the creatures' attention.

TIBIDEE (FROM VARIOUS LOCATIONS)

PELIKKI (FROM NABOO)

INSECTS

While insects like the slug-beetle and carrier butterfly are rather small, the can-cell can grow to be more than 3m (9ft 10in) in length. The can-cell is found on a variety of planets across the galaxy, including Kashyyyk, Rodia and Teth.

CAN-CELL (FROM
VARIOUS LOCATIONS)

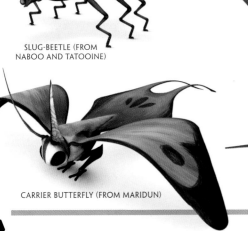

SLUG-BEETLE (FROM
NABOO AND TATOOINE)

CARRIER BUTTERFLY (FROM MARIDUN)

REPTAVIANS

These flying reptiles from across the galaxy are often large enough to ride. A notable example is the ruping, a loyal and brave species used as mounts by Saw Gerrera and the Onderon rebels during the Clone Wars.

DACTILLION (FROM UTAPAU
AND SHANTIPOLE)

Vocal cords
produce
rasping roar

Rider's saddle
and reins

BOGWING (FROM NABOO)

RUPING (FROM ONDERON)

SPACE CREATURES

Even in the cold depths of space, weird, wonderful and terrifying creatures thrive and multiply. From the mysterious purrgil to the maddening mynock, you might just come across an astonishing array of space creatures when travelling the galaxy.

Scraggly feathers

Strong beak for picking apart metal

Claws sharpened on scrap

STEELPECKER (FROM JAKKU)

ASTEROID DWELLERS

Many monstrous creatures dwell in the depths of asteroids. Space slugs are known to swallow unlucky spaceships whole, while the ferocious fyrnocks will attack their prey with sharp teeth and claws.

EXOGORTH, ALSO KNOWN AS A SPACE SLUG

FYRNOCK

TENTACLED

Purrgil are huge, whale-like creatures that travel through space in flocks. They have a reputation for accidentally colliding with starships and damaging them. When they consume enough gas known as Clouzon-36, a purrgil can travel in hyperspace.

BREZAK (FROM ZYGERRIA)

Thumb claw

Dorsal fin

Hind tentacle

Side fin

Wings can grasp and climb

Finger-like wing tips

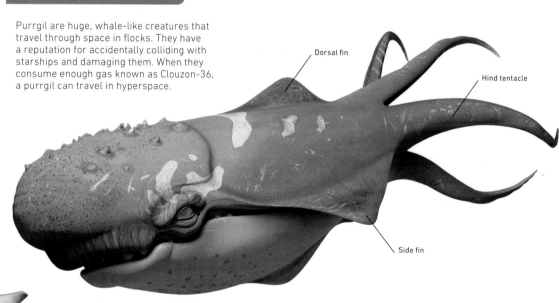

PURRGIL

WINGED

Monstrously large neebray mantas feed on gases in space, although they can also live on planets and moons. Mynocks chew on the wires of spaceships to consume electricity. It's been said that mynocks will feast on so much energy that they can get "spark-drunk".

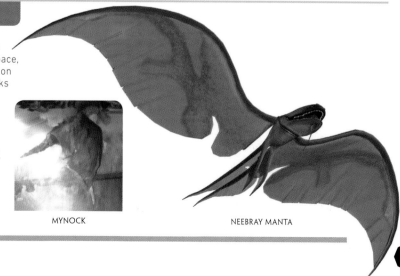

MYNOCK

NEEBRAY MANTA

BUGS, BEASTS AND INVERTEBRATES

They're creepy, crawly and come in all shapes and sizes. These nasty bugs, beasts and invertebrates are scary enough to make a Wookiee whimper. Just take one look at their biting jaws, grabbing tentacles or lanky legs and you'll see why!

GELAGRUB, ALSO KNOWN AS
FELUCIAN GROUND BEETLE (FROM FELUCIA)

INSECTS

RIDDEN AS MOUNTS

On unforgiving planets like Mustafar and Quarzite, the local population must make the most of their hardy native animal species. The Mustafarians tame lava fleas while the Kage harness milodon. Both use their local bugs as mounts.

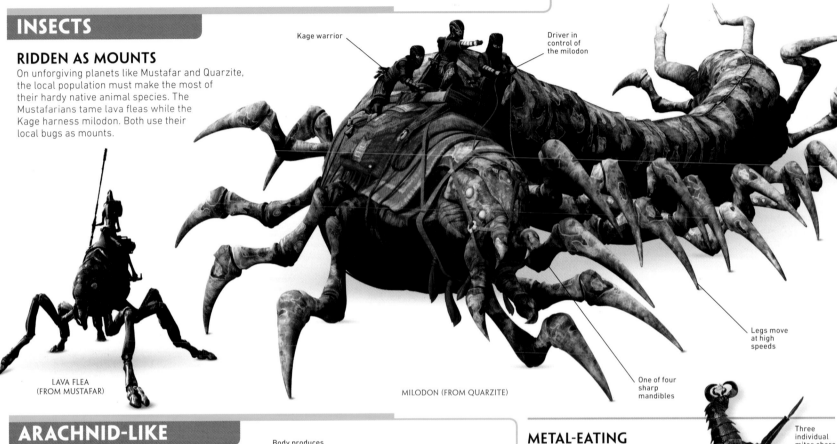

Kage warrior

Driver in control of the milodon

Legs move at high speeds

One of four sharp mandibles

LAVA FLEA
(FROM MUSTAFAR)

MILODON (FROM QUARZITE)

ARACHNID-LIKE

The krykna is a six-legged, spider-like creature found on the planet Atollon. While they primarily eat tiny dokma, they also attempt to attack the rebel crew of the *Ghost*. Like the ginntho spider from Utapau, the krykna uses strong webs to capture and hold its prey.

KRYKNA (FROM ATOLLON)

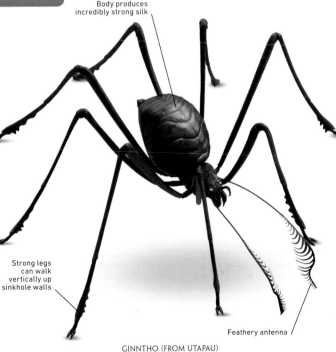

Body produces incredibly strong silk

Strong legs can walk vertically up sinkhole walls

Feathery antenna

GINNTHO (FROM UTAPAU)

METAL-EATING

Wary freighter pilots and spacers could tell you tales about the dangers that stone mites pose to anything made out of metal. With grasping claws and acidic saliva, they feed on starships and buildings alike.

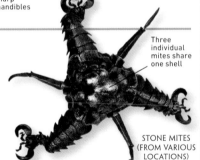

Three individual mites share one shell

STONE MITES
(FROM VARIOUS LOCATIONS)

PACK HUNTERS

Careless individuals might quickly find themselves surrounded by a pack of gutkurrs, vicious pack hunters from Ryloth. The kouhuns' victim would never see them coming though, as they silently follow body heat to find their target, then disable it with a single poisonous sting.

GUTKURR
(FROM RYLOTH)

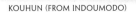

KOUHUN (FROM INDOUMODO)

SLUGS, SNAILS AND WORMS

HARD SHELLS

For slow-moving creatures, a hardened shell offers some protection from larger, faster predators. Duracrete slugs are born with soft hides, but their skin forms a hard coating as they eat – and then excrete – artificial stone, known as duracrete.

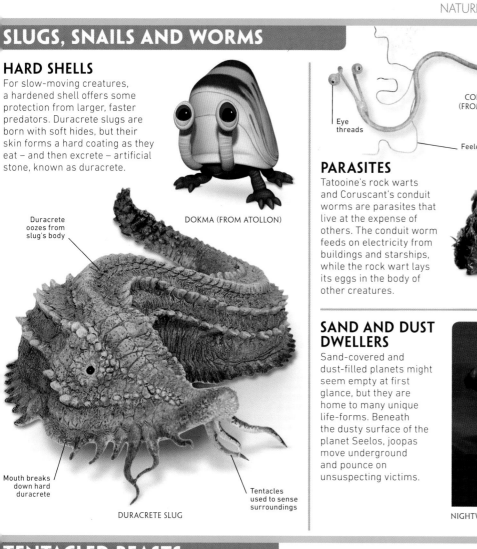

DOKMA (FROM ATOLLON)

Duracrete oozes from slug's body

Mouth breaks down hard duracrete

Tentacles used to sense surroundings

DURACRETE SLUG

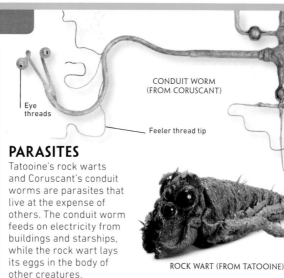

CONDUIT WORM (FROM CORUSCANT)

Eye threads

Feeler thread tip

Body core segment

Worm absorbs components as it grows along electricity conduits

Capacitor beads store energy

Resistor segment

PARASITES

Tatooine's rock warts and Coruscant's conduit worms are parasites that live at the expense of others. The conduit worm feeds on electricity from buildings and starships, while the rock wart lays its eggs in the body of other creatures.

ROCK WART (FROM TATOOINE)

SAND AND DUST DWELLERS

Sand-covered and dust-filled planets might seem empty at first glance, but they are home to many unique life-forms. Beneath the dusty surface of the planet Seelos, joopas move underground and pounce on unsuspecting victims.

NIGHTWATCHER WORM (FROM JAKKU)

JOOPA (FROM SEELOS)

TENTACLED BEASTS

Although the vixus, blixus, rathtar and sarlacc are native to different planets, they share a common ancestor. They all have tentacles, huge mouths and voracious appetites, but each has evolved differently to be a great hunter in its specific environment.

RATHTAR

BLIXUS

SARLACC (FROM TATOOINE)

VIXUS (FROM UMBARA)

IN-DEPTH ANALYSIS

The Sarlacc is the largest and least mobile of these tentacled monsters. Like an iceberg, it is mostly hidden beneath the surface. Its weak stomach acids mean that digestion is an extremely long – and for its prey, very unpleasant – process. Unable to move quickly, the Sarlacc is injured when Jabba the Hutt's sail barge explodes nearby.

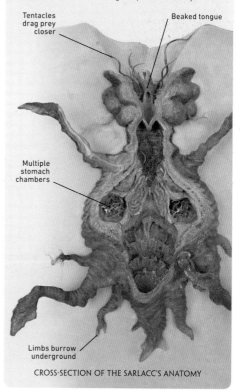

Tentacles drag prey closer

Beaked tongue

Multiple stomach chambers

Limbs burrow underground

CROSS-SECTION OF THE SARLACC'S ANATOMY

MAMMALS

These warm-blooded and often hairy creatures are sources of food, transportation, protection and even entertainment for the sentient beings of the galaxy. Some, like eopies and falumpasets, have been exported across the galaxy due to their popularity and usefulness.

MINES AND ROCKS

Puffer pigs are prized by miners for their ability to sniff out valuable mineral ore. On occupied worlds like Lothal, their use is restricted by the Empire. The pigs inflate to many times their natural size when they are startled or frightened.

PUFFER PIG (FROM VARIOUS LOCATIONS)

HERBIVORES

SWAMPS

Both the people of Naboo and the Gungans use falumpasets to pull carts. In the wild, they live in family groups. Wild motts use their horns for defence, in mating disputes and for rooting in the mud for food.

FALUMPASET (FROM NABOO)

MOTT (FROM NABOO)

DESERTS

These beasts provide vital transportation on arid worlds. On Tatooine, eopies serve weary travellers, while banthas are ridden by Tusken Raiders. Skalders give Jar Jar Binks and his squad of clone troopers a ride on Florrum, and happabores help junkers haul their finds on Jakku.

SKALDER (FROM FLORRUM)

EOPIE (FROM VARIOUS LOCATIONS)

BANTHA (FROM TATOOINE)

GRASS PLAINS AND TURF

Gungans farm bulbous shaak for their meat and skins. Wild herds of ikopi are fast runners and a favourite game animal of Naboo's hunters. Reeks are powerful, territorial beasts. Although they are usually herbivores, on Geonosis they are fed meat to make them more aggressive in the arena.

SHAAK (FROM NABOO)

Red colouring from meat diet on Geonosis

IKOPI (FROM NABOO)

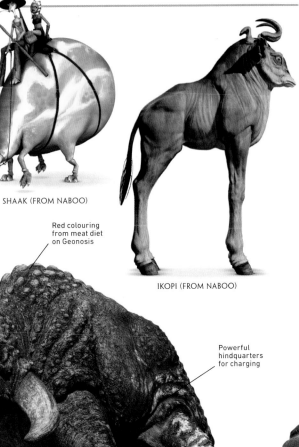

Central horn

Nose ring for handlers

Cheek horns

Powerful hindquarters for charging

REEK (FROM VARIOUS LOCATIONS)

Armoured hide protects from sun and predators

Large snout aids in finding and digging tubers

HAPPABORE (FROM DEVARON AND JAKKU)

CARNIVORES

ICE

Carnivorous diets are common in cold environments, where plants are in short supply. Wampas roam the snowy plains of Hoth, where they catch and eat tauntauns. Fearsome narglatches are tamed and ridden by the Talz of Orto Plutonia.

WAMPA (FROM HOTH)

NARGLATCH (FROM ORTO PLUTONIA)

PETS

Tookas are a popular pet on many worlds because they eat unwanted pests. The Loth-cat is a wild relative that hunts Loth-rats in the grasslands of Lothal. Although they look monstrous, barghests are loyal protectors of their masters.

LOTH-CAT (FROM LOTHAL)

TOOKA (FROM VARIOUS LOCATIONS)

DESERTS

Packs of anoobas stab their prey with chin tusks and then tear them apart with long claws and fangs. Gundarks are vicious creatures from Vanqor, renowned for their strength and ferocity.

GUNDARK
(FROM VANQOR)

ANOOBA (FROM THE
OUTER RIM TERRITORIES)

BARGHEST (NAMED IZBY, WITH
OWNER GWELLIS BAGNORO)

FORESTS

Six-limbed momongs are aggressive hunters, preying on convorees in the forests of Wasskah. The nexus' fierce reputation has made them popular animals for gladiator matches. On their homeworld of Cholganna, they use their second pair of eyes to sense the body heat of their prey.

Whip-like
double tail

Defensive mane
of spines

Four eyes give the
nexu excellent sight

NEXU
(FROM CHOLGANNA)

MOMONG (FROM WASSKAH)

Large claws for
climbing trees

AMPHIBIANS AND REPTILES

Although some amphibians make great snacks, like the gorgs gobbled by Jabba the Hutt, usually it's amphibians and reptiles who are at the top of the food chain. This makes them popular in the Geonosian Arena, and as war mounts.

MOUNTS

Their great strength and hardiness means that these reptiles are well suited for use as transportation. On Hoth, thick-skinned tauntauns are one of the few species able to survive the icy conditions, and are used by the rebels as mounts, while the deserts of Tatooine are patrolled by stormtroopers on dewbacks.

DEWBACK (FROM TATOOINE)

TAUNTAUN (FROM HOTH)

AMPHIBIANS

Amphibians slip between water and land with ease. Tatooine may be a desert planet, but plenty of amphibious creatures like the gorg and worrt can be found there. On Naboo, the Gungans use massive fambaa to carry deflector shield generators.

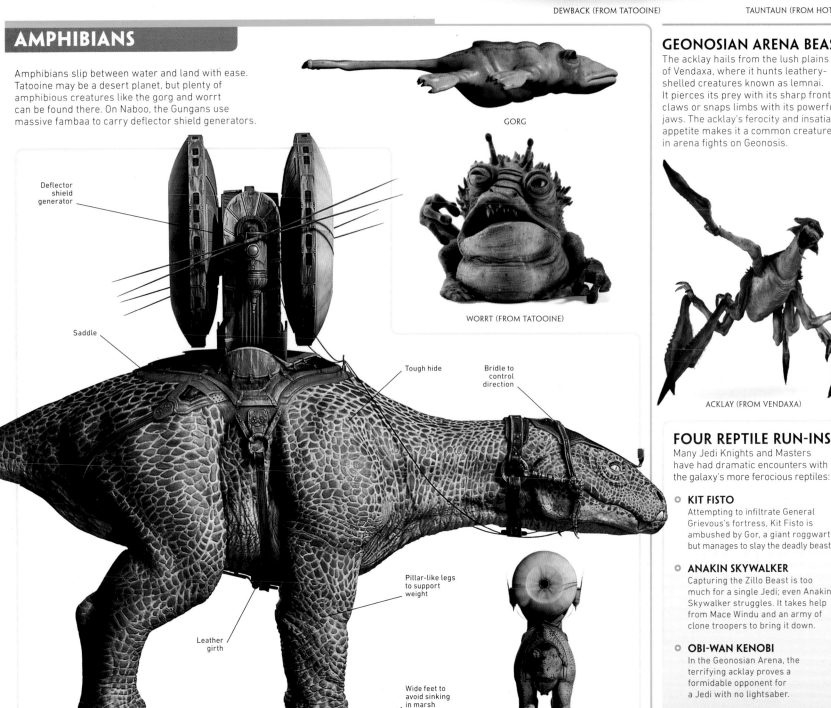

GORG

WORRT (FROM TATOOINE)

Deflector shield generator

Saddle

Tough hide

Bridle to control direction

Pillar-like legs to support weight

Leather girth

Wide feet to avoid sinking in marsh

FAMBAA (FROM NABOO AND ONDERON)

FRONT VIEW

GEONOSIAN ARENA BEAST

The acklay hails from the lush plains of Vendaxa, where it hunts leathery-shelled creatures known as lemnai. It pierces its prey with its sharp front claws or snaps limbs with its powerful jaws. The acklay's ferocity and insatiable appetite makes it a common creature in arena fights on Geonosis.

ACKLAY (FROM VENDAXA)

FOUR REPTILE RUN-INS

Many Jedi Knights and Masters have had dramatic encounters with the galaxy's more ferocious reptiles:

- **KIT FISTO**
  Attempting to infiltrate General Grievous's fortress, Kit Fisto is ambushed by Gor, a giant roggwart, but manages to slay the deadly beast.

- **ANAKIN SKYWALKER**
  Capturing the Zillo Beast is too much for a single Jedi; even Anakin Skywalker struggles. It takes help from Mace Windu and an army of clone troopers to bring it down.

- **OBI-WAN KENOBI**
  In the Geonosian Arena, the terrifying acklay proves a formidable opponent for a Jedi with no lightsaber.

- **LUKE SKYWALKER**
  Luke Skywalker avoids the fate of many before him in Jabba's rancor pit, when he uses a massive blast door to smash the beast's skull.

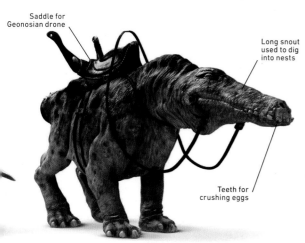

Saddle for Geonosian drone

Long snout used to dig into nests

Teeth for crushing eggs

ORRAY (FROM GEONOSIS)

RONTO (FROM TATOOINE)

UNTAMABLE BEASTS

Nobody can tame the most fearsome reptiles. After being caught by Mace Windu and Anakin Skywalker, the huge Zillo Beast escapes and rampages through Coruscant. On Dagobah, a dragonsnake tries to eat R2-D2, but after finding his metal body inedible, decides to spit him back out again!

GUARD

Massiffs have been domesticated to guard Tusken Raider villages. They use their sharp spines for defence, and thanks to their large eyes, they can see well in the dark. During the Clone Wars, the Republic Army trains massiffs to track the enemy.

DANGEROUS PETS

For those seeking extreme pets, reptiles offer some exciting choices. General Grievous calls his pet roggwart Gor, and uses it to guard his fortress. Jabba the Hutt enjoys watching his rancor, Pateesa, devour those that offend him!

RANCOR (NAMED PATEESA)

Size of spines indicates age

rmoured hide

MASSIFF (FROM VARIOUS LOCATIONS)

Mechanical arms attached to Gor's body

Flesh-tearing fangs

Powerful leg muscles

ROGGWART (NAMED GOR)

Tail can impale attackers

ZILLO BEAST (FROM MALASTARE)

DRAGONSNAKE (FROM DAGOBAH AND NAL HUTTA)

REPTAVIANS

Exhibiting traits of both reptiles and birds, reptavians are swift animals. Kaadu carry Gungan warriors into battle, and to tame one is a sign of reaching adulthood. Varactyls are fearless steeds, willing to jump down perilous slopes f asked by their rider.

KAADU (FROM NABOO)

VARACTYL (NAMED BOGA, FROM UTAPAU)

PIKOBI (FROM VARIOUS LOCATIONS)

WET HABITAT SENTIENTS

Most sentient beings need water to thrive, but some need more access to it than others. The majority of sentients live on land, where frequent rain sustains lush forests, gardens and grassy plains. Some species hail from worlds covered in water.

FORESTS AND JUNGLES

Woodlands are cradles of life for many diverse beings. Sharp claws help Trandoshans and Wookiees climb tall trees; Ithorians tend forest gardens; and Gamorreans chop down forests to clear land for farming.

PHINDIAN (MORALO EVAL)   TRANDOSHAN (BOSSK)

AQUATIC/AMPHIBIOUS

MOST COMFORTABLE UNDER WATER

Certain species prefer to be immersed in liquids, but they can also survive in airy environments without environmental suits or breathing apparatus. They are identified by crusher claws, flippers and fins, gills, flailing tentacles, beaks or bulbous eyes.

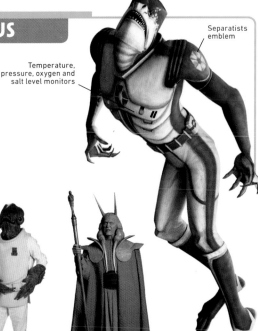

Separatists emblem

Temperature, pressure, oxygen and salt level monitors

EWOK   GAMORREAN (GHANA GLEEMORT)   TROIG (FODE AND BEED)

ISHI TIB (WAKS TRODE)   QUARREN (ZIL TOPUR)   MON CALAMARI (ADMIRAL ACKBAR)   CHAGRIAN (MAS AMEDDA)   KARKARODON (GENERAL RIFF TAMSON)   SELKATH (MANTU)   PATROLIAN (ROBONINO)   NAUTOLAN (KIT FISTO)

ON WATER

Kaminoans like Lama Su live in cities on the ocean's surface. They travel between cities on the backs of flying whales called aiwhas. They only concern themselves with off-worlders if the opportunity is profitable.

ON, UNDER AND AROUND WATER

The lives of some species revolve around water, but they don't necessarily need it to thrive. Gungans of Naboo, Bivall of Protobranch and Aqualish of Ando build cities on, under or near water, but they can settle far away from it.

ANKURA GUNGAN (BOSS NASS)

SWAMPS

Species that make their homes in bogs need to cope with a variety of conditions. Pads on Rodian fingers help them climb aquatic vegetation; Pa'Lowick snouts can act as snorkels; and Hutt tails propel them through muck, where legs would just get stuck.

PA'LOWICK (SY SNOOTLES)

An unfortunate chuba being eaten as a snack

Tail supported by skeletal spine

HUTT (JABBA)

LARGE KAMINOAN EYES

KAMINOAN (PRIME MINISTER LAMA SU)

AQUALISH (NANK TUN)   BIVALL (SIONVER BOLL)   GUNGAN (CAPTAIN TARPALS)   RODIAN (DAR WAC)

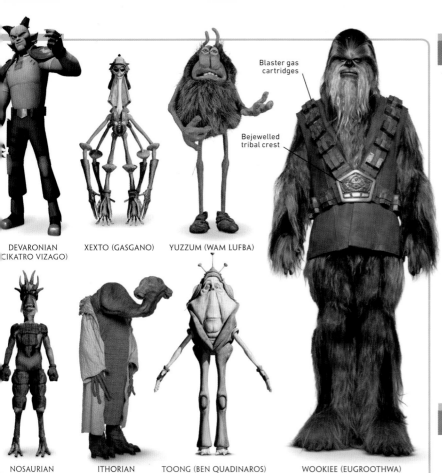

DEVARONIAN
(CIKATRO VIZAGO)

XEXTO (GASGANO)

YUZZUM (WAM LUFBA)

Blaster gas
cartridges

Bejewelled
tribal crest

GARDENS

Some garden species have
very interesting anatomies.
Cereans have binary brains
which let them consider
both sides of any issue,
simultaneously. Quermians
have a secondary brain
inside their torso,
which also supports
an often-hidden,
second pair of arms!

QUERMIAN (YARAEL POOF)

CEREAN (KI-ADI-MUNDI)

NOSAURIAN
(CLEGG HOLDFAST)

ITHORIAN

TOONG (BEN QUADINAROS)

WOOKIEE (EUGROOTHWA)

MARSHES AND TUNDRAS

Pantorans live in elegantly
sombre cities, amidst dreary,
marshy tundra stretching away
beneath overcast skies. Artiodacs
are native to the cold, swampy
world of Artiod Minor – but their
planet was overrun by Zygerrian
slavers, who scattered the
Artiodacs across the galaxy.

PANTORAN
(BARON PAPANOIDA)

ARTIODAC
(STRONO "COOKIE" TUGGS)

PLAINS AND GRASSLANDS

Felucians are peaceful farmers,
growing nysillim and other crops.
Lurmen are peace-seeking
immigrants to the plains of
Maridun, pulled into the Clone
Wars by the Jedi and Separatists.
Amani are also immigrants,
to the planet Utapau, where
they live as hunter-gatherers.

LURMEN (TUB)

FELUCIAN (CASISS)

AMANI (AMANAMAN)

ICE AND SNOW

The Whiphids of Toola and the Talz
of Orto Plutonia are protected from
freezing weather with shaggy fur
coats. Ortolans fend off the cold by
eating their way to a blubbery body.
Many Snivvians simply escape their
icy world by working as gangsters
and bounty hunters on other planets.

ORTOLAN (MAX REBO)

WHIPHID (J'QUILLE)

SNIVVIAN (GEEZUM)

TALZ (THI-SEN)

DRY HABITAT SENTIENTS

Many intelligent beings live in dry ecosystems and rocky habitats. Their ability to survive in difficult environments helps them adapt more easily off-world. Many of these species are also physically and intellectually suited to becoming Jedi.

Loose skin on neck inflates for mating calls

The latest fashion on Coruscant

Hind limbs used as arms and hands

Forelimbs used as legs and feet

DUG (SEBOCA)

DESERTS AND WASTELANDS

Species living in dry environments need protection from the sun. Some, such as Kitonaks, are protected by tough skin, while Tusken Raiders and Jawas have to wear protective clothing. Geonosians take shelter inside their hives.

Missing right eye

Insect-like wings

GEONOSIAN (SUN FAC)

KITONAK (DROOPY McCOOL)

KADAS'SA'NIKTO (J'OOPI SHÉ)

KAJAIN'SA'NIKTO (MA'KIS'SHAALAS)

TUSKEN RAIDER

TWI'LEK (OOLA)

JAWA

SWOKES SWOKES (GRAGRA)

UGNAUGHT (YOXGIT)

MIRIALAN (LUMINARA UNDULI)

MOUNTAINS, ROCKS AND HEIGHTS

MOUNTAINS AND HIGH ELEVATION

Wings allow Toydarians to hover high above the mud flats of their home planet. Both they and the Bardottans perch their palaces on tall peaks. Muun construct their empire high amidst snowy mountains. Togruta immigrants build colonies in the cliffs on Kiros in pursuit of art and beauty.

TOYDARIAN (WATTO)

BARDOTTAN (QUEEN JULIA)

MUUN (SAN HILL)

TOGRUTA (SHAAK TI)

ROCKY

Some species have claws to make climbing in rocky environments easier. A Thisspiasian's long tail lets them slither over rocks with ease. Aleena build homes among the rocks, but must be careful not to disturb the creatures of the underworld below.

Thick hair deters biting cygnat swarms

Second pair of arms hidden beneath robes

Seated on coiled serpent-like lower half

THISSPIASIAN (OPPO RANCISIS)

ZYGERRIAN (ATAI MOLEC)

ALEENA (RATTS TYERELL)

IKTOTCHI (SAESEE TIIN)

TEEDO

KLATOOINIAN (BARADA)

WEEQUAY (HONDO OHNAKA)

LAVA

Mustafarians come in two forms: stocky southerners and tall, thin northerners. Both have tough, blaster-resistant skin, but they still need armour to protect themselves while they work around lava.

SOUTHERN MUSTAFARIAN

NORTHERN MUSTAFARIAN

ADAPTIVE SENTIENTS

Despite the huge size of the galaxy, some species manage to explore and settle in alien worlds with conditions that are very different from their own. Genetic variations can help them survive in new lands, and technology may make the colonisation process more comfortable.

BREATHING FILTERS REQUIRED

Explorers from different atmospheres harness technology to survive on other planets. Kel Dors breathe a helium mixture unique to their world, while Gands breath ammonia. Dybrinthe offworlders and Skakoans wear suits to simulate the higher pressures and temperatures that they are used to.

GAND (ZUCKUSS)

KYUZO (EMBO)

EASILY MISTAKEN FOR PESTS

Surprising visitors sneak into palaces and starships, where they reside in the shadows. They may look like vermin, but these intelligent beings survive by earning the favour of their new masters – or by taking advantage of them!

SIC-SIX

KOWAKIAN MONKEY-LIZARD (SALACIOUS CRUMB)

HOOVER (ATTARK)

ANACONDAN (MORLEY)

FROG-DOG (BUBOICULLAAR/BUBO)

WOL CABASSHITE (GHOEL)

SKAKOAN (WAT TAMBOR)

DYBRINTHE (ATHGAR HEECE)

KEL DOR (PLO KOON)

DARKNESS AND CAVES

Even on dark worlds and in dim caves, intelligent beings have adapted and developed. On Utapau, Pau'an and Utai live peacefully in shadowy sinkhole cities. Elom live in frozen grottos, while sophisticated Sullustans dwell in underground cities, surrounded by lava. Umbarans have taken this evolutionary challenge to the extreme – living on a world locked in eternal night.

PAU'AN (LAMPAY FAY)

UMBARAN (SLY MOORE)

SULLUSTAN (NIEN NUNB)

ELOM (TANUS SPIJEK)

UTAI (SENIN VANT)

UNKNOWN

Some species are so secretive that much about them remains a mystery. Clawdites are difficult to find due to their shape-shifting abilities. Yaddle and Yoda are the only two known examples of their species.

CULISETTO (DENGUE SISTER)

CLAWDITE (ZAM WESELL)

MIKKIAN (TIPLAR)

BESALISK (DEXTER JETTSTER)

SPECIES UNKNOWN (YADDLE)

VURK (COLEMAN TREBOR)

DELPHIDIAN (DURTEEL HAZA)

COLONIAL

Some species have migrated and adapted to dominate many worlds, perhaps because they lost their own homeworlds – or they merely enjoy exploring. Humans are one of the most successful and their diverse cultures include Mandalorian, Naboo, Ming Po, Corellian and Alderaanian.

Duros faces have no noses

HUMAN
(HERMIONE BAGWA)

DEVELOPED CLONE

BITH (FIGRIN D'AN)

KOORIVAR
(PASSEL ARGENTE)

NEIMOIDIAN
(LUFA DANAK)

LASAT (GARAZEB
"ZEB" ORRELIOS)

FALLEEN (ZITON MOJ)

DUROS (CAD BANE)

THEELIN
(LATTS RAZZI)

ABEDNEDO (ELLO ASTY)

GRAN (MAWHONIC)

CHEVIN (EPHANT MON)

BARAGWIN (HERMI ODLE)

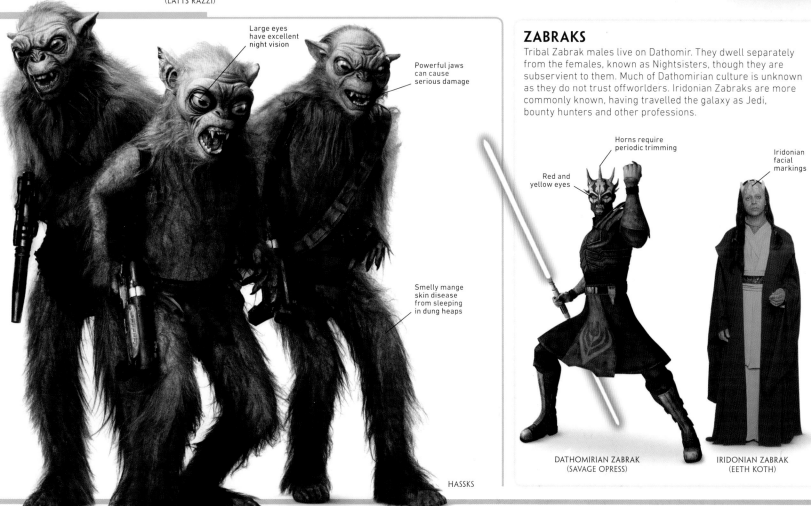

Large eyes have excellent night vision

Powerful jaws can cause serious damage

Smelly mange skin disease from sleeping in dung heaps

HASSKS

ZABRAKS

Tribal Zabrak males live on Dathomir. They dwell separately from the females, known as Nightsisters, though they are subservient to them. Much of Dathomirian culture is unknown as they do not trust offworlders. Iridonian Zabraks are more commonly known, having travelled the galaxy as Jedi, bounty hunters and other professions.

Horns require periodic trimming

Iridonian facial markings

Red and yellow eyes

DATHOMIRIAN ZABRAK
(SAVAGE OPRESS)

IRIDONIAN ZABRAK
(EETH KOTH)

41

PLANTS

There is a wide variety of plant life across the galaxy, and each species has evolved to suit its surroundings. As well as being a source of food for many life-forms, plants can also help maintain a planet's atmospheric balance, by producing oxygen and other gases.

A DAY ON MORTIS
On Mortis, the flow of the Force is particularly strong and greatly affects plant life. Through the day, the abundant and flourishing landscape becomes wilted and withered by the dark side of the Force. At nightfall, violent storms remove the last traces of greenery, but with dawn comes the light side of the Force. This renews the vegetation and the cycle of life begins again.

SHRUBS

Shrubs live on surface water, growing in open areas and under sparse tree cover. In the highlands of Onderon, tee-musses feed on purple kings' crown. Blue Hutt's tongue collects water in conical fronds, which form protected pools used by breeding amphibians.

PURPLE KINGS' CROWN (BACKGROUND), BLUE HUTT'S TONGUE (FOREGROUND), HIGHLAND SCRUB, ONDERON

SKELETON WEED, ONDERON

JUNGLE UNDERGROWTH, ONDERON

TREES

Trees can stabilise soil, prevent erosion, filter pollution and produce breathable air. They also provide homes and nesting opportunities for many species. On Balnab, umbrella trees play host to troops of hesten, the native primates. Greater cake trees fill with flocks of starklebirds taking shelter on Saleucami.

TORRENT WISP TREES, CONCORDIA

GREATER CAKE TREE, SALEUCAMI

UMBRELLA TREE, BALNAB

ARBOZOIC TREE, ALEEN

ORNAMENTAL

Gardens are a popular way to create peaceful, reflective spaces in busy cities. The trees of the Royal Academy on Mandalore are pruned to resemble the architecture of the capital city, Sundari. They are much older than their small size suggests.

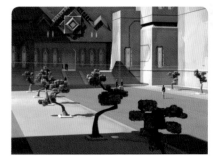

TREES OF TE ANI'LA, ROYAL ACADEMY, MANDALORE

CROPS

Common crops like medicinal nysillim and calarantum root grow across the galaxy. The Clone Wars cut off agricultural trade between many systems. Confiscation of farmland by the Empire also results in shortages and price rises.

CUT LAWQUANE'S FARM, SALEUCAMI

NYSILLIM CROPS, FELUCIA

SLAVE SHADE, ZYGERRIA

FLOWERS

Flowers are essential to plant reproduction. Some flowers are actually edible: Marina Rung flowers form a part of the momong's varied diet on Wasskah. Towering Bith may smell unpleasant, but their buds vibrate in charming harmony for several hours before they open.

MARINA RUNG FLOWERS, WASSKAH

TOWERING BITH, SALEUCAMI

QUEENS' HEARTS, NABOO

SPINY PLANTS

Rancor bramble is native to Trandosha's Wasskah Moon. It is host to many parasitic plants, and is a habitat for momongs, convorees and other creatures. On Dathomir, burial pods of deceased Nightsisters hang from the woody barbs of Grave Thorn.

RANCOR BRAMBLE FOREST (NIGHT), WASSKAH

RANCOR BRAMBLE FOREST (DAY), WASSKAH

GRAVE THORN, DATHOMIR

CORAL

ABOVE GROUND

Coral forests are hot and dry environments, where reptiles and insects thrive. Rugosan coral forests are nurseries for neebray, which fly into space when they are adults. Atollon coral provides roosts for convorees and hiding places for dokma.

RUGOSAN KING CORAL, RUGOSA

PLATED TREE CORAL, ATOLLON

TRIDENT CLUSTER CORAL, RUGOSA

UNDERWATER

On the marine planet Mon Cala, coral grows in large colonies. Their hard skeletons form reefs that provide shelter, breeding and feeding grounds for varied sea life. Reefs tend to thrive in areas bathed in the light of Mon Cala's twin suns. However, some hardier species live deep below the surface.

CORAL REEF, MON CALA

DEEP SEA REEF, MON CALA

TAKE COVER

When Jedi Master Yoda must sign a treaty with the Toydarian king on Rugosa, Count Dooku arranges an ambush to disrupt their plans. The dense maze of coral forests provide excellent cover for Asajj Ventress and her battle droids to spring the ambush and prove their worthiness as allies to the king.

WEIRD AND WONDERFUL

TENTACLED

Some plants have evolved tentacles, which allow plants to collect pollen or nutrients, uproot themselves and even defend themselves. Umbara's flora is especially aggressive – not many have escaped the tendrils of death's embrace.

DIANOGA'S KISS, BALNAB

DEATH'S EMBRACE, UMBARA

BIOLUMINESCENT

Some plants are bioluminescent, which means they can create light. These species thrive in environments where light is limited, such as caverns or deep sea beds. Bioluminescence attracts pollinators, or even prey, in the darkness. Bioluminescent plants are common on Umbara, a world in perpetual shadow or in the deepest, darkest depths of Mon Cala's oceans.

ZABRAK SPINES, UMBARA

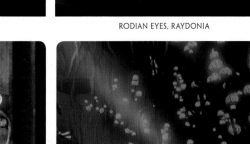

RODIAN EYES, RAYDONIA

CARNIVOROUS

Carnivorous plants tend to grow in soils with poor nutrients. Reeksa survive in low-light environments at the bottom of canyons by capturing live prey and digesting them. The reeksa root is an essential ingredient in the cure for the Blue Shadow Virus.

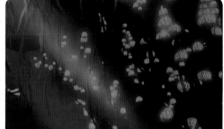

POOLA BLOSSOMS, RODIA

KWAZEL CANDY, RODIA

REEKSA PLANT, IEGO

HISTORY

Galactic history tells a story of political scheming, duelling factions, powerful militaries and ancient orders. The decades that follow the Battle of Naboo are a particularly tumultuous time. This period is marked both by grand events on a galactic scale, as well as personal stories of triumph and betrayal. As the fate of the entire galaxy hangs in the balance, these events show us that just a few individuals have the power to change the course of history forever.

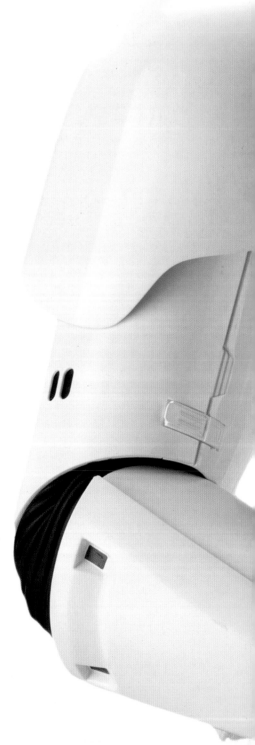

FIRST ORDER
STORMTROOPER

TIMELINE

The reemergence of the Sith changes the course of history in the galaxy. Darth Sidious manipulates politics to bring about the devastating Clone Wars. An Empire rises, but the fire of rebellion burns in those that they oppress. Decades later, the First Order rises from the Empire's ashes...

CRISIS ON NABOO
Tensions mount as the Trade Federation blockades the planet of Naboo.

SITH SIGHTING
The first Sith is spotted in 1,000 years when Darth Maul appears on Tatooine.

RACE FOR FREEDOM
Against all odds, child slave Anakin Skywalker wins his freedom in the Boonta Eve Classic podrace.

APPRENTICE VS MASTER
Vader is gravely injured in a duel with Obi-Wan on Mustafar.

A NEW EMPIRE
Palpatine becomes Emperor of a harsh new regime.

ORDER 66
Clone troopers slaughter "treacherous" Jedi across the galaxy.

ARISE DARTH VADER
Thanks to Darth Sidious, Anakin's fall to the dark side is complete.

UTAPAU CHASE
Obi-Wan tracks down General Grievous and kills him on Utapau.

CAPITAL KIDNAP!
The Jedi rescue Chancellor Palpatine during the Battle of Coruscant. Anakin slays Dooku.

TWINS FOR PADMÉ
A newborn boy, Luke, and a girl, Leia, are taken separately into hiding after their mother passes away.

JEDI HUNTERS
The Emperor forms the Inquisitorius, a new group for tracking down Force-sensitives.

SEEDS OF REBELLION
Separate cells of rebel fighters begin to form, including the crew of the *Ghost*.

FULCRUM UNMASKED
Ahsoka Tano reveals herself to be the fledgling rebels' spymaster, Fulcrum.

DUEL ON MALACHOR
Ahsoka must face her old mentor again in a savage battle with Vader.

THRAWN ON THE HUNT
Grand Admiral Thrawn is tasked with eliminating the Lothal rebels.

SLAYING THE GIANT
Ewoks and rebels defeat Imperial soldiers and destroy the Death Star's shield generator on Endor.

SECOND SUPERWEAPON
The rebels realise the Empire is building a second Death Star.
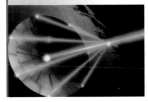

END OF AN ERA
Yoda breathes his last and becomes one with the Force. He is the last of the Republic's Jedi Order to pass away.

RESCUING HAN
Leia saves Han from Jabba's palace with the help of the other rebels.

FATHER AND SON
Luke is shocked to discover that Vader is his father!

A FROZEN PRIZE
The captive Han Solo is frozen in carbonite on Cloud City and delivered to Jabba the Hutt.

BACK INTO THE LIGHT
Darth Vader chooses to save his son, Luke, and slays the Emperor, but cannot save himself.

VICTORY AT ENDOR
The destruction of the second Death Star marks a turning point in the Galactic Civil War.

PEACE TREATY
After the Battle of Jakku, the Empire surrenders and signs a peace treaty. The New Republic is established and restores democracy.

NEW ENEMIES
The First Order rises from the ashes of the Empire to reclaim power from the New Republic.

NEW FRIENDS
Rey saves the droid BB-8 on Jakku. First Order runaway Finn joins them and they escape together.

AWAKENING IN THE FORCE
Supreme Leader Snoke senses a powerful new Force user.

REPUBLIC TRIUMPH
The Republic scores a victory over the droid army at the Battle of Naboo.

DEATH OF A JEDI
Jedi Master Qui-Gon Jinn is slayed by Darth Maul, before Obi-Wan Kenobi defeats him.

ASSASSINATION ATTEMPT
Bounty hunter Zam Wesell tries and fails to assassinate Senator Padmé Amidala with kouhuns.

CLONE ARMY DISCOVERY
Obi-Wan discovers a secret army of clones being built on Kamino.

STATE OF EMERGENCY
Chancellor Palpatine gains emergency wartime powers from the Senate.

ARENA RESCUE
The surprise arrival of the Clone Army saves the Jedi and the Republic at the Battle of Geonosis.

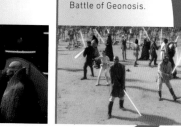

AHSOKA IS FRAMED!
Ahsoka faces the death sentence for plotting to bomb the Jedi Temple. She is pardoned but chooses to leave the Jedi Order.

NIGHTSISTER MASSACRE
Mother Talzin and Asajj Ventress survive a devastating attack on the Nightsister clan on Dathomir.

SENATE CRISIS
Bounty Hunter Cad Bane holds senators hostage. Jedi intervention prevents too much bloodshed.

SUCCESS FOR SNIPS
Anakin's new Padawan Ahsoka Tano proves herself in the Battle of Christophsis.

SECRET WEDDING!
The secret union between Anakin and Padmé breaks the Jedi Code.

BEGUN THE CLONE WAR HAS
Yoda rescues Obi-Wan and Anakin, but Count Dooku evades capture.

SECRET WEAPON UNMASKED
Plans for a terrifying new Imperial superweapon are uncovered by rebels.

STANDING FIRM
Vader interrogates Princess Leia Organa over the location of the stolen Death Star plans.

A GOOD DAY'S TRADING FOR JAWAS
Owen Lars and Luke Skywalker buy two droids, R2-D2 and C-3PO, on Tatooine.

MISSION ACCOMPLISHED!
The Death Star plans reach Obi-Wan, thanks to R2-D2's determination.

EXTERMINATION OF ALDERAAN
The Death Star destroys the planet of Alderaan, Leia's homeworld.

NOBLE SACRIFICE
Obi-Wan is defeated in a duel with Darth Vader and becomes one with the Force.

DINNER WITH DARTH VADER
Han, Leia and Chewie are betrayed by Lando Calrissian and captured by Vader on Bespin.

SURPRISE ON DAGOBAH
Luke discovers Jedi Master Yoda and begins his Jedi training.

OVERWHELMED
The rebels must flee Hoth after the Imperials launch an attack.

SPOTTED!
An Imperial probe locates the secret rebel base on the icy planet of Hoth.

CHAIN REACTION
Luke destroys the Death Star in his X-wing during the Battle of Yavin.

DEATH STAR ESCAPE
Luke, Han Solo, Leia and Chewbacca escape the Death Star with R2-D2 and C-3PO.

LIGHTSABER DISCOVERY
Rey finds Luke's lightsaber in Maz Kanata's castle on Takodana.

HORROR ON HOSNIAN
The entire Hosnian system is destroyed by a First Order superweapon, Starkiller Base.

RESISTANCE SAVES THE DAY
Poe Dameron leads the Resistance to defeat the First Order on Takodana.

PATRICIDE!
Kylo Ren slays his father, Han Solo.

STARKILLER KILLED
The Resistance destroys the First Order superweapon.

LUKE FOUND
Rey tracks down Luke Skywalker and returns his lightsaber.

GALACTIC POLITICS

In a galaxy brimming with countless people, there are many conflicting political viewpoints. When two sides cannot find enough common ground, like the Separatists and Republic, or the First Order and the Resistance, one outcome is inevitable – war.

SUNSETS ON DEMOCRACY

For countless generations, the Republic and the Jedi Order have maintained peace. But as the evil Sith manipulates galactic events, both the Republic and the Jedi's very existences are threatened and war consumes the galaxy.

| THE REPUBLIC | VS | THE SEPARATISTS |

| THE EMPIRE | VS | THE REBEL ALLIANCE |

| THE RESISTANCE | VS | THE FIRST ORDER |

REPUBLIC ERA → **IMPERIAL ERA** → **NEW REPUBLIC ERA**

REPUBLIC ERA

THE REPUBLIC

The Republic has existed for over a thousand years and is the dominant political institution in the galaxy. It is a representative parliament that governs the galaxy from Coruscant. The Chancellor is the Republic's leader and is elected by the senators.

SYMBOL OF THE REPUBLIC

THE SENATE

Hundreds of elected senators, who represent various worlds, sectors or trade groups across the galaxy, hold seats in the Galactic Senate. This body mediates disputes between its members and votes on laws.

GRAND ARMY OF THE REPUBLIC

Unknown to the Republic, the Kaminoans create a clone army on the order of a maverick Jedi, who foresaw that the Republic would need a military force. The clones protect the Republic from the Separatists.

THE SEPARATISTS

Following the Naboo Crisis, a number of planets declare their independence from the Republic. Known as the Separatists, they object to excessive taxes and rampant corruption in the Senate. The Separatists' cause is funded by massive corporations, including the Trade Federation.

SYMBOL OF THE SEPARATISTS

SEPARATIST LEADERSHIP

The charismatic Count Dooku leads the Separatists and is their Head of State. Dooku sits on the secret Separatist Council with representatives from each of the greedy businesses that contribute credits to the cause.

SEPARATIST ARMY

In stark violation of Republic laws, the Separatists' droid army is made up of a variety of deadly droid models. The Separatists use it to wage war against the Republic, but are ultimately defeated and their units are deactivated.

THE JEDI ORDER

The Jedi Order is a group of Force-sensitives that follow the light side of the Force and have existed for thousands of years. They uphold peace and democracy in the galaxy primarily through diplomacy, but will occasionally resort to lightsabers.

SYMBOL OF THE JEDI ORDER

JEDI GENERALS

Guardians of peace for the Republic, the Jedi become leaders of the clone army during the Clone Wars. While the war rages, the Jedi have no time to consider whether this role is truly the will of the Force. Few survive the Jedi Purge at the war's end.

THE SITH

The Force-sensitive Sith are the Jedi's ancient enemies. They follow the dark side of the Force and have two main aims: rule the galaxy and wipe out the Jedi. While the Jedi believed them to be extinct, they have been plotting in secret to carry out their evil goals.

SYMBOL OF THE SITH

DARTH SIDIOUS

During the Clone Wars, the Sith Lord Darth Sidious poses as the caring Republic leader, while his apprentice, Count Dooku, leads the Separatists. By the war's end, the Jedi and the Separatist leadership have been destroyed and the Republic has become a Sith dictatorship.

IMPERIAL ERA

THE EMPIRE

In contrast to the democratic Republic, the Empire is a dictatorship with ultimate power resting in the hands of the Emperor. On a regional level, sector governors, called Moffs, oversee different areas. They exploit these planets for resources to construct Imperial vehicles and weapons.

SYMBOL OF THE EMPIRE

THE SITH

After the near annihilation of the Jedi Order in the Jedi Purge, the Sith now rule the galaxy. While Darth Sidious rarely leaves Coruscant, he unleashes his ferocious apprentice, Darth Vader, to hunt down any enemy Force users or rebel insurgents.

IMPERIAL ARMY

The faceless uniformity of the Imperial Army is an awe-inspiring sight. Regular displays of military might are meant to make citizens feel secure and stop any rebellious ideas from taking root. Those who do oppose the Empire are swiftly silenced by the Imperial Army.

THE REBEL ALLIANCE

Formed by Mon Mothma and Bail Organa in secret, the Rebel Alliance is an organisation dedicated to restoring democracy to the galaxy. Not only do they wage a civil war against the Empire, they also assist civilian populations suffering under Imperial oppression.

SYMBOL OF THE REBEL ALLIANCE

JEDI

Not all Jedi die during the Jedi Purge, and some actively fight the Empire. Two Jedi Council members, Obi-Wan Kenobi and Yoda, survive and hide in the hope that one of Anakin Skywalker's hidden children can be trained as a Jedi and restore balance to the Force.

REBEL ALLIANCE MILITARY

Humans and aliens from many different ways of life and political views fight side by side in the Rebel Alliance's military. Operating a wide array of starfighters and weapons, they must work together to overcome the superior might of the Empire.

NEW REPUBLIC ERA

THE NEW REPUBLIC

Soon after their victory at Endor, the Rebel Alliance forms a new democratic government called the New Republic. Rebel leader Mon Mothma serves as the first Chancellor. The Galactic Civil War ends when a peace treaty is signed with the remaining Imperial forces.

SYMBOL OF THE NEW REPUBLIC

NEW REPUBLIC SENATE

Like the Old Republic, the New Republic elects senators and a Chancellor, but its capital also shifts by election. The Senate was based on Hosnian Prime until the Senate, as well as the system, are wiped out by the First Order.

> " WHAT WE'VE DISCOVERED SHOULD TRANSCEND PETTY POLITICAL BICKERING "
> **SENATOR LEIA ORGANA**

THE FIRST ORDER

The First Order arises from the remains of the Empire. It begins politically as part of the New Republic, but its growing military might is hidden in the Unknown Regions. Led by the enigmatic Supreme Leader Snoke, they bide their time, building a new military force and formulating a plan for galactic domination.

SYMBOL OF THE FIRST ORDER

DARK FORCES

While the Sith were destroyed at the Battle of Endor, other dark side Force users have arisen. Snoke corrupts Darth Vader's grandson, Ben Solo. Ben, now known as Kylo Ren, wipes out the fledgling Jedi Order – only his uncle, Luke Skywalker, remains.

FIRST ORDER ARMY

Compared to the Imperial Army, the First Order operates a smaller force. The First Order army uses more advanced weaponry and vehicles than its predecessors. Its troops are also incredibly skilled and have been training since birth.

THE RESISTANCE

Formed by General Leia Organa, the Resistance is a small military force that answers to no government. It is comprised of valiant volunteers, who are deeply concerned about the growing power of the evil First Order.

SYMBOL OF THE RESISTANCE

RESISTANCE FORCES

The Resistance military is intended to monitor the First Order and battle them if they threaten to break the peace treaty. The Resistance comprises Rebel Alliance veterans and new volunteers who are eager to protect the New Republic.

THE FORCE

Although the galaxy is again without a Jedi Order and the shroud of darkness has descended, hope is not lost. It exists in good people who still believe in the Jedi. Through them, the Force burns like a beacon in the night, and with it the hope that democracy will prevail.

THE SENATE

The Republic is a representative democracy, with the capital located on Coruscant. Member worlds send senators there to vote on all manner of issues, and elect a Supreme Chancellor to lead. While some politicians are genuine in their desires to make improvements, others are altogether corrupt and seek only personal gain.

The Senate Building houses the Galactic Senate Chamber, countless smaller meeting rooms, senatorial offices (including those of the Chancellor) and other administrative facilities. A docking bay along the side of the building allows easy access for diplomats.

SYMBOL OF THE GALACTIC SENATE

AT THE TIME OF THE BATTLE OF NABOO

SUPREME CHANCELLOR

Supreme Chancellor Finis Valorum deliberates during the blockade of Naboo but fails to act. Queen Amidala blames him for the invasion of her world, and is easily manipulated by Senator Palpatine of Naboo, to push for a vote of no confidence in Valorum.

SUPREME CHANCELLOR VALORUM

SENATORIAL AIDES

The careers of aides are closely tied to their senators, unless they can eventually replace them. When Valorum is ousted, Sei Taria loses her position, even after attempts to join Palpatine.

LIANA MERIAN, ALDERAAN AIDE

AGRIPPA ALDRETE, ALDERAAN AIDE

STONROY SOMA, ALDERAAN AIDE

SEI TARIA, VALORUM'S AIDE

IANAD CISMA, CONSORT TO TOONBUCK TOORA

SENATORS

Member worlds, systems, sectors or other political alliances may send representatives to the Senate. Amplifying microphones, droid hovercams and automatic translators guarantee that their concerns may be heard – but not that anything will necessarily be done about them.

Horns intimidate political foes

Hands folded in determined manner

VICE CHAIR MAS AMEDDA

SHEEV PALPATINE

AKS MOE

HOROX RYYDER

EDCEL BAR GANE

ORN FREE TAA

TOONBUCK TOORA

LOTT DOD

YARUA

MOT-NOT RAB

PASSEL ARGENTE

IN-DEPTH ANALYSIS

The Senate Chamber is the centre of political activity. Debates involving the entire Senate are held here, as is voting. Every political body has a delegation, as do some of the many influential guilds, clans and federations that carry out business with the Senate.

THE SENATE CHAMBER

HOVERPODS

The Senate Chamber is lined with 1,024 repulsorlift hoverpods, arranged in concentric circles. The delegation from Naboo uses their pod to address the assembly. It can detach from the wall and travel around the chamber. Sometimes delegations must share, but a central podium is reserved for the Supreme Chancellor and the Vice Chair to address the chamber and preside over meetings.

AT THE OUTBREAK OF THE CLONE WARS

SUPREME CHANCELLOR

Once Palpatine achieves his goal of becoming Supreme Chancellor, he continues to manipulate and scheme to gain greater influence. He orchestrates the Clone Wars as an excuse to build his own army, weaken the Jedi and accumulate more political power.

ALL AN ILLUSION

Darth Sidious secretly controls both sides of the Clone Wars, as Supreme Chancellor of the Republic, and as the secret Sith Master directing Count Dooku, leader of the Separatist Alliance. No matter which side wins, Palpatine will remain in control of the galaxy. Dooku doesn't realise that he is just a disposable pawn in Palpatine's treacherous game.

SUPREME CHANCELLOR PALPATINE

JUNIOR REPRESENTATIVE

While senators serve entire worlds or sectors, Junior Representatives act on behalf of a specific minority. Jar Jar Binks proves himself a hero during the Battle of Naboo, and so is elected to represent the Gungans as part of the Naboo delegation.

JAR JAR BINKS

SENATORS

The Clone Wars are a trying time for the Senate. Some delegations, such as the Quarren, Aqualish and Koorivar senators, withdraw from the Republic and join the Separatists. Other senators remain in the Republic – some are still loyal, but a few make secret deals that undermine the failing democracy.

PADMÉ AMIDALA

ISTER PADDIE

LEXI DIO

PO NUDO

ORN FREE TAA

TUNDRA DOWMEIA

ASK AAK

PASSEL ARGENTE

SENATORIAL AIDES

In difficult times, rivalries spring up between aides, even those working for the same senator. Supi and Pampy are loyal aides to Orn Free Taa, but there is a bitter rivalry between them, with both vying for the favour of the senator. It is has been said that Sly Moore can influence others through the power of her mind. This may be true, but could equally be mere rumour, circulated by lesser aides who are jealous of her growing power.

SUPI, ORN FREE TAA'S AIDE

PAMPY, ORN FREE TAA'S AIDE

SLY MOORE, SENIOR ADMINISTRATIVE AIDE

WARTIME SENATE

As the Clone Wars rage on, senators and representatives continue to govern from deep within the massive Senate Building on Coruscant. Divisions form between them as they debate the merits of the ongoing conflict, but little do they know they are all pawns in Palpatine's sinister game!

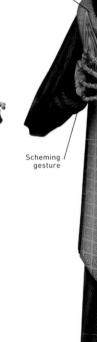

Senatorial mitre worn proudly

Neimoidian hat represents the wearer's position and stature

LOYAL TO THE CONFEDERACY

SENATORS

The senators who support Supreme Chancellor Palpatine – elected a decade before the Clone Wars, and staying far longer than his original term – have become greedy and selfish. They use their positions to serve their own interests. Some seek profit in war or political opportunities in working with the Separatists, while others are bribed or blackmailed into promoting the Chancellor's goals.

Mantle of the supreme representative

Scheming gesture

GUME SAAM

TAL MERRIK

PASSEL ARGENTE

PO NUDO

RUSH CLOVIS

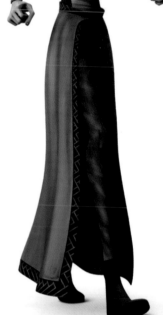

NIX CARD

LOTT DOD

PRO-WAR

Steady supporters of the Chancellor, these pro-war senators vote in favour of expanding the Grand Army of the Republic. They claim to be patriotic to the Republic, and will question or threaten other senators who do not support the war.

MOT-NOT RAB

MEE DEECHI

ASK AAK

FEMA BAAB

HALLE BURTONI

AIDES

Assisting selfish senators means working behind the scenes. The aides write drafts, send sneaky messages and manage secret meetings of the politicians they serve.

NANK TUN

RUTE GUNNAY

DENARIA KEE

MEMBERS OF THE DELEGATION OF 2,000

SENATORS

The senatorial representatives known as the Delegation of 2,000 grow concerned with how Palpatine conducts the war. They want him to revoke his emergency powers so that the Senate may once again fully oversee the Republic.

MON MOTHMA   FANG ZAR   BAIL ORGANA   CHI EEKWAY   MEENA TILLS   TANNER CADAMAN   SWEITT CONCORKILL   IVOR DRAKE   GIDDEAN DANU

PADMÉ AMIDALA   TUNDRA DOWMEIA   NEE ALAVAR   MALÉ-DEE   BANA BREEMU

DIFFICULT DISCUSSION

The leaders of the Delegation of 2,000 meet with Chancellor Palpatine in his office to discuss their concerns. Palpatine is very popular among most of the Senate, so they must be careful in how they approach the conversation, as questioning his conduct could be seen as unpatriotic, or even traitorous.

AIDES

Aides to senators in the Delegation of 2,000 must be loyal, willing to keep many secrets and be ready to protect their politicians during these dark and dangerous times.

SATEEN VESTSWE, BAIL ORGANA'S AIDE   SHELTAY RETRAC, BAIL ORGANA'S AIDE   CELLHEIM ANUJO, TUNDRA DOWMEIA'S AIDE

OTHER ALLIES OF SENATOR AMIDALA

SENATORS

Senator Amidala earns the admiration and friendship of many other politicians during her time in the Senate. After her untimely and mysterious death, many attend her funeral ceremony on Naboo to pay their respects.

JUNIOR REPRESENTATIVE

If a senator is unable to perform their duties in the Senate, they can appoint a representative. Lolo Purs is a dedicated servant for her planet of Rodia, and serves alongside Senator Onaconda Farr.

SILYA SHESSAUN   KHARRUS   GEM SIRROM

Antenna detects vibrations

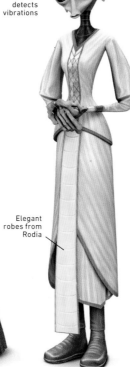

Elegant robes from Rodia

OPPOSITION TO ENHANCED PRIVACY INVASION BILL

A small group of senators want to stop a vote on the Enhanced Privacy Invasion Bill. This would give the Chancellor unprecedented ability to spy on citizens who are suspected Separatists.

DANGEROUS MEETING

Members of the opposition, led by Bail Organa and including Padmé Amidala and Philo, meet to discuss the upcoming bill. But things don't go quite to plan – during the meeting, they are held hostage by bounty hunter Cad Bane.

VEEDAAZ AWMETTH   NEB CREIP   EEUSU ESTORNII   LOLO PURS   KIN ROBB   PHILO (LEFT) AND JAKKER-SUN (RIGHT)   ONACONDA FARR   DANTUM ROOHD   RIYO CHUCHI

THE JEDI COUNCIL

The Jedi Council serves as the highest authority within the Order. Its members are chosen from among the most respected Jedi. There are always 12 members – when one member dies, another Jedi is chosen to replace them.

JEDI TEMPLE

The Jedi Order answers to the Republic, and so the Order maintains its headquarters on Coruscant, close to the Chancellor and Senate. The temple is where younglings are brought to be trained in the ways of the Force. It also houses a vast archive of ancient knowledge.

JEDI COUNCIL MEMBERS

AT THE TIME OF THE BATTLE OF NABOO

Grand Master Yoda and Jedi Master Mace Windu serve as the Council's senior members. During the invasion of Naboo, another of Yoda's species, Yaddle, sits on the Council. She is joined by legendary Jedi warriors such as Even Piell and Saesee Tiin, as well as noble thinkers Yarael Poof and Ki-Adi-Mundi. Qui-Gon Jinn is not a council member, but after his death, the Council decide to honour his wish to train Anakin Skywalker – a fateful decision.

YODA   MACE WINDU   PLO KOON   KI-ADI-MUNDI   SAESEE TIIN

AT THE TIME OF THE BATTLE OF GEONOSIS

By the time the Clone Wars erupt between the Republic and Separatists, the Council has undergone a few changes. Yaddle steps down, and Yarael Poof perishes on a mission. To replace them, the Togruta Jedi Shaak Ti joins as a new member, alongside Coleman Trebor. Trebor's membership of the Council is only brief, however, as he is killed in the Battle of Geonosis.

YODA   MACE WINDU   PLO KOON   KI-ADI-MUNDI   SAESEE TIIN

AT THE TIME OF THE JEDI PURGE

Years of brutal battles cut a swath through the Jedi Council. Although some members still hold the seats they have held since the Invasion of Naboo, with the fighting in its third year, many others have been promoted to the Council to replace fallen masters. New members include Obi-Wan Kenobi, the Nautolan Kit Fisto and Anakin himself – appointed against the wishes of the Council, but at the insistence of Supreme Chancellor Palpatine.

YODA (ESCAPES TO EXILE ON DAGOBAH)   MACE WINDU (PERISHES ON CORUSCANT)   PLO KOON (PERISHES ON CATO NEIMOIDIA)   KI-ADI-MUNDI (PERISHES ON MYGEETO)   SAESEE TIIN (PERISHES ON CORUSCANT)

IN-DEPTH ANALYSIS

The Council Chamber is situated atop a high tower of the Jedi Temple. Large windows allow in natural sunlight, bathing the Council in the light of the Force. In the round room, the Jedi Council sits in a circle. This arrangement fosters a sense that all 12 masters on the Council have equal importance.

Grand Master Yoda's chair

JEDI COUNCIL CHAMBER

FORCE TESTS

Jedi Master Mace Windu tests the young Anakin Skywalker. Mace looks at the rotating images on his viewscreen; Anakin must state what the master sees. Strong in the Force, Anakin's answers are correct, but initially the Jedi Council refuses to train him. Mace senses a conflict within the boy that makes him uneasy.

YADDLE

EVEN PIELL

OPPO RANCISIS

ADI GALLIA

YARAEL POOF

EETH KOTH

DEPA BILLABA

SHAAK TI

EVEN PIELL

OPPO RANCISIS

ADI GALLIA

COLEMAN TREBOR

EETH KOTH

DEPA BILLABA

SHAAK TI
(PRESUMED KILLED)

OBI-WAN KENOBI
(ESCAPES TO EXILE
ON TATOOINE)

ANAKIN SKYWALKER
(FALLS TO THE DARK SIDE)

STASS ALLIE
(PERISHES ON SALEUCAMI)

KIT FISTO
(PERISHES ON CORUSCANT)

AGEN KOLAR
(PERISHES ON CORUSCANT)

COLEMAN KCAJ
(PRESUMED KILLED)

THE JEDI

For over a thousand generations, the Jedi Knights are the guardians of peace and justice in the Republic. This ancient order follows a disciplined way of life, shunning both family and romantic attachments, and the desire for personal wealth and power.

IN-DEPTH ANALYSIS

The Jedi Temple Archives form a vast warehouse of knowledge. Historical records span thousands of years and the map collection covers the entire known galaxy. Electronic and holographic information is stored on standard devices, as well as within precious Jedi holocrons. The holocrons are kept in a secure vault and watched over by temple guards.

LIBRARIAN JOCASTA NU HELPS OBI-WAN FIND INFORMATION

KEEPING THE PEACE

The Jedi serve as negotiators to defuse hostile situations and find peaceful resolutions. Although Qui-Gon and Obi-Wan fail with the Trade Federation, they successfully negotiate with the good-natured Gungans. Jedi mind tricks serve as temporary solutions, but only persuasive arguments bring long-term results.

NON-COUNCIL MEMBERS

JEDI MASTERS

Normally a Jedi must attain the rank of master in order to sit on the High Council, except in the unusual case of Anakin Skywalker. Not all serve on the Council though – some are regularly sent off-world on sensitive and sometimes dangerous missions.

QUI-GON JINN

LUMINARA UNDULI

AAYLA SECURA

BOLLA ROPAL

CIN DRALLIG

HALSEY

QUINLAN VOS

SHADDAY POTKIN

JEDI KNIGHTS

Knights are the first level of mature Jedi, after they have completed their trials and proven their devotion to the light side of the Force. Although they are meant to be keepers of the peace, they become military generals during the Clone Wars.

ANAKIN SKYWALKER

BULTAR SWAN

MELIK GALERHA

MA'KIS'SHAALAS

FALLEN JEDI

Sometimes Jedi go astray, such as former Jedi Master Count Dooku. He begins training as Yoda's apprentice, and becomes master of Qui-Gon, but later abandons the Jedi to serve Sith Lord Darth Sidious. Meanwhile, in a bout of evil madness, Pong Krell leads his own troops to slaughter in the hope of joining the Sith, too.

Hand-woven tunic made on Vjun

Clasp of Serenno silver

COUNT DOOKU

Wattle of adult Besalisk

Upper arms are dominant over lower ones

PONG KRELL

CONSULAR JEDI

Some Jedi devote themselves to the study of science or diplomacy, and withdraw from duties concerning combat and warfare. Doctor Rig Nema is dedicated to medicine. Jocasta Nu serves as the Chief Librarian of the Jedi Temple Archives.

JOCASTA NU

DOCTOR RIG NEMA

JEDI-IN-TRAINING

PADAWANS

Padawans are taken on as apprentices by Jedi and receive personal instruction. They may wear a Padawan braid as a symbol of their status. Padawans typically accompany their masters on missions for a number of years to gain vital practical experience.

OBI-WAN KENOBI

IMA-GUN DI

TIPLEE

TIPLAR

ANAKIN SKYWALKER

AHSOKA TANO

TERA SINUBE

LUKE SKYWALKER

J'OOPI SHÉ

BARRISS OFFEE

EZRA BRIDGER

NAHDAR VEBB

PABLO-JILL

KANAN JARRUS

YOUNGLINGS

Younglings leave their families to join the Jedi and begin their training in classroom settings. They must pass a series of tests, and some complete a rite of passage known as "The Gathering", in which they find a kyber crystal and construct their first lightsaber.

SAYLIND DONELS

IN-DEPTH ANALYSIS

A Jedi's duty is to pass on what he or she has learned. Younglings become Padawans when they are ready for combat training and intensive studies. A Padawan must pass a series of trials to become a Jedi Knight. A knight must attain their full potential to become a master. The oldest and wisest Jedi holds the title of Grand Master, humbly teaching the most junior members of the Order – the younglings.

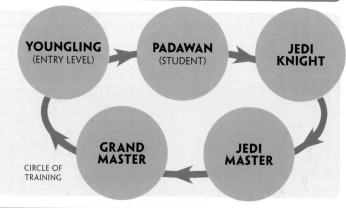

YOUNGLING (ENTRY LEVEL) → PADAWAN (STUDENT) → JEDI KNIGHT → JEDI MASTER → GRAND MASTER →

CIRCLE OF TRAINING

YOUNGLINGS RETURN FROM "THE GATHERING" TO MAKE THEIR OWN LIGHTSABERS

THE SITH

Shrouded in mystery, this ancient line of Force users have hidden themselves for over 1,000 years, working in the shadows. Their strength is drawn from the dark side of the Force by harnessing hate, anger and fear. Sith Masters demand loyalty from their apprentices, but betray them if stronger potential is sensed in another.

Traditional Sith red blade

Vestigial horn

Undertunic

Sith clothing allows freedom of movement

SITH WARRIORS

Limitless strength, power and victory – these are the values that each Sith warrior upholds, as part of the Sith Code. They must be willing to do anything to achieve their goals as a Dark Lord of the Sith. In ancient times, Sith Lord Darth Bane created his own streamlined Sith Order, to control ambitious infighting. His descendants, such as vicious apprentice, Darth Maul, continue to strike fear in the hearts of other beings.

Protective gloves

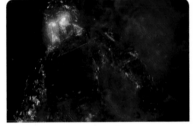

DARTH BANE

DARTH SIDIOUS

Double-bladed lightsaber

" LET THE HATE FLOW THROUGH YOU "
DARTH SIDIOUS

Loose-fitting trousers for high kicks

Heavy-action boots

DARTH TYRANUS (AKA COUNT DOOKU)

DARTH VADER

DARTH MAUL

THE PATH TO THE DARK SIDE

Younger apprentices make ideal candidates for Sith Masters to turn to the dark side, as they lack the emotional control of a fully trained Jedi Knight. Inexperienced youth is easier to taint and twist to the purposes of the Sith. Both Anakin Skywalker and his son Luke were trained at an older age than most Jedi, but they make very different choices when facing the temptations of Darth Sidious.

DARTH SIDIOUS WITH LUKE SKYWALKER

DARTH SIDIOUS WITH ANAKIN SKYWALKER

ALWAYS TWO THERE ARE...
Darth Bane's Rule of Two creates a powerful dynamic by limiting the Sith to only one master and one apprentice at any one time. The master holds the power, and the apprentice craves it. With Count Dooku dead at Anakin Skywalker's hands, the way is clear for Darth Sidious to take a new apprentice: Anakin kneels to pledge himself to his new master, and rises as Darth Vader. Sith don't always follow this rule though; some have been known to take their own apprentice while they still have a master.

IN-DEPTH ANALYSIS
Maul is the first known apprentice of Sidious, until he disappears on Naboo. After quitting the Jedi Order, Dooku becomes Sidious's next protégé. Dooku trains several successive apprentices, before Sidious orders Anakin Skywalker to kill Dooku. Eventually, Anakin takes Dooku's place and becomes Darth Vader.

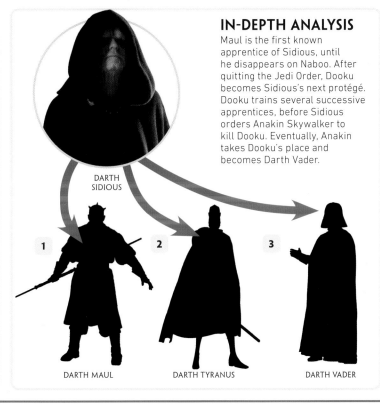

DARTH SIDIOUS

1 DARTH MAUL   2 DARTH TYRANUS   3 DARTH VADER

THE DARKNESS SHOWS
As windows to the soul, eyes reflect the emotions harnessed by the Sith. When rage and anger seethe inside a dark side user, their eyes may burn yellow with a fiery-red rim. On Mustafar, Darth Vader's eyes glow as he massacres the Separatist leaders, but return to normal when his wife Padmé Amidala arrives.

SIDIOUS'S TRANSFORMATION
As Darth Sidious becomes more deeply embroiled in his plot to control of the galaxy, his changing face shows the strain of leading a double life. When Jedi Master Mace Windu deflects Sidious's Force lightning back at him, his face is forever transformed. The disfigurement further fuels Sidious's hatred for the Jedi, as it serves as a reminder of his own weakness and mortality.

 SENATOR PALPATINE

 SUPREME CHANCELLOR PALPATINE

 DARTH SIDIOUS

 EMPEROR PALPATINE

THE SEPARATISTS

The Confederacy of Independent Systems, known by some simply as the Separatist Alliance, is a union of planets and sectors who declare independence from the Republic. During the Clone Wars, the Separatists try to topple the Republic, but collapse once the Empire seizes control.

DROID ARMY
For waging war with the Republic, the Separatists use an enormous metal army, supplied by the Techno Union and led by the cyborg, General Grievous. These disposable droids swarm across Republic planets, exerting the will of their masters through military might.

HEAD OF STATE

Darth Sidious leads the Separatist group from behind the scenes. Count Dooku may be the head of state and public face of the Separatists throughout most of the Clone Wars, but he secretly follows his master Sidious's orders.

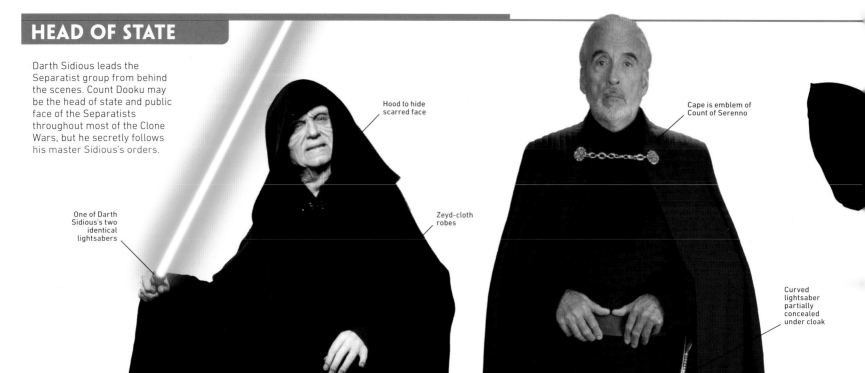

Hood to hide scarred face

Cape is emblem of Count of Serenno

One of Darth Sidious's two identical lightsabers

Zeyd-cloth robes

Curved lightsaber partially concealed under cloak

DARTH SIDIOUS

COUNT DOOKU

SEPARATIST PARLIAMENT

During the Clone Wars, Count Dooku sets up a civilian group of law-makers to govern the Alliance's growing number of worlds and deal with civil matters. Separatist Congress Leader Bec Lawise presides over the Parliament, which meets on the planet Raxus. Mina Bonteri joins Padmé Amidala to press for peace, but is thwarted by Dooku's plots and schemes.

BEC LAWISE, SEPARATIST CONGRESS LEADER

SENATOR BY BLUSS

SENATOR VOE ATELL

MINA BONTERI, SENATOR FOR ONDERON

LUX BONTERI, SENATOR FOR ONDERON AFTER HIS MOTHER MINA'S DEATH

SEPARATIST COUNCIL

The Separatist Council is the secret group behind the Separatist Parliament and deals with military operations and funding. Mostly fuelled by self-interest and greed, these members represent big businesses. Leaders of the Trade Federation, the Techno Union, the InterGalactic Banking Clan, the Corporate Alliance and the Commerce Guild are all attracted to the Separatist cause. However, they are all ultimately destroyed by it.

GENERAL GRIEVOUS, COMMANDER OF THE DROID ARMY

NUTE GUNRAY, VICEROY OF THE TRADE FEDERATION

RUNE HAAKO, SETTLEMENT OFFICER FOR THE TRADE FEDERATION AND LIEUTENANT TO NUTE GUNRAY

ARCHDUKE POGGLE THE LESSER OF GEONOSIS

WAT TAMBOR, FOREMAN OF THE TECHNO UNION

SAN HILL, CHAIRMAN OF THE INTERGALACTIC BANKING CLAN

SHU MAI, PRESIDENT OF THE COMMERCE GUILD

PO NUDO, FORMER REPUBLIC SENATOR

Cranial horn

Crocheted hood

Brooch of Luristan

Shimmerbird tongue robe

PASSEL ARGENTE, MAGISTRATE OF THE CORPORATE ALLIANCE (LEFT), AND HIS AIDE DENARIA KEE

REGIONAL POLITICS

The galaxy contains countless planets, civilisations and factions, each with its own unique set of complex political structures and political figures. When war breaks out throughout the galaxy, it forces these local leaders to choose sides and stand up for their people!

NABOO ROYALTY

A king or queen rules Naboo, serving a short term while assisted by a council of trusted advisors. Multiple queens rule in the final years of the Old Republic, and monarchs continue to serve throughout the days of the Empire.

QUEEN AMIDALA

QUEEN JAMILLIA

NATIONAL LEADERS

REPUBLIC ALLIES

Unlike senators who gather on Coruscant to represent their people, these leaders are primarily focused on governing their local planet. Some, like King Katuunko of Toydaria, must be convinced to join the Republic's cause during the Clone Wars.

CHIEF TARFFUL OF KASHYYYK

QUEEN APAILANA

QUEEN NEEYUTNEE

PRIME MINISTER LAMA SU OF KAMINO

CHIEFTAIN THI-SEN OF A TALZ TRIBE ON ORTO PLUTONIA

PRINCE LEE-CHAR OF MON CALA

DUCHESS SATINE KRYZE OF MANDALORE

KING KATUUNKO OF TOYDARIA

KING MANCHUCHO OF ALEEN

CHAIRMAN CHI CHO OF PANTORA

CHAIRMAN PAPANOIDA OF PANTORA

GUNGAN LEADERSHIP

Below the oceans of the planet Naboo, the chief leader of the Gungans is known as a Boss and is head of the Gungan High Council. They have the power to send their army to war or banish trouble-making citizens.

BOSS NASS

BOSS LYONIE

SEPARATIST ALLIES

Some local leaders see the rise of the Separatists as an opportunity to gain power or reclaim former glory. King Rash of Onderon is just a puppet for the Separatists, while Queen Scintel of Zygerria hopes to rebuild her illegal slave empire.

NOSSOR RI OF THE QUARREN ISOLATION LEAGUE

KING SANJAY RASH OF ONDERON

QUEEN MIRAJ SCINTEL OF ZYGERRIA

QUEEN KARINA THE GREAT OF GEONOSIS

ARCHDUKE POGGLE THE LESSER OF GEONOSIS

REBEL ALLIES

The Empire makes enemies of local leaders as it expands its grip on the galaxy. Alien species are poorly treated under Imperial rule, forcing many of them to flee to the Outer Rim or join the Rebellion to fight back.

NEUTRAL

Some cultures attempt to remain neutral, preferring to avoid galactic politics and war. Tee Watt Kaa leads a pacifist colony on Maridun. Big Hay-Zu does not care about galactic politics and will do or say almost anything to remain dictator of the Patitites on Patitite Pattuna.

CHIEF CHIRPA OF BRIGHT TREE VILLAGE ON ENDOR

GOVERNOR RYDER AZADI OF LOTHAL

BARON ADMINISTRATOR LANDO CALRISSIAN OF CLOUD CITY ON BESPIN

MOTHER TALZIN, LEADER OF THE NIGHTSISTERS

TEE WATT KAA, LEADER OF THE LURMEN PEOPLE

PIETER, CHIEFTAIN OF A MING PO TOWN ON CARLAC

JABBA THE HUTT, LEADER OF THE HUTT GRAND COUNCIL ON TATOOINE

QUEEN JULIA OF BARDOTTA

KING RAMSIS DENDUP OF ONDERON

BIG HAY-ZU, LEADER OF THE PATITITES ON PATITITE PATTUNA

BESPIN BETRAYAL

Lando Calrissian is forced to temporarily side with the Empire and give up Han, Leia and Chewbacca to Darth Vader. It is a tough choice that Lando must make in order to protect the people of Cloud City. Only after he orders the city's evacuation can Lando reveal his true loyalty to his friends and attempt to save them.

LEADERS OF POLITICAL MOVEMENTS

While all of these leaders are passionate about their cause, few have fought as long, or sacrificed as much, as Cham Syndulla. The head of the Twi'lek resistance on Ryloth, Cham and his people wage war with the occupying Separatists, and later the Imperials.

PRE VIZSLA OF THE DEATH WATCH

CHAM SYNDULLA OF THE TWI'LEK RESISTANCE

KRISMO SODI OF THE KAGE WARRIORS

SAW GERRERA OF THE ONDERON REBELS

STEELA GERRERA OF THE ONDERON REBELS

THE EMPIRE

Officially, the Empire seeks to instill order, control and rule of law to a chaotic galaxy. Secretly, the Empire is a part of a plot by a Dark Lord of the Sith, who seeks unlimited power to destroy the Jedi, overthrow the Republic and rule the galaxy with an iron fist.

LET ME SEE YOUR IDENTIFICATION!
As the Empire expands, citizens on occupied planets must adapt to the harsh reality of rule. Compulsory parades, taxes, propaganda, heavily armed garrisons and forced relocations become a formidable part of daily life. Obi-Wan Kenobi and Luke Skywalker experience security checks by armed stormtroopers firsthand on the remote planet Tatooine.

LEADERS

Emperor Sheev Palpatine is the undisputed head of the New Order. He appoints political leaders, known as Moffs, to manage his Empire. Darth Vader serves as his apprentice and enforcer, fulfilling any number of secret requests for the shadowy Sith Lord.

MOFF TIAAN JERJERROD

GRAND MOFF WILHUFF TARKIN

EMPEROR PALPATINE

DARTH VADER

IMPERIAL ORGANISATIONS

THE IMPERIAL SECURITY BUREAU
The ISB is a secretive agency tasked with investigating matters of Imperial security and loyalty. There are ISB agents on most ships in the Imperial fleet, ready to arrest and question anyone who they suspect of treason. ISB interrogators are said to have a 95 percent success rate in extracting information.

COLONEL WULLF YULAREN

AGENT KALLUS

> " I LIVE ONLY TO SERVE THE EMPEROR, AS DO WE ALL. "
> ## DARTH VADER

THE INQUISITORIUS
Darth Vader leads a small and mysterious order known as the Inquisitors, who aim to hunt down the remaining Jedi after Order 66. Chief among them is the Grand Inquisitor, a former Jedi temple guard who now serves the dark side. Other Inquisitors are simply titled brother or sister. The Inquisitors also seek out other Force-sensitive individuals who might threaten the Emperor's rule. If they refuse to serve the Empire, they face elimination!

GRAND INQUISITOR

SEVENTH SISTER

FIFTH BROTHER

EIGHTH BROTHER

RIVALRY IN THE RANKS
When Admiral Konstantine and Agent Kallus fail to capture the rebel crew of the *Ghost* on Seelos, the Inquisitors are only too ready to step in and finish what the Navy and ISB started. Palpatine encourages competition within his own ranks – as long as they achieve his desired result.

REBELS

Outnumbered and against all odds, heroic people band together in an ever-growing rebellion that seeks to end the tyrannical Imperial rule. For almost all of them, their fight is personal. They've experienced firsthand how terrible the Empire can be, and they have an inspiring reason to fight back.

EARLY REBEL MOVEMENT

REBELS

The crew of the starship *Ghost* begins challenging the Empire long before they learn about a larger rebel organisation. While fighting back on the planet Lothal, their defiant deeds come to the attention of rebel leaders – who are uniting patchwork cells into a more formal Rebel Alliance.

EZRA BRIDGER

KANAN JARRUS

GARAZEB "ZEB" ORRELIOS

HERA SYNDULLA

SABINE WREN

CHOPPER

REBEL ALLIES

The Rebel Alliance can't afford to be choosy about who it works with. To stand a chance against the Empire, it comes to accept the help and firepower of those such as Jedha civilians Chirrut Îmwe and Baze Malbus, and even the hacking and piloting skills of Empire defector Bodhi Rook.

THE REBEL ALLIANCE

LEADERSHIP

Mon Mothma is a longtime opponent to Palpatine and serves as a civilian leader in the Alliance. She works alongside military leaders like Admiral Ackbar, who focus their efforts on building a fighting force that can stand up to the enormous Imperial war machine.

MON MOTHMA

ADMIRAL ACKBAR

KEY REBELS

Although they don't always agree at first, these rebels put their differences aside during some of the rebellion's most impossible missions. Working together, they destroy two Death Star space stations, disrupt one of the largest Imperial weapons factories on Cymoon 1 and even hijack an Imperial Star Destroyer, the *Harbinger*.

JYN ERSO

CASSIAN ANDOR

K-2SO

LUKE SKYWALKER

PRINCESS LEIA ORGANA

R2-D2

HAN SOLO

C-3PO

CHEWBACCA

BODHI ROOK

CHIRRUT ÎMWE

BAZE MALBUS

REBEL BASES

The Alliance tries to stay one step ahead of the Imperials by concealing their bases within the natural surroundings of each planet they inhabit. The Empire takes a very different approach, preferring their buildings to be uniform and imposing – recognisable displays of Imperial might.

REBEL ALLIANCE'S ECHO BASE, HOTH

A NEW ERA

At the end of the Galactic Civil War, a New Republic is formed and a peace treaty – the Galactic Concordance – is signed with the last remnants of the Empire. The new Senate then passes the Military Disarmament Act, which leaves them woefully unprepared when the sinister First Order emerges from the Unknown Regions.

THE NEW REPUBLIC SENATE

Led by Chancellor Villecham, the Senate's main concern is preserving peace in the New Republic. It is no longer based on Coruscant; instead it convenes on different member worlds, chosen in elections. Unfortunately, the Republic is naïve to the First Order's ambitions.

CHANCELLOR LANEVER VILLECHAM

SENATOR BRASMON KEE OF ABEDNEDO

SENATOR ANDRITHAL ROBB-VOTI OF TARIS

SENATOR GADDE NESHURRION OF UBARDIA

SENATOR THANLIS DEPALLO OF COMMENOR

SENATOR NAHANI GILLEN OF UYTER

SENATOR THADLÉ BERENKO OF NABOO

SENATOR ZYGLI BRUSS OF CANDOVANT

THE FIRST ORDER

SUPREME LEADER

Snoke is the leader of the First Order. He is aligned with the dark side of the Force, and encourages Kylo Ren, his most promising apprentice, to utilise the teachings of both the light and dark sides of the Force to his advantage.

SUPREME LEADER SNOKE

LEADERS OF HATE

This trio carry out Snoke's orders. Captain Phasma's stormtroopers spread violence and hate. General Hux has spent his life learning to hate the New Republic, and Kylo Ren has embraced the dark side. He and Hux are now rivals for power within the First Order.

CAPTAIN PHASMA

GENERAL ARMITAGE HUX

KYLO REN

RALLY ON STARKILLER BASE

General Hux rallies his troops with enthusiasm, making a show of unwavering patriotism and commitment. This bolsters the morale of his troops, who are about to watch the First Order annihilate billions of innocent beings.

ATTACK ON JAKKU

Service to the First Order requires total devotion. Stormtroopers must never question Phasma's orders, even when it means massacring helpless villagers. For Phasma, loyalty is the most important quality.

THE RESISTANCE

LEADERSHIP

Although Leia Organa helps build the New Republic, she is labelled a fear monger by her political rivals because of her warnings about the emerging First Order threat. As founder and general of the Resistance, she returns to her old role as freedom fighter.

RESISTANCE FIGHTERS

For some, it is friendship, loyalty and love that draws them to the Resistance, rather than a political cause. Han Solo and Chewbacca reunite with Leia after falling in with Rey, Finn and BB-8. Han's ultimate motivation is to save Rey and his son, Ben – the man who became Kylo Ren.

GENERAL LEIA ORGANA

BB-8

REY

FINN

POE DAMERON

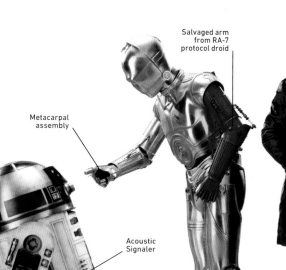

R2-D2

Metacarpal assembly

Salvaged arm from RA-7 protocol droid

Acoustic Signaler

C-3PO

HAN SOLO

CHEWBACCA

IN COMMAND

Years of conflict and political manoeuvring have turned General Organa into an expert strategist. At the Resistance command centre on D'Qar, she monitors operations during the attack on Starkiller Base, just as she did from Yavin 4 and Hoth in previous battles. Admiral Statura stands by her side, as does her protocol droid C-3PO and long-time friend and ally, Admiral Ackbar.

HUNT FOR LUKE

Poe Dameron is sent on a special mission by General Organa to find her brother, Luke Skywalker. The First Order is looking for Luke too, making Poe's mission a very treacherous one. Poe's journey leads him to a strange culture known as the Crèche on the planet Ovanis, then to Grakkus the Hutt, before meeting with the traveller Lor San Tekka on Jakku. San Tekka finally gives Luke's location to Poe.

MILITARY OFFICERS

No matter in which division they serve, all officers must exhibit leadership qualities, earn the respect of their troops and be confident, even in the face of great difficulties. These brave men and women must be prepared to make life-or-death decisions on behalf of the troops they command.

THE GRAND ARMY OF THE REPUBLIC

ADMIRALS

Admirals Yularen and Kilian are fine examples of the Republic Navy's best officers. Both demonstrate bravery: Yularen's long career includes being wounded at the Battle of Ryloth, while Admiral Kilian valiantly stays with his battle cruiser as it crash-lands on Vanqor.

ADMIRAL YULAREN

ADMIRAL KILIAN

CLONE COMMANDERS

Kaminoan cloners and bounty hunter trainers handpick clone soldiers with high potential to become commanders. These leaders form strong bonds, both with their men, and with the Jedi generals whom they serve.

COMMANDER CODY

COMMANDER NEYO

COMMANDER WOLFFE

COMMANDER GREE

COMMANDER BLY

COMMANDER BACARA

CAPTAIN REX

THE SEPARATISTS' DROID ARMY

COMMANDERS

Living commanders act as the highest leaders of the Separatist droid army. Many are skilled tacticians who study the fighting style of their Jedi opponents. General Grievous and Riff Tamson are brutal combatants who will fight face-to-face if necessary.

GENERAL GRIEVOUS

COMMANDER RIFF TAMSON

BATTLE DROID COMMANDER

GENERAL LOK DURD

CAPTAIN MAR TUUK

ADMIRAL TRENCH

GENERAL WHORM LOATHSOM

THE IMPERIAL MILITARY

NAVY OFFICERS

Of all of the Imperial Navy's highest-ranking officers, perhaps the most thoughtful is Grand Admiral Thrawn. One of the few non-humans to rise in the Empire's ranks, he studies both the art of war and the cultures of the enemies he hunts.

GRAND ADMIRAL THRAWN

ADMIRAL KENDAL OZZEL

ADMIRAL FIRMUS PIETT

CAPTAIN LORTH NEEDA

ADMIRAL KASSIUS KONSTANTINE

ARMY OFFICERS

The Imperial Army – with hordes of stormtroopers, walkers and other ground troops under its command – is unparalleled in galactic history. Its officers must be ruthless and willing to do whatever it takes to ensure Imperial victory.

GENERAL CASSIO TAGGE

GENERAL MAXIMILIAN VEERS

COMMANDANT CUMBERLAYNE ARESKO

TASKMASTER MYLES GRINT

THE REBEL ALLIANCE

CHANCELLOR

Mon Mothma – once a senator and leader of the Rebel Alliance – becomes the first new Chancellor in decades following the Emperor's defeat. She has the difficult task of rebuilding the Galactic Senate, which was disbanded before the Battle of Yavin.

MON MOTHMA

ADMIRAL

Admiral Ackbar begins his distinguished career as a captain in the military on his home planet of Mon Cala. Decades later, he serves as admiral in the Rebellion, leading his mighty MC80 starcruiser flagship, the *Home One*.

ADMIRAL ACKBAR

GENERALS

Alliance generals play a vital role in planning the Rebellion's strategy to combat the Empire. General Dodonna is one of the ranking officers at Base One on Yavin. After its discovery, he leads the Alliance's efforts to find a new planet suitable for another hidden base.

GENERAL CARLIST RIEEKAN

GENERAL JAN DODONNA

GENERAL AIREN CRACKEN

GENERAL CRIX MADINE

THE FIRST ORDER

SENIOR OFFICERS

General Hux serves as the leading strategist for the First Order and Captain Phasma commands its stormtroopers. Kylo Ren sits outside the formal command structure, but wields great power as Snoke's apprentice.

GENERAL ARMITAGE HUX

CAPTAIN PHASMA

KYLO REN

OFFICERS

Though very few of them remember life during the Empire, officers of the First Order are deeply devoted to restoring stability to the galaxy. They are trained in secret, deep within the Unknown Regions of the galaxy.

COLONEL DATOO

LIEUTENANT DOPHELD MITAKA

LIEUTENANT RODINON

CHIEF PETTY OFFICER UNAMO

PETTY OFFICER THANISSON

IN-DEPTH ANALYSIS

Uniform armbands display the First Order's nostalgic rank insignia system, emblazoned with the names of famous individuals and units from the Empire. These are written in Aurebesh, and include the name "Tarkin" for the rank of major, "Kaplan" for the rank of colonel and "Dillon" for the rank of captain.

GENERAL RANK INSIGNIA

ADMIRAL RANK INSIGNIA

COLONEL RANK INSIGNIA

MAJOR RANK INSIGNIA

CAPTAIN RANK INSIGNIA

LIEUTENANT RANK INSIGNIA

SERGEANT RANK INSIGNIA

SQUAD LEADER RANK INSIGNIA

THE RESISTANCE

COMMANDERS

General Organa recruits her most trusted military allies to help her lead the Resistance. While many younger citizens do not remember the Emperor's terrible reign, these commanders know firsthand how dangerous the First Order could be for the New Republic.

GENERAL LEIA ORGANA

ADMIRAL STATURA

ADMIRAL ACKBAR

MAJOR TASLIN BRANCE

MAJOR CALUAN EMATT

DOCTOR HARTER KALONIA

IN-DEPTH ANALYSIS

The rank insignia of the Resistance is simple and streamlined. Red indicates officers in the army, while blue indicates rank in the Resistance navy. When officers in the New Republic join the Resistance, their rank often carries over. Technicians, dispatchers and other lower-ranking Resistance personnel at the main base on D'Qar wear no visible rank insignia at all.

GENERAL RANK INSIGNIA

COLONEL RANK INSIGNIA

CAPTAIN RANK INSIGNIA

MAJOR RANK INSIGNIA

LIEUTENANT RANK INSIGNIA

COMMANDER RANK INSIGNIA

SOLDIERS

Whether you call them soldiers, ground troops, infantry or "grunts", these proud and loyal fighters put themselves in harm's way in order to serve their cause. They must rely on their equipment and training for survival, almost as much as they rely on one another.

Phase I helmet design

DC-15 rifle

CLONE FLAMETROOPER

Utility belt carries spare blaster magazines

Stark white plates show Kaminoan design aesthetics

THE REPUBLIC'S CLONE ARMY

PHASE I CLONE TROOPERS

When the Republic's Clone Army takes to the battlefields at the start of the Clone Wars, they wear standardised armour known as Phase I. Infantry spend most waking hours in their armour, which is issued to them during their training on Kamino.

CLONE (WITHOUT ARMOUR)

CLONE RIOT TROOPER

PHASE I CLONE TROOPER

CLONE SCUBA TROOPER

CLONE GUNNER

THE REBELS

Rebel infantry groups are equipped with a vast array of stolen, smuggled or cobbled-together equipment. Combat in different environments on countless worlds across the galaxy means that rebel units rarely look alike. On Hoth, rebel troops don padded snow gear, while on Scarif, camouflage is a necessity for the rogue rebel commando team.

REBEL HOTH TROOPER

CORPORAL TONC

PHASE II CLONE TROOPERS

As the Clone Wars drag on, troopers become more specialised, and the Republic upgrades them with increasingly advanced armour types, known collectively as Phase II. In most units, clones customise their new armour with colour patterns signifying their personalities, and the units in which they proudly serve.

PHASE II CLONE TROOPER

SHOCK TROOPER

ADVANCED RECON COMMANDO

501ST LEGION TROOPER

21ST NOVA CORPS GALACTIC MARINE

Large visor offers excellent visibility

Woodland camouflage pattern

Pouches hold supplies for extended missions

Tall boots protect legs in tall vegetation

41ST ELITE CORPS SCOUT TROOPER

THE IMPERIAL ARMY

When the Republic becomes the Galactic Empire, the soldiers who serve in its army change as well. Rather than manufacturing clone soldiers, the Empire uses propaganda and conscription to recruit human soldiers from across the galaxy.

DASHING DISGUISE

Trapped on board the Death Star, Han Solo and Luke Skywalker use deception to evade the Imperials. In a daring ruse, they hide in plain sight using stormtrooper armour. The sneaky rebels move freely around a battle station filled with thousands of the Empire's finest troops.

Throttle and boost controls

Scout trooper trained for speeder piloting

SANDTROOPERS

Powerful engine accelerates to speeds greater than 360 kph (224 mph)

SCOUT TROOPER RIDING A 74-Z SPEEDER BIKE

LOTHAL ACADEMY FOR YOUNG IMPERIALS

For young cadets on Imperial-governed planets, it is a great honour to join academies like those on Lothal or Arkanis. While the best prospects are trained to be pilots, less capable recruits are sent to the stormtrooper corps.

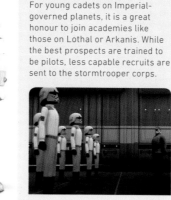

STORMTROOPER SNOWTROOPER

DEATH TROOPER TANK TROOPER SHORETROOPER

THE RESISTANCE

The small but brave band of Resistance soldiers must make do with whatever gear they can get. While not officially supported by the government of the New Republic, much of their equipment is secretly given to the Resistance as surplus.

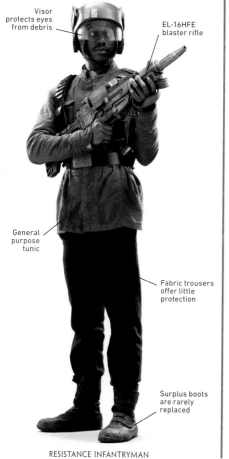

Visor protects eyes from debris

EL-16HFE blaster rifle

General purpose tunic

Fabric trousers offer little protection

Surplus boots are rarely replaced

RESISTANCE INFANTRYMAN

THE FIRST ORDER'S ARMY

Thanks to a training regime developed by Commandant Brendol Hux, and continued by his son Armitage, the soldiers of the First Order are as well trained as they are equipped. These white-armoured warriors gain a fearsome reputation wherever they go.

MEGABLASTER HEAVY ASSAULT TROOPER   RIOT CONTROL STORMTROOPER

SNOWTROOPER   FLAMETROOPER

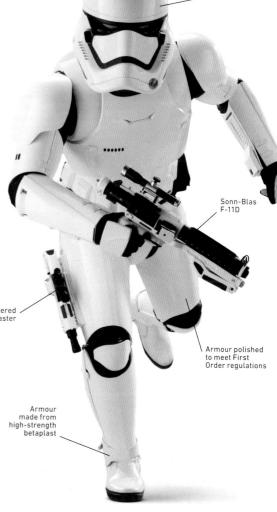

Standard First Order stormtrooper helmet

Sonn-Blas F-11D

Holstered backup blaster

Armour polished to meet First Order regulations

Armour made from high-strength betaplast

STORMTROOPER

PILOTS

Pilots are a crucial component of any military force. Whether the operation is in space or on a planet, these courageous men, women and droids take to their vehicles to fight for what they believe in – or for what they have been programmed to do.

SEPARATISTS

Many Separatist starfighters are piloted by their own internal droid brain rather than by a separate pilot. However, the Separatists do use pilots to operate other starships. Pilot battle droids are equipped with specialised programming, while Neimoidians fly the Trade Federation's numerous warships.

PILOT BATTLE DROID

NEIMOIDIAN TRADE FEDERATION BATTLESHIP PILOT

THE REPUBLIC'S CLONE ARMY AND ALLIES

WALKER PILOT

Specialised clones, named Advanced Recon Force (ARF) Troopers, pilot All Terrain Recon Transports (AT-RTs). Compared to regular troops, ARF troopers are cleverer and more adept at surviving behind enemy lines. AT-RTs are nimble walkers that can easily traverse difficult terrain.

AT-RT DRIVER

SPACESHIP PILOTS

Starships often require multiple pilots to handle flight duties. Captain Maoi Madakor works in tandem with her copilot to transport Qui-Gon Jinn and Obi-Wan Kenobi to the Trade Federation during the Naboo Crisis.

CAPTAIN MAOI MADAKOR

CAPTAIN RAYMUS ANTILLES

CAPTAIN COLTON

STARFIGHTER PILOTS

While clones fill many of the pilot positions in the Republic Army, some Jedi generals, like Plo Koon, lead their squadrons personally into battle. Naboo has its own Space Fighter Corps. This small force is instrumental in defeating the blockade of Naboo by the Trade Federation.

NABOO PILOT DINEÉ ELLBERGER (BRAVO FIVE)

STEALTH CLONE PILOT

CLONE PILOT

PLO KOON

IMPERIAL MILITARY

STARFIGHTER PILOTS

Imperial pilots fly an array of TIE-series fighters, which often lack shields. Pilots are forced to rely on the manoeuvrability of their lightweight fighters in order to survive. Mandalorian allies support the Imperial Navy in their hunt for rebels.

TIE PILOT

BARON VALEN RUDOR

FENN RAU, MANDALORIAN PILOT SKULL LEADER

TECHNICIAN

While pilots fly the gargantuan Star Destroyers, a crew of Imperial weapons technicians identify and destroy their targets. Often manning powerful turbolasers, the technicians work in teams to ensure that weapons always operate at peak efficiency.

WALKER PILOTS

The Empire uses a variety of walkers in their operations. Towering over their Imperial subjects, they are used to terrorise local populations and to maintain control. AT-AT pilots believe themselves to be unstoppable, but rebel cells have proved otherwise!

AT-DP PILOT

AT-AT PILOT

AT-ST PILOT

IMPERIAL WEAPONS TECHNICIAN

EARLY REBEL MOVEMENT

The early rebellion consists of loosely connected rebel cells. These rebels fly an assortment of ships, from cargo freighters to B-wing prototypes, and everything in between. Hera Syndulla leads the Lothal cell and makes death-defying moves in her ship called the *Ghost*.

PHOENIX
SQUADRON

HERA SYNDULLA

SABINE WREN

C1-10P "CHOPPER"

REBEL ALLIANCE

Many pilots fighting for the Rebel Alliance, like Wedge Antilles, have defected from the Empire. Others, like Nien Nunb, are smugglers who have decided to pursue nobler goals. Regardless of their origins, a great number of brave pilots sacrifice their lives for Rebel Alliance victories.

LUKE SKYWALKER

BIGGS DARKLIGHTER

WEDGE ANTILLES

GRIZZ FRIX

JEK PORKINS

KEIR SANTAGE

DEREK "HOBBIE" KLIVIAN

GARVEN DREIS

JON VANDER

DEX TIREE

DAVISH "POPS" KRAIL

DOROVIO BOLD

DAK RALTER

ZEV SENESCA

WES JANSON

TEN NUMB

NIEN NUNB

THE FIRST ORDER'S NAVY

STARFIGHTER PILOTS

In contrast to the Empire, the First Order does not view its pilots as expendable. While all First Order pilots are highly trained from childhood, only the elite become Special Forces pilots. The narrow red stripes on their helmets denote their superior status.

TIE PILOT

SPECIAL FORCES TIE PILOT

TECHNICAL STAFF

The First Order's fleet engineers perform a variety of tasks to keep their ships flying. From turbolasers to missile launchers, these engineers maintain the vast assortment of weaponry required for the First Order's military operations.

CHIEF PETTY OFFICER UNAMO

FLEET ENGINEER

THE RESISTANCE

STARFIGHTER PILOTS

General Leia Organa personally recruits pilots for the Resistance. While Nien Nunb is Leia's trusted ally from the days of the Rebel Alliance, other pilots leave the New Republic's navy to join the Resistance's ranks.

POE DAMERON

TEMMIN "SNAP" WEXLEY

JESS "TESTOR" PAVA

ELLO ASTY

NIEN NUNB

GROUND CREW

Working with limited supplies and funding, Chief Vober Dand leads the Resistance's Ground Logistics Division. This highly skilled team of volunteers works tirelessly to keep the Resistance's starfighters in operation.

VOBER DAND

BOLLIE PRINDEL

GOSS TOOWERS

KAYDEL KO CONNIX

PAMICH NERRO GOODE

WAR

Galactic history is marked by more conflicts than can be counted. The blockade of Naboo is a single event that sets into motion the Clone Wars, the rise of the Galactic Empire, the ascent of the New Republic and the foundation of the First Order. These weren't the first conflicts in the galaxy – and they certainly won't be the last!

THE CLONE WARS

BATTLE OF NABOO

The Trade Federation's invasion of Naboo increases hostilities between Separatists and the Republic during the build up to the Clone Wars. In this multiphase battle, a Naboo victory is only secured when Anakin Skywalker blows up the control ship, knocking out the droid forces on the ground.

GUNGANS BATTLE DROIDS ON THE GREAT GRASS PLAINS.

ONLY OBI-WAN KENOBI WALKS AWAY FROM A DEADLY BATTLE WITH DARTH MAUL.

QUEEN AMIDALA'S STRIKE FORCE RETAKES THE PALACE OF THEED.

FIRST BATTLE OF GEONOSIS

The first Battle of Geonosis marks the start of the Clone Wars. Although the Republic is victorious, slippery Separatist leader Count Dooku escapes when Yoda is forced to choose between saving Anakin and Obi-Wan's lives, or capturing Dooku.

JEDI ARE SURROUNDED BY BATTLE DROIDS ON GEONOSIS.

THE NEW CLONE ARMY ARRIVES TO SAVE THE JEDI.

THE JEDI DUEL DOOKU – UNTIL HE FLEES.

BATTLE OF CORUSCANT

In one of the final battles of the Clone Wars, the Separatists kidnap Chancellor Palpatine. Obi-Wan and Anakin are recalled to the capital where they defeat Dooku, duel with General Grievous and rescue the Chancellor.

OBI-WAN AND ANAKIN BATTLE THEIR WAY TO CORUSCANT.

PALPATINE IS RESCUED BY THE JEDI.

OBI-WAN BATTLES HIS WAY THROUGH TO ATTACK GRIEVOUS.

THE JEDI PURGE

Palpatine brands all Jedi as traitors. He issues Order 66, and across the galaxy clone troopers turn on their Jedi generals. The clones unquestionably obey the command, thanks to a control chip implanted into their brains. Only a scattered number of Jedi are lucky enough to survive the attack.

DURING THE BATTLE OF KASHYYYK, YODA FIGHTS OFF HIS ATTACKERS AND FLEES IN TIME.

ON MYGEETO, GALACTIC MARINES KILL JEDI KI-ADI-MUNDI.

THE 327TH STAR CORPS KILL JEDI AAYLA SECURA ON FELUCIA.

TROOPS ATTACK JEDI STASS ALLIE ON SALEUCAMI.

JEDI PLO KOON IS SHOT DOWN ABOVE CATO NEIMOIDIA.

DARTH VADER LEADS A MASSACRE IN THE JEDI TEMPLE.

THE REBELLION

BATTLE OF SCARIF

A rogue band of rebels, headed by Jyn Erso, leads the mission to steal the Death Star plans from the planet Scarif. Against all odds, they infiltrate the shield station and, with backup from Yavin 4, engage in battle with the resident Imperials. Jyn transmits the plans to the Rebel Alliance just in time.

REBEL PATHFINDERS INFILTRATE IMPERIAL PLANET SCARIF.

IMPERIALS COUNTER THE INCURSION WITH AT-ACTS.

THE REBELS' SHIP – AND ROUTE OFF SCARIF – IS DESTROYED.

BATTLE OF YAVIN

After analysing the plans to the Death Star superweapon, rebel technicians discover a single weakness in its design. Rebel pilots mount an attack on it, and with the help of smuggler Han Solo, manage to destroy the technological terror before it strikes again.

REBEL X-WINGS APPROACH THE DEATH STAR.

DARTH VADER'S TIE FIGHTER CHASES REBELS IN THE DEATH STAR TRENCHES.

A REBEL PROTON TORPEDO CAUSES TOTAL DESTRUCTION.

BATTLE OF HOTH

When the Empire discovers the Rebel Alliance's base on the ice planet of Hoth, Sith Lord Darth Vader himself leads a crushing siege. Thanks to the pilots of Rogue Squadron, many of the rebels are able to escape before the Empire storms the base.

THE REBELS ATTEMPT TO DEFEND THE SNOWY BASE.

LUKE BRINGS AN IMPERIAL AT-AT DOWN WITH A CABLE.

THE REBELS FLEE ECHO BASE UNDER IMPERIAL FIRE.

BATTLE OF ENDOR

Emperor Palpatine plans to trap and destroy the Rebel Alliance, but he does not foresee the rebels overcoming his forces – nor the betrayal of his apprentice, Vader. The battle ends with the destruction of the second Death Star and the Emperor along with it.

THE REBELS FALL INTO A TRAP, BUT EWOKS HELP THEM FIGHT.

THE ALLIANCE FLEET ATTACKS THE SECOND DEATH STAR.

PALPATINE ATTACKS LUKE – THEN VADER FIGHTS BACK.

THE RESISTANCE

BATTLE ON TAKODANA AND ASSAULT ON STARKILLER BASE

The First Order movement finally reveals itself to the wider galaxy, displaying their ruthlessness on the planets Jakku and Takodana, as they seek out the map to find Luke Skywalker. The Resistance destroys the weaponised planet, Starkiller Base, but not before it lands a terrible blow against the New Republic.

FIRST ORDER FORCES ATTACK CIVILIANS IN THE BATTLE ON JAKKU.

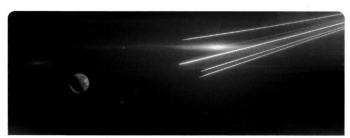
STARKILLER BASE SHOWS OFF ITS POWER, WIPING OUT THE HOSNIAN SYSTEM IN ONE GO.

ON TAKODANA, THE FIRST ORDER LAYS SIEGE TO MAZ KANATA'S CASTLE AND REY IS CAPTURED.

THE RESISTANCE DESTROYS STARKILLER BASE.

CRIMINAL ORGANISATIONS

Gangsters band together in their struggle for dominance over the criminal underworld. Lawless groups, such as the Kanjiklub and Broken Horn Syndicate thrive in areas neither the Republic nor the Empire are able to fully control.

DARTH MAUL

INTERGALACTIC ORGANISATIONS

THE SHADOW COLLECTIVE

Darth Maul creates a criminal empire in order to overthrow both the Republic and the Separatists. He gathers various underground groups, such as the Black Sun, the Pyke Syndicate and the Death Watch, with the ultimate goal of usurping his former master, Darth Sidious. He directs the Shadow Collective from Mandalore, hiding behind a puppet government.

NIGHTBROTHERS

PYKE SYNDICATE

DEATH WATCH

SAVAGE OPRESS

ZYGERRIAN SLAVE EMPIRE

The Zygerrian empire is a cruel one, built entirely upon slavery. Its queen, Miraj Scintel, aligns with the Separatists, but when she refuses to let Count Dooku execute her Jedi captives, he murders her and frames Anakin Skywalker.

QUEEN MIRAJ SCINTEL   DARTS D'NAR   ZYGERRIAN JAILER   ATAI MOLEC

BLACK SUN

THE HUTTS

The Hutts are notorious gangsters and swindlers, often trading in slaves, spice, weapons and other illegal ventures. There is much infighting and scheming among them – such as when Ziro kidnaps Rotta, the son of his nephew, Jabba, as part of a scheme to align the Hutts with Dooku.

MAMA THE HUTT

ZIRO THE HUTT

THE GRAND HUTT COUNCIL

The Hutt Council is led by the heads of five powerful crime families. Jabba and Gorga join the Shadow Collective reluctantly, after Maul attacks the Hutt Council and kills Oruba.

GARDULLA THE HUTT

JABBA THE HUTT   GORGA THE HUTT

FRONTIER ORGANISATIONS

Cikatro Vizago's Broken Horn Syndicate is based on Lothal, while Unkar Plutt and his gang operate on Jakku. Other fine examples of scum and villainy, such as Azmorigan, the Guavian Death Gang and the Kanjiklub, are treacherous marauders who travel to find the richest pickings.

GUAVIAN DEATH GANG

BROKEN HORN SYNDICATE

AZMORIGAN

UNKAR PLUTT'S GANG

UNKAR PLUTT   THUGS

KANJIKLUB

TASU LEECH   VOLZANG LI-THRULL   CROKIND SHAND   RAZOO QIN-FEE

PIRATE CREWS

HONDO OHNAKA'S CREW

Hondo Ohnaka and his gang of Weequay pirates are based on Florrum. Hondo considers Obi-Wan Kenobi and Ezra Bridger to be his friends, though his loyalties seem to shift in whichever direction has the biggest profit to be made.

PILF MUKMUK

PEG LEG PIIT   TURK FALSO   HONDO OHNAKA

SIDON ITHANO'S CREW

The Delphidian pirate, Sidon Ithano, is known by several aliases, including the Red Raider, the Blood Buccaneer and the Crimson Corsair. He and his first mate, Quiggold, fly the *Meson Martinet* freighter, and are known to harbour at a cantina on Ponemah Terminal.

PRU SWEEVANT   QUIGGOLD   CAPTAIN SIDON ITHANO

AROK THE HUTT

ORUBA THE HUTT

MARLO THE HUTT

THE COUNCIL FALTERS

When the Shadow Collective comes to negotiate with the Grand Hutt Council on Nal Hutta, the situation turns violent. Darth Maul and his gang are attacked by the Hutts' bounty hunters. Meanwhile, Marlo and Arok flee to Jabba's palace on Tatooine, where Gorga is also waiting.

CRIMINAL PROFESSIONS

In a galaxy full of warring sides and corrupt governments, there are lots of opportunities for illegal activities. Some criminals work on their own, while others have accomplices. They may even work for government officials or the Sith.

Potent drink

Protruding stomach peeks through gaping shirt

GRUMMGAR

BOUNTY HUNTERS

Most bounty hunters have no morals and will do anything for the right price. They are hired to hunt, capture or eliminate a valuable target depending on the wishes of their clients. They are loyal only to themselves – and the highest bidder.

BOBA FETT

JANGO FETT

ZAM WESELL

AURRA SING

Sturdy sofa supports immense bulk

ASAJJ VENTRESS

DERROWN

ONCA

EMBO

JAKOLI

KIERA SWAN

MANTU

GREEDO

THE BOX
Twelve bounty hunters are invited to take part in a competition held by Count Dooku at his home on Serenno. They enter "The Box", a deadly, maze-like device created by criminal mastermind, Moralo Eval. Only five bounty hunters escape alive – and are then hired to assassinate Chancellor Palpatine.

DENGAR

BOUSHH

ATHGAR HEECE

BOSSK

ZUCKUSS

TRICKSTERS AND MOLES

CON ARTISTS AND FORGERS

These criminals trade in tricks, secrets and information. The Ubdurian brothers, Prashee and Cratinus, are gamblers who use their identical appearance to their advantage. Gwellis Bagnoro is an Onodone document forger. Young Ezra Bridger lives on the streets of Lothal's Capital City, running scams to survive.

GWELLIS BAGNORO AND HIS PET BARGHEST

EZRA BRIDGER

PRASHEE AND CRATINUS

SPIES

When it comes to keeping an eye on someone, these agents are the best around. Garindan is a Kubaz spy for the Empire on Tatooine, and Bazine Netal for the First Order. But not all spies are part of the struggles of the galaxy. J'Quille is stationed in Jabba's palace in order to spy on the Hutt for one of his many rivals.

GARINDAN

J'QUILLE

BAZINE NETAL

CONTRABAND VENDORS AND THIEVES

SMUGGLERS

Smugglers sneak all sorts of illegal merchandise into forbidden areas for profit. Any law that stands in their way will be broken, regardless of who made it. They may sell the goods on the black market, deliver them to employers or use the contraband themselves.

LOBOT

TEE VA

CHEWBACCA

LANDO CALRISSIAN

DOCTOR EVAZAN

PONDA BABA

HAN SOLO

DEALERS

When restricted goods have made it past government officials to their destinations, well-connected traders take over distribution. Car Affa, Ephant Mon and Sarco Plank all work as illegal weapons dealers. Elan Sleazebaggano tours nightclubs on Coruscant, selling addictive death sticks.

EPHANT MON

CAR AFFA

SARCO PLANK

ELAN SLEAZEBAGGANO

THIEVES

Coruscant is a hustling, bustling, planet-wide city, with a shady underworld full of dark alleys. With so many people about, including many tourists from quieter planets, the conditions are ideal for sneaky thieves to prosper. Cassie Cryar uses her natural agility to steal Ahsoka Tano's lightsaber.

BANAMU

CASSIE CRYAR

IONE MARCY

CULTURE

Culture is the ideas, arts and customs of a particular group of people. From an opulent Naboo royal gown and a cantina band's lively melodies, to a Mandalorian's customised armour and a child's tooka doll, galactic culture is rich and varied. The arrangement of furniture in a Chancellor's office and the simple interior of a farmer's homestead reflect their differing cultural backgrounds. Culture also shines through in popular pastimes, such as podracing spectators rooting for a favourite winner in the arena – or gamblers making and losing their fortunes in a game of sabacc.

ROYAL OUTFITS

Monarchs' gowns are rich with symbolic embellishments, highlighting the unique culture of the planets they rule. During galactic visits, the luxurious fabrics, statement headdresses and costly jewels of queens and their handmaidens make a lasting impression.

NABOO

QUEENS

The queen represents the Naboo human population; her elaborate gowns reflect their culture. Bright red gowns project authority, whereas travelling gowns are more subdued, and showcase the planet's array of fabrics.

CLOAK AND HEADDRESS, QUEEN JAMILLIA

Feather-crested Shiraya fan headdress

Mourning beads symbolise Naboo's tears

Funeral gown

Trim embossed with royal emblem

Underdress

BACK VIEW

MOURNING DRESS, QUEEN APAILANA

Hair fashioned to resemble the horns of a guarlara creature

Hairtip ornament

Orange-shot gold silk taffeta

SENATE OUTFIT WITH CLOAK, QUEEN AMIDALA

SENATE OUTFIT WITHOUT CLOAK, QUEEN AMIDALA

BACK VIEW

Ivory organza with hand-stitched floral pattern

Red silk with gold embroidered motifs

THRONE ROOM GOWN, QUEEN AMIDALA

PARADE GOWN, QUEEN AMIDALA

Velvet shoulder decoration

Elaborate embroidered silk

Metallic thread and beads

TRAVELLING GOWN, QUEEN AMIDALA
(WORN BY SABÉ IN DISGUISE)

TRAVELLING GOWN (TO NABOO),
QUEEN AMIDALA

LILAC VISITATION OUTFIT,
QUEEN AMIDALA

FOREIGN RESIDENCE GOWN,
QUEEN AMIDALA

HANDMAIDENS

Handmaidens are the queen's advisors and personal bodyguards. Matching outfits and hoods conceal their identities, while billowing cloaks help to hide weapons used to protect the queen in the event of an attack.

TAILORED DRESS
AND COAT, DORMÉ

GREEN VELVET ROBES, MIRÉ

HOODED CLOAK, HOLLÉ

FLAME-COLOURED
ROBES, RABÉ

SHORT CAPE AND
PLEATED DRESS, MOTEÉ

PATTERNED RED
CLOAK, UMÉ

BLUE DRESS WITH
BODICE, TECKLA

ALDERAAN

Alderaan's monarchy tend to dress modestly, with relatively simple designs in muted colours. Queen Breha's blue and bronze gown mirrors the planet's beautiful oceans and tranquil valleys. Princess Leia awards medals to rebel heroes in a simpler flowing white dress.

BLUE SLASH-SLEEVED DRESS,
QUEEN BREHA

HANGING-SLEEVED DRESS,
PRINCESS LEIA

OCCASION WEAR

A chance to escape from their everyday routines, galactic citizens dress up for special occasions. A night out at the Coruscant Opera or Outlander Club offers a chance to show off personal flair. Conversely, a sombre funeral requires understated, respectable attire.

EVENING WEAR

DINNER WEAR

For an intimate dinner with Anakin Skywalker, Padmé Amidala wears a striking evening gown. The black leather corset, matching full-length gloves and sleek lace skirt create a memorable look.

Dramatic jet collar necklace

SIDE VIEW

Fingerless gloves

Melodie skirtline

BACK VIEW

BLACK CORSET DRESS WITH METALLIC-EFFECT SKIRT, PADMÉ AMIDALA

NIGHTCLUB WEAR

A night at a club allows individuals to relax and leave behind their worries. Clothing is designed to grab attention on the dance floor or at the gambling tables. Eye-catching colours and sheer or metallic fabrics are always popular.

SUIT, NIGHTCLUB PATRON

HAND-DYED BODYSUIT, AYY VIDA

SEQUINNED PLAYSUIT, NIGHTCLUB PATRON

BACK VIEW

FLAMBOYANT OUTFITS, NIGHTCLUB PATRONS

OPERA HOUSE WEAR

A visit to the opera or ballet is an opportunity for patrons to stand out from the crowd. Luxurious cloaks, elaborate headdresses, bold prints, form-fitting dresses – when it comes to the opera house, the more extravagant the better!

GREEN CLOAK WITH HOOPSKIRT HEM, JANU GODALHI

FUR-TRIMMED COAT AND SILK SHIRT, ULFOR BOMBAASA

OPERA COAT, DUKE TETA

Convor feather collar

PANTORAN COAT, BARON PAPANOIDA

FUR CLOAK, BEYTOLIM

CHUNKY CAPE, RYSTÁLL SANT

GOLDEN GOWN, OPULA DEGET

BEJEWELLED WHITE DRESS, KOYI MATEIL

FUNERAL WEAR

ROYAL

For Padmé Naberrie Amidala's funeral, her parents and sister wear dark tones to reflect their sadness and mourning of her death. In tribute to her sister, Sola's cloak and dress closely resemble Queen Amidala's royal wardrobe.

BLACK MOURNING CLOAK, JOBAL NABERRIE

DARK BURGUNDY OUTFIT WITH GOLDEN DETAIL, SOLA NABERRIE

SOMBRE ROBE, RUWEE NABERRIE

JEDI

Jedi do not value worldly possessions, nor do they fear death. Their lives of service are remembered in humble funerals, with most Jedi attendees wearing their usual daily attire. Non-Jedi guests, even honourable ones, show respect with modest clothing.

OBI-WAN KENOBI'S FAKE FUNERAL

QUI-GON JINN'S FUNERAL

BRIDAL WEAR

Although she is to be married in a secret ceremony, Padmé Amidala selects a beautiful, one-of-a-kind dress. Completely hand-sewn, the matching lace overdress flows out in a train behind the bride.

Hand-sewn pearl details

Sheer sleeves with intricate pattern

Lace overdress

WEDDING DRESS, PADMÉ AMIDALA

NIGHTWEAR

Senator Padmé Amidala has an extensive wardrobe that includes luxury nightwear. Fine materials help to maintain a comfortable body temperature while sleeping. Robes provide extra warmth before bedtime.

SILK NIGHTDRESS, PADMÉ AMIDALA

BACK VIEW

NIGHTDRESS AND ROBE, PADMÉ AMIDALA

AQUA GEORGETTE NIGHTGOWN, PADMÉ AMIDALA

IN-DEPTH ANALYSIS

Even clothes that are worn to sleep make a statement about the wearer. As a young woman in love, Padmé Amidala prefers romantic sleepwear, such as her aqua georgette nightgown. The detailing harks back to her time as queen of Naboo, with royal-inspired patterns made of hand-stitched seed beads and delicate shells.

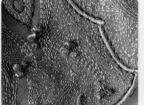

INTRICATE EMBROIDERY WITH SHELL AND BEAD DETAIL

EVERYDAY WEAR

From weather to wealth, many factors affect a person's choice of clothes. An outfit to suit the dirty depths of Coruscant will be vastly different to that worn for a picnic in a flower-filled meadow on Naboo. Looking at the way someone dresses can offer many clues about their life and where they live.

JAKKU

Clothes are not something to waste money upon when nourishment and water cost a premium. Settlers and war refugees cobble together clothes from recycled material they scavenge. The layers of Rey's outfit can be rewrapped to protect her skin from the elements.

MULTI-LAYERED OUTFIT, REY

DESERT WEAR

TATOOINE

Tatooine is a harsh planet, with whipping sandstorms and dangerously high daytime temperatures. Most individuals keep skin covered with practical materials that wick away sweat and limit exposure to harmful ultraviolet radiation from Tatooine's twin suns.

LIGHT ROBES, BERU WHITESUN   BACK VIEW

TRADITIONAL CLOTHES, TUSKEN RAIDER (FEMALE)   BACK VIEW

PRACTICAL OVERALLS, SPACERS

LOOSE-FITTING CLOTHES, MOS ESPA SETTLERS

ROUGH WRAPPINGS, TUSKEN RAIDER (MALE)

GREEN ROBES, ILCO MUNICA   SLEEVELESS OVERCOAT WITH BLUE DRESS, DASHA PROMENTI

IN-DEPTH ANALYSIS

Padmé Amidala's simple outfit still reflects her important position as a Naboo senator. Handstitched details and silk ribbons on the deep blue overdress might seem out of place for most on Tatooine, but are understated for a former queen. The lightweight pleated gown keeps her cool in Tatooine's hot climate.

PEASANT DRESS DISGUISE, PADMÉ AMIDALA

EMBROIDERED OVERCOAT, PADMÉ AMIDALA

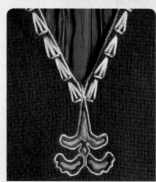

EMBROIDERED DETAIL ON NECKLINE   SATIN STITCH DECORATION

WEATHER-WORN CLOAK, SARCO PLANK

BAGGY GREEN TROUSERS, "CRUSHER" ROODOWN

CITY WEAR

CORUSCANT

Coruscant's sprawling urban landscape holds thousands of city levels filled with a myriad of alien and humanoid species. Clothing is as diverse as the population, ranging from the green-spiked cloak of an immigrant to the all-black outfit of a vigilante.

CHEAP SUIT, UNDERLEVEL BITH

SIMPLE OVERALLS, WAKS BURR

DARK, ARMOURED OUTFITS, UNDERLEVEL VIGILANTES

VEST WITH SPELLSAYER TEARDROP EMBLEM, FREIGHTER TRAMPER　SIDE VIEW

SPIKED GREEN CLOAK, NAR HIDA

NAVY OVERALLS, ELA TIPS

BURGUNDY OVERALLS, FORCH GOMOU

FLOOR-LENGTH ROBE, HAT LO

LOOSE GARMENTS, UNDERLEVEL KADAS'SA'NIKTO

RADDAN VERMIN-KILLER VEST, FREIGHTER TRAMPER

Rose-accented headband

Shoulder strap

Embroidered tulle shawl

BESPIN

The controlled environment of Cloud City means people don't have to worry about the weather. Baron Administrator Lando Calrissian flaunts his wealth with an extravagant cape and offers Leia Organa a refined leisure suit during her visit.

NABOO

Naboo's human inhabitants value culture and beauty. This is reflected in their everyday attire; even children like Pooja Naberrie wear graceful clothes made of natural material. Padmé Amidala's golden dress is accented with hand-sewn roses.

TRADITIONAL CHILDREN'S DRESS, POOJA NABERRIE

SIDE VIEW

TUNIC AND DELICATE CLOAK, LEIA ORGANA

HIGH-QUALITY SUIT, LANDO CALRISSIAN

TEXTURED TUNIC, THEED CIVILIAN

DRAPED PURPLE DRESS, HELA BRANDES

BACK VIEW

SUMMER MEADOW DRESS, PADMÉ AMIDALA

WORK CLOTHING

Clothes create an important statement in the work environment. A senator's formalwear will reflect the culture of their homeworld, but can also command respect while they negotiate deals. Jedi robes present an air of serenity, while Sith garbs are designed to instill fear.

GIGOT-SLEEVED ROBES, SUPREME CHANCELLOR PALPATINE

BACK VIEW

OFFICE WEAR

POLITICIANS

Many senators proudly wear the traditional garments of their people. However, others use their status and the significant budgets of their offices to pay for lavish clothing. They wear elaborate creations made by the most famous designers on Coruscant, using the finest imported fabrics.

ORNATE VELVET OVERCLOAK, CHANCELLOR VALORUM

ELABORATE CLOAK, SENATOR PALPATINE

Glossy hand-woven Tyrian shimmersilk

CHANDRILAN TUNIC AND MANTLE, SENATOR MON MOTHMA

GOLDEN ROBES WITH VELVET OVERCLOAK, SUPREME CHANCELLOR PALPATINE

DIAMOND-PATTERNED LILAC ROBES, SENATOR FANG ZAR

CORUSCANTI ROBES, SENATOR ORN FREE TAA

SIDE VIEW

DRESS WITH HANGING SLEEVE DETAIL, SENATOR TOONBUCK TOORA

TRADITIONAL OVERCOAT, SENATOR GIDDEAN DANU

VICEROY GOWN, NUTE GUNRAY

LONG VELVET CLOAK, SENATOR EDCEL BAR GANE

ALDERAANIAN SUIT AND OVERCOAT, SENATOR BAIL ORGANA

HIGH-NECKED DRESS, SENATOR FEMA BAAB

ORNATE HALBARA OUTFIT, SENATOR ISTER PADDIE

BEADED INDIGO GOWN,
SENATOR AMIDALA

DARK VELVET DRESS WITH GOLD
PANEL, SENATOR AMIDALA

PURPLE PUFF-SLEEVED DRESS,
SENATOR AMIDALA

Naboo folk overcoat with hand-sewn voorpak wool

PEACOCK GOWN WITH BROWN
OVERCOAT, SENATOR AMIDALA

SENATORIAL AIDES

A prudent assistant will follow the lead of their senator in dressing for official duties. Others may prefer to create an intimidating presence, such as Sly Moore, in her long cloak with high collar.

UMBARAN SHADOW CLOAK,
SLY MOORE

IN-DEPTH ANALYSIS

Although she is no longer a queen, Senator Padmé Amidala still represents the culture and people of Naboo. The dresses and cloaks are less ceremonial and more practical than her royal gowns, but no less beautiful or varied.

WARDROBE, SENATOR AMIDALA'S APARTMENT

Fine Onderon silk sash

Luxurious fabric displays patterns of the House Bonteri

GREEN VELVET DRESS, SENATOR AMIDALA

BACK VIEW

CREAM DRESS AND CAPE,
SHELTAY RETRAC

DRAPED OVERCLOAK,
STONROY SOMA

RELIGIOUS ROBES

JEDI

Having adopted a simple yet strict lifestyle, most Jedi prefer to wear traditional, earth-toned robes. These are warm, comfortable and allow great freedom of movement. The Jedi also permit members to wear robes from their own homeworlds, such as Barriss Offee and Luminara Unduli's Mirialan designs.

MIRIALAN-JEDI PADAWAN
HYBRID OUTFIT, BARRISS OFFEE

JEDI MASTER ROBE WITH
TABARD, LUMINARA UNDULI

JEDI KNIGHT OUTFIT,
BULTAR SWAN

JEDI MASTER OUTFIT,
MACE WINDU

JEDI PADAWAN OUTFIT,
ANAKIN SKYWALKER

JEDI MASTER ROBES, ADI GALLIA

SITH

While in hiding, the Sith don clothing that obscures their identity. As Palpatine rises to power, he wears cloaks more in keeping with Sith traditions, though his taste in lavish, comfortable fabrics does not lessen. The emblem on his red robes is reminiscent of the serpents of the Sith planet, Moraband.

CLOAK, DARTH SIDIOUS

SERENNO CAPE,
COUNT DOOKU

SITH ROBE, DARTH MAUL

RED ROBES, EMPEROR PALPATINE

SIDE VIEW

PROTECTIVE CLOTHING

The galaxy is a dangerous, dirty place where mechanics, guards, pilots and others must wear specialised clothing to protect themselves during the course of their work. From regal uniforms to dirty aprons, these outfits have seen some action!

Cap bears Naboo Security crest

MECHANIC OVERALLS

Mechanics help keep the galaxy moving as they turn wrenches, wield welders and work on machines of all types. Overalls made of durable fabrics protect them from dirt and oil, and their many pouches and pockets hold the tools their wearers need for work.

THEED HANGAR GROUND CREW OVERALLS

CORUSCANT LANDING PAD CREW OVERALLS

CORUSCANT SPACEPORT CREW OVERALLS

TATOOINE MECHANIC OVERALLS

SECURITY GUARD UNIFORMS

When keeping watch over dignitaries, royalty and other important individuals, security guards must protect themselves in order to protect others. A guard's armour alone is often enough to make would-be assassins think twice before striking a high-value target.

IMPERIAL ROYAL GUARD ROBES

NABOO PALACE GUARD ARMOUR

REPUBLIC SENATE GUARD ROBES

JEDI TEMPLE GUARD UNIFORM

GAMORREAN GUARD ARMOUR

GUAVIAN DEATH GANG SECURITY SOLDIER ARMOUR

PANTORAN GUARD UNIFORM

MANDALORIAN ROYAL GUARD ARMOUR

TOYDARIAN ROYAL GUARD UNIFORM

ZYGERRIAN ROYAL GUARD UNIFORM

Blast-damping shoulder pauldron

Traditional Naboo red colour

Bracer for hand-to-hand combat

NABOO SECURITY OFFICER ARMOUR

PILOT UNIFORMS

Pilots take flight in the unforgiving vacuum of space, requiring special protective clothing to keep them safe. Their flight suits must also carry life-support gear and survival tools to be used in case of accidents.

Space fighter corps overcoat

Flying jacket

Flying gloves

Naboo pilot-issue boots

DINEÉ ELLBERGER'S NABOO SPACE FIGHTER CORPS PILOT UNIFORM

A-WING STARFIGHTER PILOT UNIFORM

POE DAMERON'S X-WING STARFIGHTER PILOT UNIFORM

CLONE TROOPER PILOT UNIFORM

TIE FIGHTER PILOT UNIFORM

Data goggles

Neimoidian pilot tabard

CLONE TROOPER PILOT UNIFORM

LUKE SKYWALKER'S X-WING STARFIGHTER PILOT UNIFORM

PADMÉ AMIDALA'S STARFIGHTER UNIFORM DISGUISE

TEN NUMB'S X-WING STARFIGHTER PILOT UNIFORM

NEIMOIDIAN PILOT ROBES

CAMOUFLAGE CLOTHING

In contrast to the armoured troops who march directly into battle, some soldiers melt into their surroundings and strike at their enemies from the shadows. Camouflage clothing helps rebels blend in on wooded planets such as Endor, or snowy planets, like Hoth.

JABBA'S HENCHMAN'S OUTFIT

PRINCESS LEIA ORGANA'S CAMOUFLAGE OUTFIT

HAN SOLO'S CAMOUFLAGE OUTFIT

REBEL CAMOUFLAGE CLOTHING

Rebel-issue all weather vest

REBEL SNOW GEAR

LUKE SKYWALKER'S CAMOUFLAGE CLOTHING

Military snow boots with bindings

PRINCESS LEIA ORGANA'S SNOW GEAR

APRONS

For locals carrying out dirty work in kitchens and scrap yards across the galaxy, a simple apron is essential gear. Strono Tuggs, the chef better known as Cookie, wears a stained, heavy leather apron while cooking in Maz Kanata's castle.

DAVAN MARAK'S SCAVENGER APRON

STRONO "COOKIE" TUGGS'S LEATHER APRON

UNKAR PLUTT'S METAL APRON

ARMOUR

Armour must not simply protect its wearer from searing blaster bolts or deadly shrapnel – the best designs also allow the freedom of movement needed to be an effective fighter. There are many different types of armour and each piece is designed to protect a specific area of the body.

PAULDRONS

Pauldrons shield the wearer's shoulders, while allowing enough flexibility to raise a weapon to attack the enemy. Stormtrooper pauldrons come in different colours to indicate rank or affiliation. Wookiees carefully craft their decorative pauldrons; the carved patterns are based on traditional clan designs.

KANAN JARRUS'S PAULDRON

STORMTROOPER SERGEANT PAULDRON

WOOKIEE PAULDRON

FULL BODY ARMOUR

A battalion of troops in identical full body armour is an imposing sight on the battlefield. At the beginning of the Clone Wars, clone troopers were equipped with Phase I armour, but are eventually upgraded to the Phase II version. This advanced model allows for additional manoeuvrability and greater customisation of parts.

Red officer pauldron

Removing a helmet in battle violates regulations

Exposed area vulnerable to blaster fire

Ammunition container

Composite betaplast material

FIRST ORDER STORMTROOPER ARMOUR

CLONE TROOPER PHASE I ARMOUR

CLONE TROOPER PHASE II ARMOUR

IMPERIAL STORMTROOPER ARMOUR

SABINE WREN'S MANDALORIAN ARMOUR

LEG ARMOUR

Leg armour design varies according to the fighting style of the wearer. Imperial stormtroopers have a knee protector plate attached to their left leg armour, so they can kneel in a sniper position in battle.

NEIMOIDIAN GUNNER LEG ARMOUR

JANGO FETT'S LEG ARMOUR

ZAM WESELL'S LEG ARMOUR

AHSOKA TANO'S LEG ARMOUR

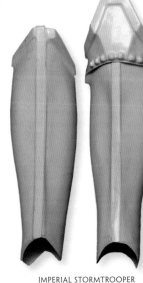

IMPERIAL STORMTROOPER LEG ARMOUR

ARM PLATES

Arm plates often do more than simply protect the limb – many contain communication devices or concealed weapons. Notorious bounty hunter Jango Fett wears gauntlets that are equipped with many inbuilt weapons and lethal gadgets to capture his targets.

SENATOR BAIL ORGANA'S ARM BRACES | INSIDE VIEW

BOBA FETT'S GAUNTLETS

CORUSCANT EMERGENCY CREW ARM BRACE

Upper shell

Darts

Wrist opening

Fuel feeder line for flamethrower

JANGO FETT'S GAUNTLET

ZAM WESELL'S ARM BRACES

BODY PLATES

A warrior can survive losing a limb, but injury to the torso is often deadly. A gorget protects the neck and its vulnerable arteries. Snowtroopers have heating controls built into their chest plates, so they can regulate the temperature inside their armour.

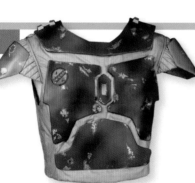

BOBA FETT'S CHEST PLATE

JANGO FETT'S CHEST PLATE

WOOKIEE CHEST PLATE

DARTH VADER'S GORGET

FIRST ORDER SNOWTROOPER CHEST PLATE

IMPERIAL SNOWTROOPER CHEST PLATE

SERIPAS'S ARMOUR

Bounty hunter Seripas may be small, but his mechanised suit of armour makes him a formidable foe. Seated inside the suit, Seripas controls its movements and many inbuilt weapons – including a buzz saw.

INTERIOR VIEW

NEIMOIDIAN GUNNER ABDOMINAL ARMOUR

GORGET

BACK ARMOUR

ZAM WESELL'S CHEST PLATE

SERIPAS'S ARMOUR

HELMETS: INTRAGALACTIC MILITARIES

Beneath these helmets lie heroic pilots, hard-working crew members and fearless foot soldiers. From underwater troopers to starfighter pilots, helmets are specifically tailored to the vast range of roles required in galactic warfare.

WARTHOG'S PHASE I CLONE PILOT HELMET

PHASE II CLONE PILOT HELMET

NAVY

LEADERS

Even for heroic leaders in the resource-strapped Rebellion and Resistance, shiny new helmets are not a luxury they can afford. Each scrape and scratch on their well-worn helmets is a reminder of hard-earned victories.

HERA SYNDULLA'S B-WING HELMET

RED SQUADRON LEADER GARVEN DREIS'S HELMET

LUKE SKYWALKER'S X-WING HELMET

STARFIGHTER PILOTS

Though decades separate the Republic, Rebellion and Resistance, their pilots' helmets share one defining feature: each reflects its owner's personality. This is in stark contrast to the identical TIE fighter helmets worn by Imperial pilots and their First Order successors.

B-WING PILOT HELMET

Y-WING PILOT HELMET

NIEN NUNB'S X-WING HELMET

IMPERIAL TIE FIGHTER PILOT HELMET

FIRST ORDER TIE FIGHTER PILOT HELMET

IN-DEPTH ANALYSIS

Special Forces TIE fighter pilots are elite fliers, but are also skilled with blasters. Their helmets include advanced targeting sensors for both ground and space combat as well as breathing tubes connected to vital life-support gear.

INTERIOR VIEW

FIRST ORDER SPECIAL FORCES TIE FIGHTER PILOT

CREW

Behind the front lines, support troops play an important role operating military equipment. Their specially designed helmets offer some protection, and often contain vital communication technology.

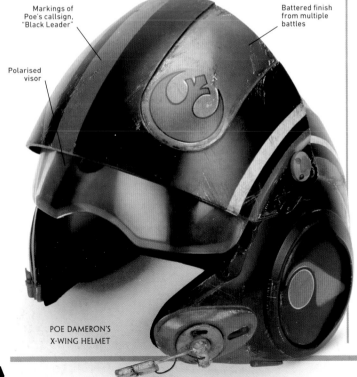

Markings of Poe's callsign, "Black Leader"

Battered finish from multiple battles

Polarised visor

POE DAMERON'S X-WING HELMET

LIBERATOR CREW MEMBER HELMET

CLONE TROOPER FLIGHT CREW HELMET

FIRST ORDER FLEET ENGINEER HELMET

ARMY

STANDARD INFANTRY

Once a welcome symbol of democracy, the white armoured helmets of clone troopers evolve alongside changes in galactic politics. Galactic citizens come to associate these helmets with the faceless stormtroopers of the tyrannical Empire and later, the ferocious First Order.

PHASE I CLONE TROOPER HELMET

PHASE II CLONE TROOPER HELMET

IMPERIAL STORMTROOPER HELMET

INSIDE VIEW

RESISTANCE COMBAT HELMET

FIRST ORDER STORMTROOPER HELMET

FINN'S FIRST ORDER STORMTROOPER HELMET

ELITE FORCES

The high credit cost of advanced equipment means that only elite forces are equipped with this gear. Republic Commandos have earned the right to wear advanced helmets offering superior protection to standard Phase I clone armour.

 CLONE MARINE HELMET

 ARC TROOPER HELMET

IMPERIAL SCOUT TROOPER HELMET

CLONE SCOUT TROOPER HELMET

REBEL COMMANDO HELMET

CLONE COMMANDO GREGOR'S HELMET

SPECIALISTS

Standard issue armour cannot always function in extreme conditions. Armour technicians forge a wide variety of helmets for specialised uses – such as underwater combat, or operations in freezing temperatures.

CLONE TROOPER SCUBA HELMET

CLONE FLAMETROOPER HELMET

FIRST ORDER FLAMETROOPER HELMET

FIRST ORDER SNOWTROOPER HELMET

IMPERIAL SNOWTROOPER HELMET

LEADERS

Clone trooper leaders often customise their helmets with additional parts, and paint them in their regimental colours. As a symbol of her rank within the First Order, Captain Phasma wears a helmet coated in chromium salvaged from Emperor Palpatine's yacht from Naboo.

CAPTAIN REX'S HELMET

COMMANDER CODY'S HELMET

CAPTAIN PHASMA'S HELMET

LEIA ORGANA'S ENDOR HELMET

COMMANDER WOLFFE'S HELMET

GROUND VEHICLE PILOTS

Though their walkers provide solid protection in combat, Imperial regulations require AT-ST and AT-DP pilots to wear helmets during operations. The AT-DP helmet contains an integrated comm system so the driver and assistant driver can communicate easily.

AT-ST PILOT HELMET

AT-DP PILOT HELMET

DEATH STAR GUNNER HELMET

DEATH STAR TROOPER HELMET

MON CALAMARI HELMET

TANTIVE IV CREW MEMBER HELMET

AT-AT PILOT HELMET

HELMETS: BEST OF THE REST

While some helmets disguise identities, others reflect their owners' roles or unique cultures. Studying the history and design of helmets gives us a fascinating insight into the remarkable people who wear them, from pirates to bounty hunters.

DARTH VADER'S HELMET

INTERIOR FACE MASK

BURNT HELMET FROM FUNERAL PYRE

DARK SIDE

The imposing, terrifying helmets that are worn by dark side Force users reflect their wearers' twisted personalites. Darth Vader needs his helmet to keep him alive. His mask and collar contain his voice processor, nutrient feeding tube and body temperature controls. In contrast, Kylo Ren's mask is more symbolic. The silver markings mimic the style of the battle gear worn by the Knights of Ren.

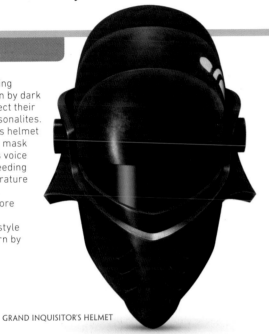

GRAND INQUISITOR'S HELMET

FIFTH BROTHER'S HELMET

SEVENTH SISTER'S HELMET

EIGHTH BROTHER'S HELMET

KYLO REN'S HELMET

MANDALORIAN

Iconic Mandalorian helmets are so well made that even non-Mandalorians like Jango Fett find ways to acquire them for their own needs. Their helmets are often customised to show the wearer's clan affiliation.

MANDALORIAN SUPER COMMANDO HELMET

BOBA FETT'S HELMET

JANGO FETT'S HELMET

PRE VIZSLA'S HELMET

BO-KATAN KRYZE'S HELMET

SABINE WREN'S HELMET

WOOKIEE

Traditional Wookiee armour serves just as well while hunting in the wild forests of Kashyyyk, as it does on the battlefields of the Clone Wars. The high crest of this handcrafted helmet makes a towering Wookiee look even taller!

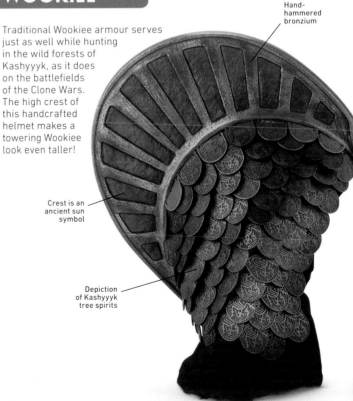

Hand-hammered bronzium

Crest is an ancient sun symbol

Depiction of Kashyyyk tree spirits

WOOKIEE HELMET

SECURITY GUARDS

A guard's helmet is perhaps the most intricate and stately part of their uniform. Do not let their regal look fool you: under these helmets are loyal fighters who are willing to sacrifice their lives for those they protect.

TOYDARIAN ROYAL GUARD HELMET

NIKTO SKIFF GUARD HELMET

NEIMOIDIAN GUNNER HELMET

LANDO CALRISSIAN'S SKIFF GUARD HELMET

SENATE GUARD HELMET

BLUE SENATE COMMANDO HELMET

CAPTAIN ARGYUS'S HELMET

MANDALORIAN ROYAL GUARD HELMET

Guards rarely clean their helmets or change clothes

Shaped to fit around a Gamorrean's horns

Tough leather material

JEDI TEMPLE GUARD HELMET

IMPERIAL ROYAL GUARD HELMET

CLONE SHOCKTROOPER HELMET

GAMORREAN GUARD HELMET

TRAINING

Helmets can be a useful tool for teaching students. Young clones wear helmets that aid their visual learning. A Jedi student must learn to trust the Force; they wear helmets that shield their eyes so they cannot see during lightsaber training.

JEDI YOUNGLING HELMET

PILOT HELMET WITH BLAST SHIELD

IMPERIAL ACADEMY HELMET

BOUNTY HUNTERS

While many bounty hunters don a helmet, Embo does not just wear his on his head. The Kyuzo hunter uses his curved helmet as a throwing weapon, a shield against blaster bolts and even as a sledge to ride down hills on snowy planets!

BOUSSH'S HELMET

EMBO'S HELMET

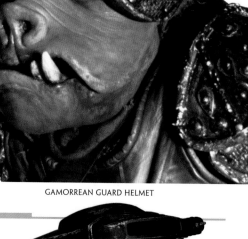

ZAM WESELL'S HELMET

CLONE TROOPER EVEN-CLASS TRAINING HELMET

PIRATES

Sidon Ithano, the Crimson Corsair, is a man of few words whose blood-red, Kaleesh helmet only adds to his mystery. The veteran pirate Hondo Ohnaka is rarely seen without a dashing helmet – quite possibly stolen from one of his many unlucky victims.

HONDO OHNAKA'S HELMET

SIDON ITHANO'S HELMET

SECRET SERVICE

Agent Kallus's Imperial Security Bureau helmet is designed for riot control situations and heavy combat. It features a heavily armoured shell and plastoid composite cheek guards.

AGENT KALLUS'S HELMET

ACCESSORIES

From fashion statements to practical enhancements, accessories complete a look. Natural materials are common for personal items, such as the japor Anakin Skywalker uses to carve a lucky charm. Military items, such as insignia, are made from durable synthetics.

CIVILIAN HATS

Hats can be worn for warmth, but they usually signify status. Senators, Trade Federation leaders and Imperial dignitaries all don hats. Extra height, an unusual shape or a splash of colour make them stand out from the crowd!

SENATOR GIDDEAN DANU'S HAT

IMPERIAL DIGNITARY HAT   NEIMOIDIAN HAT

JEWELLERY

For some, jewellery represents an individual's culture, or that they are married or belong to a specific clan. For others, jewellery can signify status, or show religious beliefs, such as Lor San Tekka's Chain of Wisdom.

PADMÉ AMIDALA'S WAIST PENDANT

NABOO BROOCH WITH FISH MOTIF

NABOO BROOCH OF ORGANIC CHIF STONE

NABOO BROOCH WITH ZOORIF FEATHER MOTIF

PADMÉ AMIDALA'S NECKLACE

NABOO GOLD BEADS

PADMÉ AMIDALA'S BROOCH

NABOO BROOCH WITH WING MOTIF

PADMÉ AMIDALA'S LUCKY CHARM (A JAPOR SNIPPET)

MAZ KANATA'S BRACELETS

CHIEF CHIRPA'S MEDALLION OF POWER

LOR SAN TEKKA'S CHAIN OF WISDOM

NABOO BROOCH WITH SPIDER MOTIF

MILITARY HATS

Military hats indicate service and rank, and the colour or style allows commanders to recognise units during battle. The First Order cap has more severe edges and a larger emblem than the Imperial version from which it evolved.

NABOO SECURITY OFFICER CAP

GENERAL HUX'S FIRST ORDER COMMAND CAP

HOTH REBEL HEADGEAR

STAFFS

MAS AMEDDA'S STAFF

Staffs provide assistance when walking long distances or over rough terrain, but some have additional uses. Chief Chirpa's feathered staff shows his authority as leader of his Ewok village. Yoda nibbles on his gimer stick as a source of nutrients.

UTAPAUN STAFF

IMPERIAL OFFICER CAP

IMPERIAL STORMTROOPER OFFICER CAP

UTAPAUN STAFF

YODA'S WALKING CANE

EMPEROR PALPATINE'S CANE

CHIEF CHIRPA'S STAFF

YODA'S GIMER STICK

WOOKIEE ELDER STAFF

NABOO SECURITY OFFICER CAP

HEADDRESSES

Headdresses are typically worn by royalty, including the monarchs of Naboo, and are often displayed on important occasions. For her wedding, Padmé Amidala chooses a lace veil adorned with wax drop stamens and flowers.

PADMÉ AMIDALA'S SENATORIAL HEADPIECE

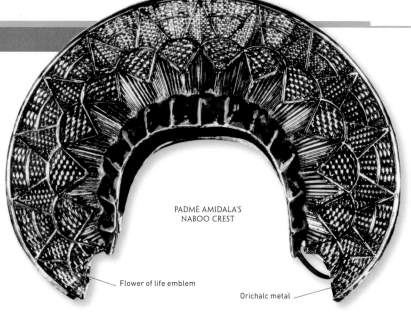

PADMÉ AMIDALA'S NABOO CREST

Flower of life emblem

Orichalc metal

PADMÉ AMIDALA'S WEDDING VEIL

PADMÉ AMIDALA'S ESCOFFIATE

PADMÉ AMIDALA'S MEADOW PICNIC HEADDRESS

GLOVES

Some wear gloves to protect their hands from harsh climates. Gloves also conceal fingerprints, making them a tool of the trade for bounty hunters like Zam Wesell.

DARTH VADER'S GLOVES

IMPERIAL OFFICER GLOVES

LUKE SKYWALKER'S GLOVE

REBEL TROOPER GLOVES

FIRST ORDER SNOWTROOPER GLOVES

CAPTAIN TYPHO'S BROWN GLOVES

ZAM WESELL'S BROWN GLOVES

ZAM WESELL'S PURPLE GLOVES

CAPTAIN TYPHO'S BLUE GLOVES

BELTS AND BUCKLES

Belts can be designed for utility or to add polish to a formal outfit. They often carry holsters for weapons or pouches for other vital items. Bail Organa's embellished buckle adds flair. Count Dooku's belt is crafted from rare rancor leather.

STORMTROOPER OFFICER BELT BUCKLE

PADMÉ AMIDALA'S PILOT DISGUISE BELT BUCKLE

IMPERIAL OFFICER BELT

BAIL ORGANA'S BELT BUCKLE

BAIL ORGANA'S AIDE'S BELT

TATOOINE MONEY BELT

CAPTAIN TYPHO'S BELT

ALDERAAN CREW BELT

COUNT DOOKU'S BELT

GOGGLES

Goggles protect eyes in dangerous situations or can enhance vision. Han Solo uses them to shield his eyes when he welds the *Millennium Falcon*. During evening raids, Steela Gerrera wears night-vision goggles to help the Onderon resistance fighters.

HAN SOLO'S WELDING GOGGLES

STEELA GERRERA'S NIGHT-VISION GOGGLES

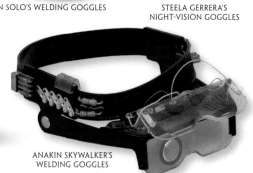

NEIMOIDIAN PILOT GOGGLES

ANAKIN SKYWALKER'S WELDING GOGGLES

INSIGNIA

Militaries use rank insignia to identify the chain of command. Various arrangements of red, blue and yellow rectangles appear on officer rank badges. Outside the military, insignia can denote membership in elite groups.

FIRST ORDER RANK CYLINDER

ZAM WESELL'S MABARI CAPE SEAL

BAIL ORGANA'S IDENTITY TAG

IMPERIAL OFFICER RANK PLAQUE

IMPERIAL OFFICER RANK PLAQUE

MUSICAL INSTRUMENTS

From the raucous rhythms of a cantina to the soulful songs of an opera, musical instruments are as diverse as the beings of the galaxy. String and wind instruments provide the melody, while percussion keeps the beat going. Some instruments use multiple parts to create their own unique sound.

Music is produced with string instruments from the sound of vibrating strings, which can be plucked by hand or with a pick, or used with a bow. Sudswater Dillifay Glon prefers to play his hallikset with a bow when his band performs at Maz's castle.

SEVEN-STRING HALLIKSET

PERCUSSION

Musicians play percussion instruments by striking or scraping with a hand or a beater, such as a Gungan drumstick. The kasta drum creates very simple beats, unlike the xyloxan, which weaves complex melodies.

GUNGAN DRUMSTICKS

Screamer gong

Tryna chime

O'Tawa cymbals

Optional centressar strings

DRUMHELLER HARP

GUNGAN DRUM

KASTA DRUM

RED BALL JETT ORGAN

Bodhar bones

Amosian gourd

Stand doubles as sled

XYLOXAN

WIND

A wind instrument contains a resonating tube where air is vibrated by blowing into or across a mouthpiece. A shell horn is a simple resonator. More elaborate tubes, like a floonorp, use keys, varying material and shape to create a range of sounds.

BANDFILL

MON CALAMARI SHELL HORN

CATTOROBE

DRIXFAR

SABRIQUET

FLOONORP

GALAXAPHONE

CHINDINKALU FLUTE

SPEETAMOR

GUNGAN WHISTLE

GUNGAN HORN

KLOO HORN

TOOLS

Tuners ensure that instruments maintain the correct pitch, so some musicians always keep one to hand before they start to play. To avoid hitting a sour note, a tuner ensures blissl pipes play beautiful melodies. Some instruments, however, require specialists to keep them pitch perfect.

Individual note dials

Analyser board

Sound receiver

LISSL TUNER

HYBRID

Individual performers have devised hybrid instruments that allow them to multi-task and play several parts of a musical composition. Many of these eclectic hybrids are collected by patrons – from royalty to Hutt crime lords – who appreciate rarer instruments.

SIFTERBOWZER

STOMPSQUEEZER

GROWDI HARMONIQUE

PODPORT BANDFILL

KETTLEBOX BLOWER BELL

BONTORMIAN KLESPLONG

MUSICIANS AND ENTERTAINERS

Talented artists keep spirits high and moods light in cantinas, palaces and castles around the galaxy – even in times of war. While they don't carry blasters, these musicians and entertainers are armed with booming voices, elegant dance moves and finely tuned musical instruments.

Mouth tube

Peel rods

FIGRIN D'AN AND THE MODAL NODES

Although the audience may think these Bith musicians look almost identical, they can be told apart by the distinct musical instrument that each band member plays. The seven-member group performs across Tatooine and is often found in Mos Eisley Cantina.

DOIKK NA'TS PLAYING A DORENIAN BESHNIQUEL

NALAN CHEEL PLAYING A BANDFILL

TECH MO'R PLAYING AN OMMNI BOX

TEDN DAHAI PLAYING A FANFAR

FIGRIN D'AN PLAYING A KLOO HORN

SLAVE DANCERS

Vile gangster Jabba the Hutt enjoys the performances of enslaved dancers. Both Oola and Yarna d'al' Gargan were kidnapped from their homes and have no choice but to dance for this evil villain.

OOLA

YARNA D'AL' GARGAN

SHAG KAVA

A patron of the arts among other activities, Maz Kanata offers free board at her castle to travelling musicians. The Shag Kava quartet consists of Taybin Ralorsa, Ubert "Sticks" Quaril, Infrablue Zedbeddy Coggins and Sudswater Dillifay Glon. This group plays songs with Huttese lyrics, including "Jabba Flow" and "Dobra Doompa".

SHAG KAVA BAND PLAYING AT MAZ KANATA'S CASTLE

MAX REBO BAND

INSTRUMENTALISTS

The rocking musicians led by Max Rebo play for the crowd of scoundrels and criminals in Jabba the Hutt's dark palace, or aboard his travelling sail barge, the *Khetanna*. Much to the outrage of his bandmates, Max Rebo happily accepted a lifetime gig from Jabba that only pays in free meals.

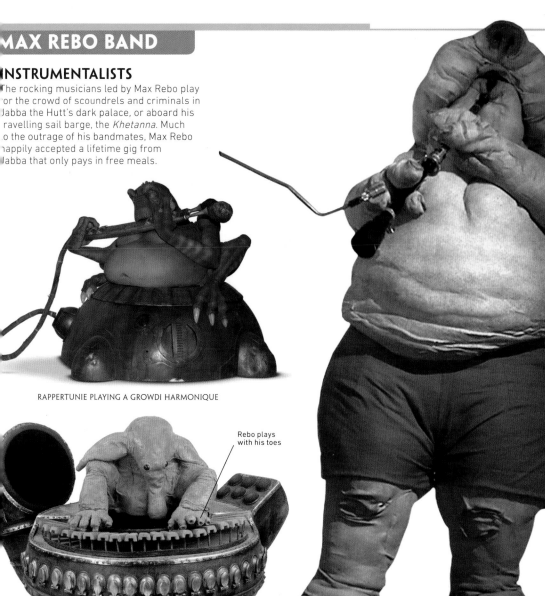

AK-REV PLAYING A DRUM

UMPASS-STAY PLAYING A DRUM

RAPPERTUNIE PLAYING A GROWDI HARMONIQUE

Rebo plays with his toes

MAX REBO PLAYING A RED BALL JETT ORGAN

DROOPY McCOOL PLAYING A CHINDINKALU FLUTE

VOCALISTS AND DANCERS

Five vocalists round out the twelve-member Max Rebo band. For many of their hits, the lead singers are Joh Yowza and Sy Snootles – a soulful singer whose career working for, and with, the Hutts spans decades.

JOH YOWZA

GREEATA

RYSTÁLL SANT

LYN ME

SY SNOOTLES

LEISURE

In every corner of the galaxy, citizens are looking for a way to relax. Whether played in corners of dark cantinas on Tatooine or consumed in nightclubs on Coruscant, these leisure items and activities help people to forget their worries or change their fortunes!

MIND-ALTERING SUBSTANCES

Enjoyed by high-level Imperial officials and common criminals alike, mind-altering substances trade short-term relaxation for long-term side effects. Some of the most addictive and dangerous are death sticks – narcotics that shorten their user's lifespan!

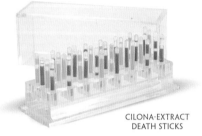

CILONA-EXTRACT
DEATH STICKS

DRINKS BAR AT THE
OUTLANDER NIGHTCLUB

JABBA THE HUTT'S HOOKAH PIPE

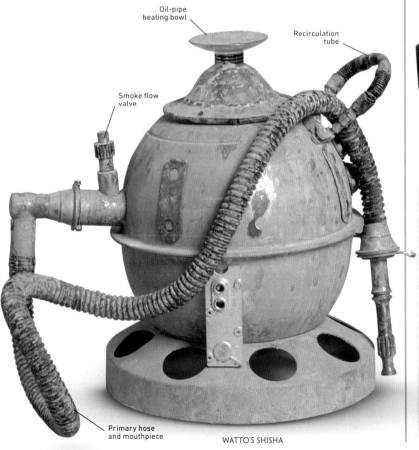

Oil-pipe
heating bowl

Recirculation
tube

Smoke flow
valve

Primary hose
and mouthpiece

WATTO'S SHISHA

SPORT

For gamblers and spectators alike, sport offers a sense of adventure and excitement. Though some competitions are friendly, others like podracing, droid boxing and arena beast battles are as dangerous for their competitors as they are exhilarating for their audiences.

ARENA BLOOD SPORTS

DROID BOXING

PODRACING

GAMES AND GAMBLING

CUBES, DICE AND MACHINES

When a decision needs to be made, some people prefer to leave it to the roll of a chance cube. Even heroes believe in luck, as Han Solo keeps a pair of lucky dice hanging in the cockpit of the *Millennium Falcon*.

WATTO'S
CHANCE CUBE

HAN SOLO'S
GOLDEN DICE

CHANCE CUBES AND
FIGHTING DROIDS

"ONE-ARMED SMUGGLER" GAMBLING MACHINE

ODDS IN THEIR FAVOUR

Prashee and Cratinus are twin brothers who frequent the chance tables in Maz Kanata's castle. When playing against others, they don't just rely on pure luck. They use their identical looks to confuse and swindle competitors – significantly improving their own chances!

"LUGJACK" GAMBLING MACHINE

TOYS

The mind of a child is truly wonderful and toys help bring their imaginations to life. Even in times of war and hardship, toys like tooka dolls and model airspeeders bring some much-needed enjoyment to younglings' lives.

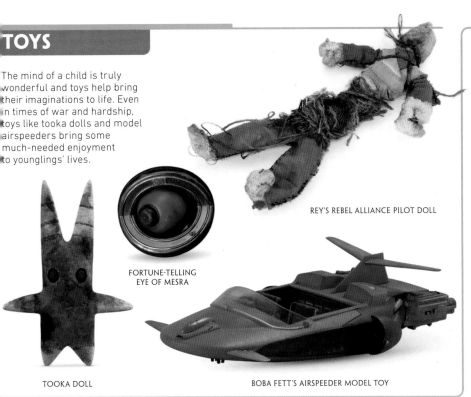

REY'S REBEL ALLIANCE PILOT DOLL

FORTUNE-TELLING EYE OF MESRA

TOOKA DOLL

BOBA FETT'S AIRSPEEDER MODEL TOY

CARD AND BOARD GAMES

Reckless gamblers will bet away great fortunes and even valuable starships in games of skill and chance. A widely played card game is sabacc, where players are always looking for the best hand, commonly known as an "Idiot's Array".

SABACC CARDS

HIGH STAKES

Feeling short of cash, Zeb plays sabacc at Old Jho's Pit Stop on Lothal against a shadowy figure, who turns out to be Lando Calrissian. Zeb ends up betting on – and losing – his ship's astromech, Chopper. In a bid to get their droid back, Zeb and his team are drawn into working for Lando in a swindle against the crime lord Azmorigan.

MONEY AND PRIZES

A gamble is only as good as the money wagered. On Republic worlds, credits are the official currency. On far-flung planets, local currencies – like wupiupi on Tatooine – are more acceptable for bets and barter. For the lucky ones, a prize box of pricey technology is always a welcome win.

PRIZE BOX

Old Huttese code of trade

WUPIUPI COINS

REPUBLIC CREDITS

GAMBLING CHITS

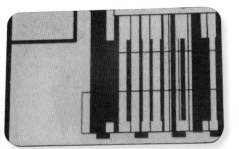

REPUBLIC CREDIT CHIP

LET THE WOOKIEE WIN

During their game of dejarik (holochess) onboard the *Millennium Falcon*, R2-D2 and C-3PO learn an unsettling fact about Wookiees: they've been known to pull people's arms out of their sockets when they lose. C-3PO wisely agrees that Chewbacca should win the game!

DEJARICK/HOLOCHESS

TRIGA GAME

DENGUE SISTERS PLAYING DEIA'S DREAM GAME

PODRACING

One of the most exciting and dangerous sports in the galaxy, podracing is extremely popular. Hordes of fans fill gigantic grandstands built at the start-finish line, or gather to watch broadcasts at cantinas and bars. Betting on the outcome is common, if risky!

IN-DEPTH ANALYSIS

Podracer pilots fly a set number of laps around an arena. With large winnings on offer, racers have no problem bumping into each other to gain any advantage. Some racers will even try and throw objects into the path of a competitor's engine.

TWO RACERS TUSSLE AT HIGH SPEED

FLAGS

As racers enter the arena, flagbearers march with them. Flags are decorated with heraldry, symbols or colours associated with the racer. The flags can also represent a sponsor who funds the team in order to gain local or galactic recognition.

PODRACE STARTING LINE

ANAKIN SKYWALKER'S FLAG

ALDAR BEEDO'S FLAG

BEN QUADINAROS'S FLAG

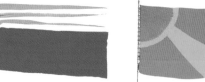

BOLES ROOR'S FLAG

ARK "BUMPY" ROOSE'S FLAG

CLEGG HOLDFAST'S FLAG

DUD BOLT'S FLAG

EBE ENDOCOTT'S FLAG

ELAN MAK'S FLAG

GASGANO'S FLAG

MARS GUO'S FLAG

MAWHONIC'S FLAG

NEVA KEE'S FLAG

ODY MANDRELL'S FLAG

RATTS TYERELL'S FLAG

SEBULBA'S FLAG

TEEMTO PAGALIES'S FLAG

WAN SANDAGE'S FLAG

COMPETITORS

Podracing requires bravado and Jedi-fast reflexes. Humans rarely possess the hand-eye coordination to compete, so Anakin Skywalker is a unique young pilot. For aliens who face discrimination in a human-centric galaxy, podracing is a lucrative career choice.

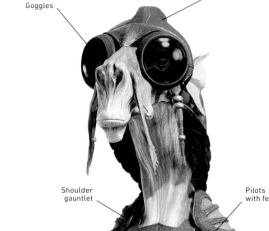

Goggles

Racing cap

Shoulder gauntlet

Pilots with feet

Stands on arms

SEBULBA

BOLES ROOR

ODY MANDRELL

CLEGG HOLDFAST

BEN QUADINAROS

SPECTATOR SPORT

AUDIENCE
The thrill of watching races full of life-threatening crashes draws enormous crowds. Podraces are often held to celebrate a holiday, like the Boonta Eve Classic on Tatooine, which fills the Grand Arena with over 100,000 spectators!

COMMENTATORS
Fodesinbeed Annodue is the perfect commentator. Red-headed Fode speaks Basic and green-headed Beed commentates in Huttese. With two heads on one body, they can keep an eye on different parts of the course and update fans with lively banter.

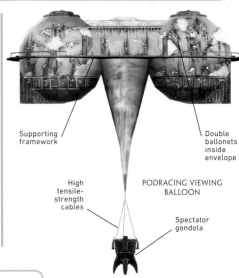

Supporting framework

Double ballonets inside envelope

High tensile-strength cables

PODRACING VIEWING BALLOON

Spectator gondola

VIEWING BALLOON
Viewing balloons are stationed over prime passing zones for brave spectators willing to pay a premium. Equipped with aerial cameras, they also project the action to the screens of audiences both in the stands and across the galaxy.

ARK "BUMPY" ROOSE

DUD BOLT

MARS GUO

MAWHONIC

ALDAR BEEDO

GASGANO

ELAN MAK

TEEMTO PAGALIES

WAN SANDAGE

NEVA KEE

EBE ENDOCOTT

RATTS TYERELL

ANAKIN SKYWALKER

FOUR ALIENS BUILT FOR PODRACING
Certain traits or physical attributes, such as extra-sensitive sensory organs, can give aliens a podracing advantage.

1 **DUG**
Strength and a cheating streak keep the Dug, Sebulba at the top of the leaderboard.

2 **ALEENA**
Small but strong, Aleena like Ratts Tyerell use their low weight as an advantage.

3 **GRAN**
Mawhonic, a three-eyed Gran, can see more of the light spectrum than most of his fellow racers.

4 **XAMSTER**
Exceptional brains give Xamsters like Neva Kee the ability to think quickly in this fast-paced sport.

FREEDOM FLIGHT
Racing in the Boonta Eve Classic, Anakin believes the fate of the stranded Jedi and their wards rests in his hands. Little does he know that Qui-Gon Jinn has bet against his master Watto. If Anakin wins he will be freed from slavery.

PODRACERS

Speeding around the racetrack at more than 800kph (497mph), podracers are the chariots of a technological age. Two or more massive engines connect to a cockpit by flexible cables. Repulsorlifts keep them hovering. These rickety-looking craft are surprisingly strong and bring hopes of sporting glory.

Podracers come in all shapes and sizes – just like the pilots who fly them. The cockpit and controls are tailored to the pilot's body, and how many arms, hands and even feet they have. Some, like Sebulba's, hide weapons.

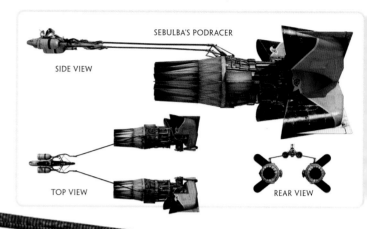

SEBULBA'S PODRACER

SIDE VIEW

TOP VIEW

REAR VIEW

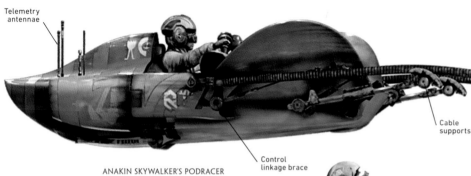

Telemetry antennae

Cable supports

Control cable

Control linkage brace

ANAKIN SKYWALKER'S PODRACER

Thrust stabiliser cone

IN-DEPTH ANALYSIS

Catastrophic engine failure is only a heartbeat away. Pilots constantly monitor engine performance to watch for overheating or pressure failure. But other crucial systems can fail, too, so warning alarms from the cockpit displays are loud enough to be heard even over the roar of the engines.

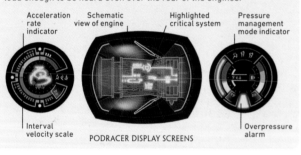

Acceleration rate indicator

Schematic view of engine

Highlighted critical system

Pressure management mode indicator

Interval velocity scale

PODRACER DISPLAY SCREENS

Overpressure alarm

ELAN MAK'S PODRACER

GASGANO'S PODRACER

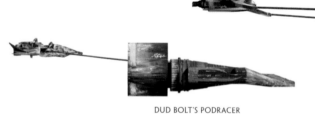

DUD BOLT'S PODRACER

ODY MANDRELL'S PODRACER

PODRACE MECHANICS

Mechanics don't get the glory, but without them the sport would not be nearly as exciting. A good mechanic can adapt a podracer to current course conditions. Expendable pit droids work on superheated engines, despite the danger.

PIT DROIDS

UNNAMED GRAN

ODIN NESLOOR

MAT RAGS

ELNICK PYE

BOK ASKOL

LANA DOBREED

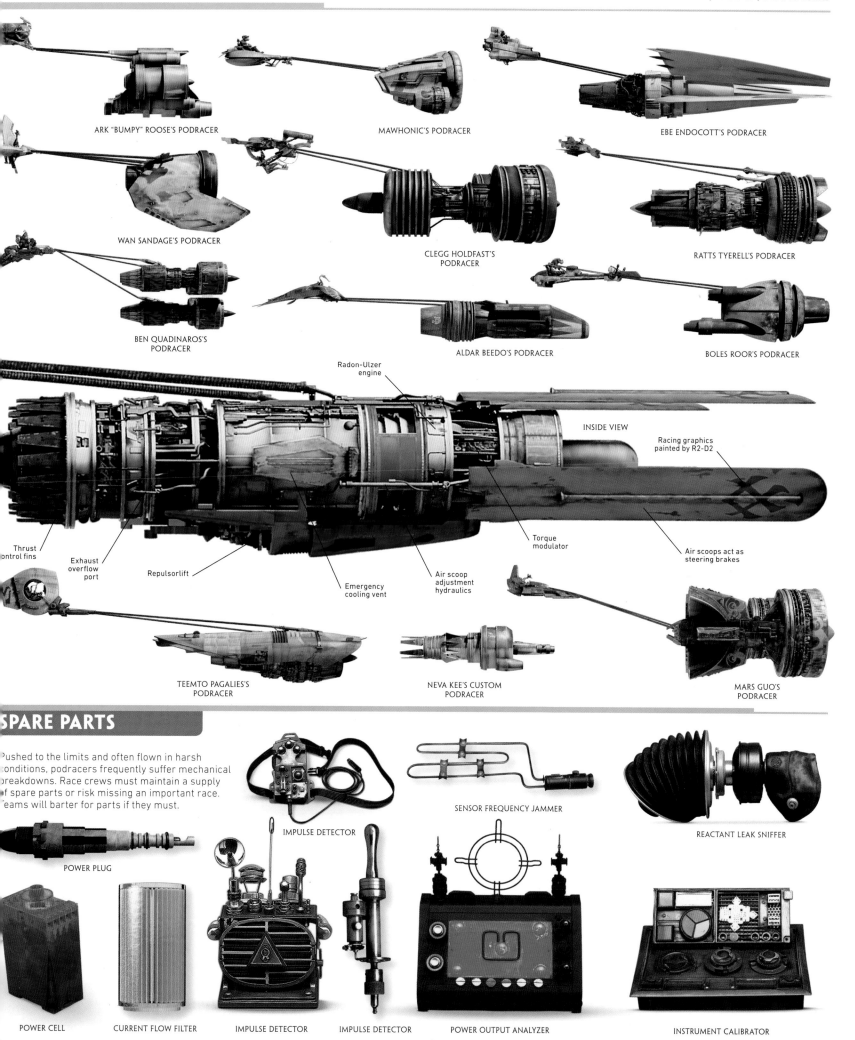

ARK "BUMPY" ROOSE'S PODRACER

MAWHONIC'S PODRACER

EBE ENDOCOTT'S PODRACER

WAN SANDAGE'S PODRACER

CLEGG HOLDFAST'S
PODRACER

RATTS TYERELL'S PODRACER

BEN QUADINAROS'S
PODRACER

ALDAR BEEDO'S PODRACER

BOLES ROOR'S PODRACER

Radon-Ulzer
engine

INSIDE VIEW

Racing graphics
painted by R2-D2

Thrust
control fins

Exhaust
overflow
port

Repulsorlift

Emergency
cooling vent

Air scoop
adjustment
hydraulics

Torque
modulator

Air scoops act as
steering brakes

TEEMTO PAGALIES'S
PODRACER

NEVA KEE'S CUSTOM
PODRACER

MARS GUO'S
PODRACER

SPARE PARTS

Pushed to the limits and often flown in harsh
conditions, podracers frequently suffer mechanical
breakdowns. Race crews must maintain a supply
of spare parts or risk missing an important race.
Teams will barter for parts if they must.

IMPULSE DETECTOR

SENSOR FREQUENCY JAMMER

REACTANT LEAK SNIFFER

POWER PLUG

POWER CELL

CURRENT FLOW FILTER

IMPULSE DETECTOR

IMPULSE DETECTOR

POWER OUTPUT ANALYZER

INSTRUMENT CALIBRATOR

FRESH FOOD

From grand banquet tables on Coruscant to street food in Mos Espa on Tatooine, food is more than just a basic necessity. Fresh food helps bring beings together and has the power to spark romance, conversation and occasionally an adventure!

SEEDS, PODS AND BARK

Scavengers and survivalists know where to find nutrition in the natural world around them. Dried seeds, flower pods and even tree bark contain essential vitamins and minerals for survival on harsh planets like swampy Dagobah.

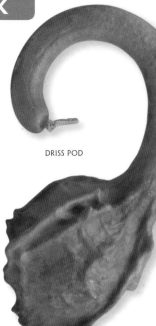

DRISS POD

DAGOBAH GALLA SEEDS

TEZIRETT SEED

DAGOBAH YARUM SEED (FOR MAKING TEA)

DAGOBAH SOHLI BARK

ANIMAL PRODUCE

MEAT

Irresistible to numerous species, meats from a variety of animals are cooked, cured and prepared as a main course for many meals. Farmers and diplomats alike enjoy fried nuna, an animal found on Naboo, Tatooine and Saleucami.

GORNT MEAT

VERKLE HUNTED BY AN EWOK

SLUG-BEETLE

PADDY FROG

NUNA

ROAST NUNA DISH

GORG

DEEP-FRIED GORG

SHAAK

MOTT

FOOD AS TRANSPORT

In some cultures, animals that might otherwise be eaten are more valuable as mounts to ride. While most in the galaxy think of banthas for their milk and steaks, Tusken Raiders ride the creatures across the desert wastes of Tatooine.

NARGLATCH

DEWBACK

BANTHA

FRUITS AND FUNGI

A prized delicacy during times of war, fruits are a popular treat eaten raw or cooked in dishes. A much-loved preparation is the jogan fruit cake, which calls for the fruit to be both baked in the batter and used as a topping.

DAGOBAH MUSHROOM SPORES

THORN PEAR

MEILOORUN FRUIT

NABOO FRUIT BOWL

PLUM

SIDI GOURD

JOGAN FRUIT AND GREEN TOPATO

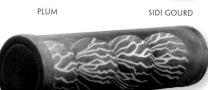

JOGAN FRUITS PACKED IN A TUBE

Unripe honey melon • Durang fruit • Oi-ois with hearthweed • Chando peppers • Muja fruit

PLATTER OF FRESH FRUIT JELLIES

STREET FOOD

CORUSCANT FOOD STALL

On the dark city streets of Coruscant, street side food stalls serve affordable, fast fare to residents of all types. Given the diversity of species inhabiting the planet, the shelves offer a wide variety of dishes to suit any palate.

SHELVED FOOD STALLS FROM CORUSCANT ENTERTAINMENT DISTRICT

TATOOINE FOOD MARKET

Local farmers and produce vendors sell their harvests directly to residents at the daily Mos Espa market. Hardworking sellers spend long days under the hot suns and only close up shop when sandstorms approach.

" HOW DO YOU GET SO BIG EATING *FOOD* OF THIS KIND? "
YODA

TATOOINE MARKET STAND SELLING FRUIT, INCLUDING GREEN PALLIES

TYPICAL MOS ESPA FOOD VENDOR'S STALL

JERKY MEATS

BRISTLEMELONS

SIDI GOURDS AND HUBBA GOURDS

BRISTLEMELONS, VAPORATOR MUSHROOMS AND DWEEZEL

SIDI GOURDS

111

PROCESSED FOOD

From the finest meals served by Coruscanti chefs to tasteless Jedi food capsules, processed foods help keep the citizens of the galaxy going. These beautiful cakes, amazing appliances and revolting rations are as interesting as those that eat them!

FOUR DRINKING CONTAINERS FROM MAZ KANATA'S CASTLE

FOOD PREPARATION

DRINK APPLIANCES AND UTENSILS

What good is a drink if you have nothing to keep it in? While simple canteens, cups or bowls are all most beings require, wealthy individuals prefer to drink from finely crafted glassware and elegant decanters.

GLASSES FROM PADMÉ AMIDALA'S APARTMENT

REY'S WATER BOTTLE

CORUSCANT DECANTER AND GLASSES SET

TATOOINE DRINKING VESSEL

WATTO'S BOWLS

ANAKIN SKYWALKER'S DRINKING BOTTLE

OUTLANDER NIGHTCLUB DRINKS CHILLER

DRINKING CANTEEN

TRAVELLER'S WATER POD

TATOOINE CUP

FOOD FOR ENTERTAINING

On the big city-planet of Coruscant, making a good impression often starts with a great meal. Serving a fine wine or delicious snack is one way to earn friends and influence on this important planet.

FOOD APPLIANCES AND UTENSILS

You wouldn't know it by looking at this old and worn meat tenderiser, but chef Strono Tuggs is an excellent cook at Maz's castle. He learned to cook at a young age by watching holovids.

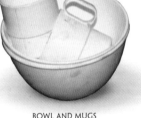
BOWL AND MUGS FROM A FREIGHTER ON CORUSCANT

FRUIT CRATE

TATOOINE MUSHROOM JAR

MEAT TENDERISER

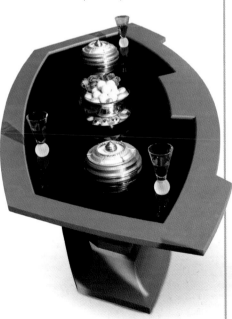
CORUSCANT TABLE SET FOR ENTERTAINING

KITCHENS

Preparing a full meal is best done in a well-stocked kitchen. While they are small and modestly appointed, kitchens for working families on Tatooine contain enough pantry space and appliances to keep a family well fed.

THE LARS FAMILY'S KITCHEN

ANAKIN AND SHMI SKYWALKER'S KITCHEN

FOOD

CONDIMENTS

Sometimes a dish could benefit from a little extra flavour – or others might need the flavour blotting out altogether. Condiments such as colourful Chadian and Ubese dressings are popular for making food more appetising.

CHADIAN AND UBESE DRESSINGS

BAKED FOOD

Whether sweet or savoury, a variety of cultures around the galaxy have recipes for delicious baked food. At Dex's Diner on Coruscant, the Sic-Six-Layer Cake is a real bargain, costing just 2.5 credits per slice.

BAKED CUSHNIPS WITH FRAL

SIC-SIX-LAYER CAKE

Haroun bread
Lamta
Spicy ahrisa
MOS ESPA FOOD BOWL

BAKER DROID HOLDING A JOGAN FRUIT CAKE

FOOD ON THE GO

On peacekeeping missions across the galaxy, you never know where your next meal is coming from. Members of the Jedi Order often carry energy capsules on their utility belts. Each contains tiny pellets with enough energy to sustain a Jedi on distant planets and long space journeys.

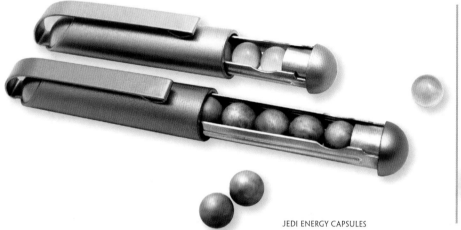
JEDI ENERGY CAPSULES

DEHYDRATED FOOD

Just add a little water to these military rations and they spring into life, becoming a bland yet nutrient rich meal for soldiers and scavengers alike. Dehydration not only saves space, but also helps to preserve food for decades.

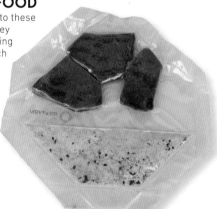
MILITARY KIT RATION PACK

VEG-MEAT

POLYSTARCH

EATING OUT

DINERS

Chefs like Dex and Borkus might seem rough and gruff, but their food is undoubtedly delicious. Each operates a diner serving up quick and hearty meals to loyal, working-class customers.

POWER SLIDERS DINER IN PONS ORA ON ABAFAR

KITCHEN PORTHOLE IN DEX'S DINER IN COCO TOWN, CORUSCANT

THE BAR IN DEX'S DINER

LUGGAGE

Whether a person is travelling from a homestead into town, or from the Core to the Outer Rim, everyone needs a way to carry precious items. Backpacks suit a traveller with only a few essentials to keep to hand. Larger luggage often reflects the wealth of its owner.

BAGS

Bags can be slung over a shoulder or attached to a belt. Tough material and secure closings help keep the articles inside safe. For some, the belongings in their bag are crucial to their survival.

LOR SAN TEKKA'S SACK

CHEWBACCA'S CARRY-POUCH

Happabore leather

Straps for salvaging gear

EWOK SHAMAN'S TALISMAN BAG

TRAMPER'S BAG

Canteen sleeve

REY'S SURVIVAL SATCHEL

SUITCASES

Travel cases can come in many shapes and sizes. Impact-resistant shells protect clothes, shoes and other personal items. For the particularly organised traveller, special shelves allow for hanging clothes or storing valuables separately.

Hanger

Storage compartment

QUEEN AMIDALA'S GARMENTCASE

NABOO SUITCASES

BACKPACKS

Backpacks are vital gear for soldiers, holding items ranging from rations to explosives. Other backpacks contain cooling apparatus, to lower the wearer's temperature on hot days.

SNOWTROOPER BACKPACK

CLONE TROOPER BACKPACK

MOS ESPA COOLTH BACKPACK

SCOUTER PACK

DESERT SURVIVAL BACKPACK

TATOOINE BACKPACK

REAR VIEW

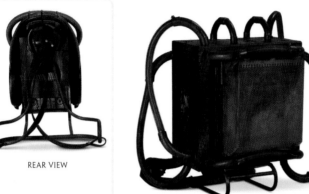

COOLING TECHNICIAN BACKPACK

WATER SIPHON CARRY PACK

YOUNG ANAKIN SKYWALKER'S BACKPACK

POWER CELL CARRY PACK

SIDE VIEW

DESERT SURVIVAL BACKPACK

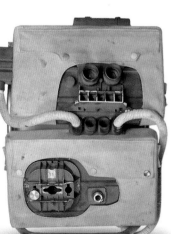

HOTH REBEL BACKPACK

ENDOR REBEL TROOPER BACKPACK

BACKPACK

Cloth protects caged animals from sun

Shoulder straps

Goods to trade at market

BOBBAJO'S HOMEMADE BACKPACK

FURNITURE

It's more than just a perch for rest, relaxation and contemplation. If furniture could talk, it would tell stories of wisdom, bravery, deception and turmoil. These objects have been witness to some of the galaxy's most pivotal events!

CHAIRS

PALACE THRONES AND CHAIRS

In the Theed Palace Throne Room, the Queen of Naboo takes council from her advisors and is never far from her trusted handmaidens. Members of her Royal Advisory Council offer their advice and expertise from modest chairs situated around the room.

COUNCIL CHAIR, THEED PALACE

Hand stitched embroidery

HANDMAIDEN CHAIR, THEED PALACE

THRONE, THEED PALACE

OFFICE AND MEETING ROOM CHAIRS

In meeting rooms and offices, leaders and politicians debate amongst themselves and set galaxy-changing strategies. In many settings, the tallest chair is reserved for the highest-ranking official.

CONFERENCE ROOM CHAIR, TRADE FEDERATION BATTLESHIP

CONFERENCE ROOM CHAIR, MUSTAFAR

CONFERENCE ROOM CHAIR, GEONOSIS

JEDI COUNCIL ROOM CHAIRS

High above the city planet of Coruscant, 12 members of the Jedi Council meet in a chamber at the peak of the Jedi Temple. The chamber's chairs must be comfortable as Council members take part in long discussions of peace and war.

JEDI COUNCIL CHAIR, AS SAT IN BY PLO KOON AND DEPA BILLABA

JEDI COUNCIL CHAIR, AS SAT IN BY YODA AND YADDLE

JEDI COUNCIL CHAIR, AS SAT IN BY MACE WINDU AND KI-ADI-MUNDI

Cushioning for long meetings

OFFICE CHAIR, BAIL ORGANA

High arching headrest represents authority

Call button for Imperial Guards

Seat-specific climate control

Rotating base

OFFICE CHAIR, SUPREME CHANCELLOR PALPATINE

RESIDENTIAL CHAIRS

In contrast to the decorative Naboo chairs, Jango Fett's furniture from his Kamino apartment is simple and understated. The basic white finish and rounded edges fit the design style of the rest of Tipoca City.

DINING ROOM CHAIR, JANGO FETT

NABOO CHAIR, PADMÉ AMIDALA

DINING CHAIR, JOBAL AND RUWEE NABERRIE

BACK VIEW

WEIRD AND WONDERFUL

For unique individuals, furniture must be built for a special purpose. Yoda's hoverchair helps the small-statured Jedi Master keep up with the long strides of taller Jedi. Sebulba's chair was designed to fit the Dug's unusual physique.

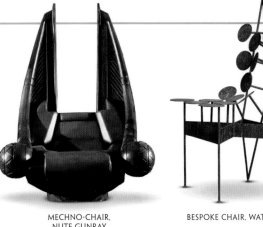

MECHNO-CHAIR, NUTE GUNRAY

BESPOKE CHAIR, WATTO

SPECTATOR CHAIR, CORUSCANT OPERA HOUSE

WALK AND TALK

Though Darth Sidious is far from the planet Naboo, he makes his presence felt by speaking to his Neimoidian pawns through a holoprojector mounted on a mechno-chair. As they stroll through the Theed palace, Sidious's projected image leads the way.

MASSAGE CHAIR, SEBULBA

HOVERCHAIR, YODA

LIGHTING

Though they all serve to illuminate dark places, some lamps are more practical than elegant. For scavengers on Jakku, oil-burning lamps provide cheap light. They extract the oil from bloggins, a species of bird famous for being panicky and loud.

Fuel fill cap

Dimmer switch activated by twisting top

High output burner

Oil pump regulator

Bloggin-oil bowl

BLOGGIN-OIL LAMP

ILLUMINATOR, PADMÉ AMIDALA

CORUSCANT OFFICE LAMP, SUPREME CHANCELLOR PALPATINE

WISH GLOBE, PADMÉ AMIDALA

SETLA LAMP, JANGO FETT

OFFICE LAMP, BAIL ORGANA

DECORATIVE PIECES

The finest residences are appointed with elegant, if unnecessary, status symbols. Citizens living on Coruscant's highest levels can afford luxuries like indoor fountains and rare birds. These collections reflect their owners' personal tastes and values.

DECORATIVE NABOO BOWL, PADMÉ AMIDALA

Brushed chromium cage

Energy field emitters confine bird

Pylat bird

GOLDEN CLOAK STAND, PADMÉ AMIDALA

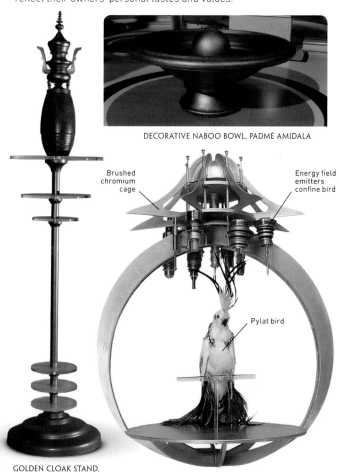

NEIMOIDIAN BIRD CAGE

INTERIOR DESIGN

The look and feel of a building is reflected in the use of space. The choice of furnishings and colour make a statement about the individuals who occupy a place. What works for a medical centre certainly won't be fit for the apartment of an important senator.

PUBLIC BUILDINGS

Large public spaces are built for a purpose and practicality rules, whether it is a power station or a hospital. An untidy space can lead to problems, and problems mean trouble!

MAZ'S CASTLE, TAKODANA

MEDICAL CENTRE, POLIS MASSA

COMMERCIAL BUILDINGS

Commercial buildings are all about business. Getting the decoration right is crucial for attracting the right customer and making them comfortable. But each building must also be functional, with plenty of storage and a range of work areas for employees.

WATTO'S JUNK SHOP, TATOOINE

DEX'S DINER, COCO TOWN, CORUSCANT

SALOON, BILBOUSA, NAL HUTTA

RESIDENTIAL BUILDINGS

Whether a working homestead or a desert dweller's hut, everyone needs a place to call home. A senator's apartment should be elegant and reflect their power, while a bounty hunter's living quarters are less a home than a place to sleep between missions.

PRINCESS LEIA'S BRIGHT APARTMENT, CLOUD CITY

JANGO FETT'S UTILITARIAN APARTMENT, KAMINO

WORK ROOM, THE LARS HOMESTEAD, TATOOINE

DINING ROOM, THE LARS HOMESTEAD, TATOOINE

BEN KENOBI'S HUMBLE HUT, TATOOINE

ANAKIN SKYWALKER'S BEDROOM, BASIC SLAVE QUARTERS, TATOOINE

LAVISH DINING ROOM, VARYKINO, LAKE COUNTRY HOUSE, NABOO

ENTERTAINING AREA, PADMÉ AMIDALA'S APARTMENT, CORUSCANT

SITTING AREA, PADMÉ AMIDALA'S APARTMENT, CORUSCANT

BEDROOM, PADMÉ AMIDALA'S APARTMENT, CORUSCANT

VERANDA, PADMÉ AMIDALA'S APARTMENT, CORUSCANT

GOVERNMENTAL AND BUSINESS BUILDINGS

If you want to hold a meeting, you need a space in which to do it. Conference rooms mix technology for communicating with distant individuals, as well as furniture for those present. A galactic leader's office offers visitors a seat to share their personal concerns – welcome or not!

THE SEPARATIST COUNCIL CONFERENCE ROOM, MUSTAFAR

TOYDARIAN MINISTRY COUNCIL, TOYDARIA

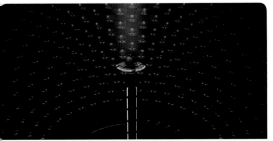

SENATE HALL, CORUSCANT

SEPARATIST CONFERENCE ROOM, GEONOSIS

THRONE ROOM, THEED PALACE, NABOO

SENATE HOLDING OFFICE, CORUSCANT

SENATOR BAIL ORGANA'S OFFICE, CORUSCANT

SENATOR CLOVIS'S OFFICE, CORUSCANT

VEHICLES

The biggest challenge when designing a spaceship is space – or lack of it! A resting nook may end up sharing space with a kitchen. Every area must have a purpose and spacious, separate rooms are a luxury for dignitaries and the wealthy.

THRONE ROOM, NABOO ROYAL STARSHIP

BRIDGE, STAR DESTROYER

BRIDGE, TRADE FEDERATION CRUISER

PASSENGER SEATING, NABOO SPEEDER BUS

SHABBY INTERIOR, *MILLENNIUM FALCON*

CONFERENCE ROOM, *TANTIVE III*

CLINICAL INTERIOR, STAR DESTROYER

RELIGIOUS BUILDINGS

Buildings for religious purposes often reveal a lot about the religion's followers. Rooms and open spaces provide areas for reflection, meditation and unity with the divine.

FUNERAL CHAMBERS, JEDI TEMPLE, CORUSCANT

GRAND HALLWAY, JEDI TEMPLE, CORUSCANT

MAIN CHAMBER, SITH TEMPLE, MALACHOR

ART

With so many rich cultures and interesting worlds across the galaxy, there is no lack of inspiration for artists. Beautiful sculpture, statuary, graffiti and illustration are captivating forms of artistic expression and important depictions of galactic history that collectors cannot resist!

ABSTRACT SCULPTURE

Shape, form and colour come together in strange, but beautiful, ways in these sophisticated art pieces. Bail Organa was a well-known collector of abstract art in the years before the destruction of Alderaan.

SCULPTURE FROM SENATOR PALPATINE'S GUEST QUARTERS

SCULPTURE

STATUES

Statues make eye-catching symbols of power for important beings. General Grievous's shrine-like lair on Vassek houses multiple statues that portray his evolution as a cyborg. As Palpatine's power grows, so does his statue and artefact collection that he considers "the spoils of war".

STATUE FROM THE JEDI TEMPLE MAIN HALLWAY

STATUE FROM SENATOR PALPATINE'S QUARTERS

STATUE FROM GENERAL GRIEVOUS'S FORTRESS

STATUE OF SHIRAYA FROM SENATOR AMIDALA'S CORUSCANT APARTMENT

STATUETTES

Small and compact, a statuette is the perfect decorative item to liven up a bedroom shelf or office. Being easy to transport and display, they are popular with wealthy collectors and common citizens alike.

STATUETTE FROM ANAKIN SKYWALKER'S CHILDHOOD BEDROOM

STATUETTE FROM SENATOR PALPATINE'S QUARTERS

SCULPTURE FROM BAIL ORGANA'S CORUSCANT APARTMENT

SCULPTURE FROM SENATOR AMIDALA'S CORUSCANT APARTMENT

SCULPTURE FROM BAIL ORGANA'S CORUSCANT APARTMENT

JEDI BUSTS

Some of the bravest and noblest Jedi are memorialised in sculpted busts cast out of the finest bronzium. Jedi relics become very rare during Imperial rule and are sought after by collectors, like obsessive Grakkus the Hutt.

BUST OF YODA

BUST OF SAESEE TIIN

BUST OF KI-ADI-MUNDI

BUST OF COUNT DOOKU

BUST OF CHON ACTRION, "ARCHITECT OF FREEDOM"

BUST OF CHERFF MAOTA

FOUR SAGES OF DWARTII

This quartet of ancient philosophers and lawmakers influenced the earliest laws in the Galactic Republic. Palpatine keeps bronzium statues of the Four Sages in his office on Coruscant and sometimes conceals his lightsabers inside the Sistros statue.

STATUE OF SISTROS

STATUE OF BRAATA

STATUE OF FAYA

STATUE OF YANJON

FRIEZE

This extremely valuable piece of art depicts an ancient battle between the forces of good and evil. The detailed carvings include terrifying war beasts and warriors engaged in a deadly conflict.

FRIEZE FROM SUPREME CHANCELLOR PALPATINE'S OFFICE

GRAFFITI

Sabine Wren and Ketsu Onyo are not only Mandalorian warriors – they are talented artists. Sabine tags walls, propaganda posters and Imperial equipment with her trademark starbird graffiti, leaving no question as to who is responsible for her rebellious acts.

SABINE WREN'S STARBIRD GRAFFITI ONBOARD THE *GHOST*

SABINE WREN'S GRAFFITI OF EZRA, ZEB AND CHOPPER ONBOARD THE *GHOST*

SABINE WREN'S GRAFFITI OF REX AND KANAN ONBOARD AN IMPERIAL SHUTTLE

TIE DYE

After Ezra Bridger and Zeb Orrelios steal a TIE fighter from the Imperials, Sabine turns it into a graffiti masterpiece. The rebels fit it with electromagnetic generators and remote flying controls that makes this unique TIE an unusual weapon in their attempt to rescue their friend, Kanan Jarrus.

SABINE WREN AMENDING IMPERIAL PROPAGANDA

KETSU ONYO'S TAG AT GAREL CITY SPACEPORT

OTHER MEDIA

HELMETS

When Kanan loses his eyesight in a duel with Darth Maul, he adopts a new custom-painted helmet. Decorated helmets are popular with the crew of the *Ghost*; both Sabine and Ezra also wear personalised headgear.

EZRA BRIDGER'S SECOND HELMET

KANAN JARRUS'S HELMET

GRAFFITIED STORMTROOPER HELMET

FLAGS AND WALL HANGINGS

The Empire uses propaganda to speak to the masses. Their posters – which only show the positive side of the Empire – are designed to influence local populations to join the cause or help stamp out rebellion.

IMPERIAL POSTER ON LOTHAL

IMPERIAL POSTER ON LOTHAL

IMPERIAL POSTER ON LOTHAL

DRAWINGS AND PAINTINGS

Family is a common subject for drawings and paintings, but not in the art favoured by Mama the Hutt. Mama adorns the walls of her swampy home on Nal Hutta with many self-portraits. She does not think highly of her son, Ziro, so she would much rather look at paintings of herself!

PAINTING OF MAMA THE HUTT

JEK LAWQUANE WITH HIS DRAWINGS

PAINTING OF THE BRIDGER FAMILY

CRIMINAL PROFILE OF BANNAMU

CHAVA THE WISE'S DRAWING OF THE LIRA SAN PROPHECY

CRIMINAL PROFILE OF BREA TONNIKA

ETHNOGRAPHY

Objects can reveal many fascinating details about a culture including its history and customs. Studying items from other cultures gives insight into what is important to them, where they come from and how they live in times of peace and war.

CULTURAL ARTEFACTS

EWOK

Although primitive by most standards, the Ewoks have a rich culture. Their history is passed down through spoken stories, while their handcrafted artefacts highlight their spiritual nature. Shaman Logray shakes his ghost rattle to ward off evil spirits during incantations.

SHAMAN LOGRAY'S GHOST RATTLE

CHURI BIRD CALLERS

SITH

Palpatine is a connoisseur of fine art, and he collects rare Sith pieces. Guests to his quarters are blissfully unaware of the origins of these relics or their dark significance, including the Jedi who frequent his offices.

SITH CHALICE

ORNATE SITH SPIRIT URN

WOOKIEE

Wookiees are renowned for their artistic skills. From a young age, Wookiees learn to craft beautiful objects made from wood, gemstones and other natural materials. Their cultural art is also often combined with advanced technology or possesses an important function – like the Kashyyyk clarion which is used to summon Wookiees to gatherings.

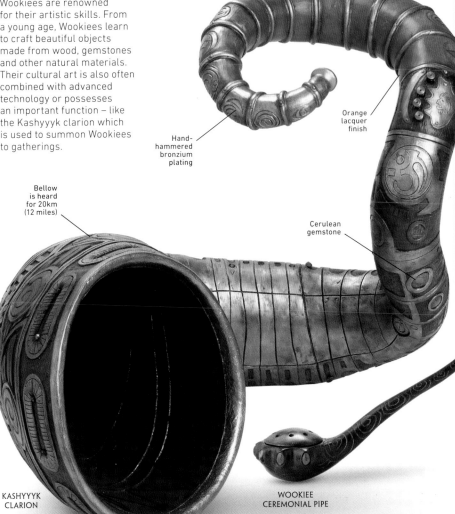

Orange lacquer finish

Hand-hammered bronzium plating

Bellow is heard for 20km (12 miles)

Cerulean gemstone

KASHYYYK CLARION

WOOKIEE CEREMONIAL PIPE

TWI'LEK

Kalikori are sacred Twi'lek family heirlooms. Each generation adds to the artwork, which may be considered an abstract representation of the Twi'lek body form. Hera Syndulla's Kalikori is passed down from her mother, but is confiscated by Grand Admiral Thrawn for his art collection.

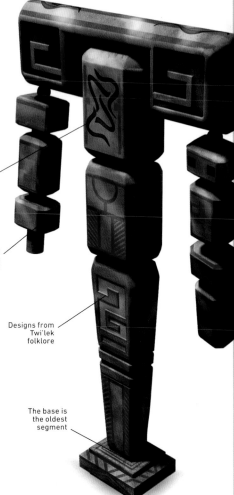

Scripts symbolise important family events

The most recent segment added to the Kalikori

Designs from Twi'lek folklore

The base is the oldest segment

HERA SYNDULLA'S FAMILY KALIKORI

TATTOOS

DATHOMIRIAN

Dathomirian tattoos represent their tribal heritage. Males have natural striping that is enhanced and embellished with tattoos. Females (Nightsisters) generally have more subtle, monochrome tattoos that contrast with their pale skin.

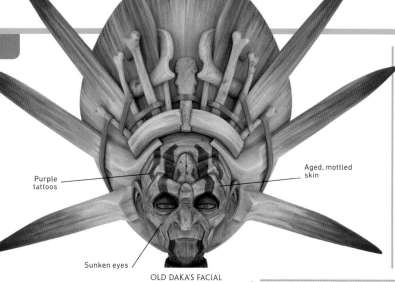

Purple tattoos

Aged, mottled skin

Sunken eyes

OLD DAKA'S FACIAL TATTOOS

ZABRAK

With thin monochrome lines on their skin, Zabrak tattoos resemble cracked soil, perhaps a reminder of their connections to the environment. Tattoo patterns vary, and may signify important events in their lives and their lineage.

EETH KOTH'S FACIAL TATTOOS

SUGI'S FACIAL TATTOOS

KARIS'S FACIAL TATTOOS

TALIA'S FACIAL TATTOOS

ASAJJ VENTRESS'S FACIAL TATTOOS

MIRIALAN

Mirialans have a flourishing spiritual culture. Their green and yellow skin tones are decorated with geometric-patterned tattoos, symbolising personal achievements such as skills gained or tasks completed.

LUMINARA UNDULI'S FACIAL TATTOOS

BARRISS OFFEE'S FACIAL TATTOOS

BARRISS OFFEE'S HAND TATTOO

DARTH MAUL'S BODY TATTOOS

BROTHER VISCUS'S FACIAL TATTOOS

SAVAGE OPRESS'S FACIAL TATTOOS

HUTTESE

Criminal behaviour is entrenched in Huttese culture. Their tattoos tend to show allegiance to crime families, organisations and gangs of ill repute. As a leader of the Black Sun, Ziro's body is covered with the syndicate's symbol.

ZIRO THE HUTT'S BLACK SUN BODY TATTOOS

JABBA THE HUTT'S DESILIJIC CRIME FAMILY TATTOO

PANTORAN

Blue-skinned Pantorans maintain an aristocratic society and sophisticated culture. Along with fine tailored clothing and elegant jewellery, they display golden facial tattoos as symbols of their status. The tattoo lines are generally simple, recalling symbology from ancient Pantoran texts.

CHAIRMAN CHI CHO'S FACIAL TATTOOS

CLONE TROOPERS

Clones of the Grand Army of the Republic are genetically identical, yet they each have distinct personalities. They express themselves by altering their hair or getting tattoos. Kix's tattoo says "a good droid is a dead one" in Aurebesh.

FIVES'S FACIAL TATTOO

JESSE'S SCALP AND FACE TATTOO

DOGMA'S FACIAL TATTOO

SENATOR CHI EEKWAY'S FACIAL TATTOOS

SENATOR RIYO CHUCHI'S FACIAL TATTOOS

HARDCASE'S SCALP, FACE AND CHIN TATTOOS

HEVY'S CHEEK TATTOOS

KIX'S SCALP TATTOO

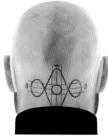

JEK'S NECK TATTOO

LANGUAGES OF THE GALAXY

Countless languages are spoken around the galaxy – C-3PO himself can converse in more than six million forms of communication! Galactic Basic is one of the most common tongues, and Bocce is spoken widely on travel and shipping routes. Languages like Huttese, Aqualish and Mando'a dominate in the systems controlled by those societies.

PHRASES

Daily life on planets that are colonised by a different species can require basic fluency in several languages. Knowing a few important phrases in a variety of languages makes galactic travel much easier, too!

" Yub nub! " *"Hooray!"* **EWOKESE**

" Elek " **MANDO'A**

" Heyo-dalee " **GUNGAN**

" Tonta tonka! " *"Tentacles up!"* **HUTTESE**

" Omu'sata! " *"Shut up!"* **TRADE TALK**

" Nyeta " **JAWAESE**

SCRIPTS

The written word can come in many forms. Some languages may use more than one script, such as Naboo. Other tongues may adopt alphabets from foreign languages – for example, the spoken language, Galactic Basic, uses both the Aurebesh and Outer Rim alphabets for its written form.

NUMBERS

Mando'a, Trade Federation, Aurebesh and Outer Rim scripts use base 10 (or decimal) number systems. Things get more complicated on Tatooine however, where Jawas use a base 9 scheme and Hutts use a base 8 system. Hutts count on their fingers, (of which they have only 8) and their numbers jump from 7 to 10 (skipping 8 and 9). This may be a reason why financial deals always seem to be in their favour!

NUMBER 3 IN AUREBESH

NUMBER 3 IN MANDO'A

NUMBER 3 IN OUTER RIM

NUMBER 7 IN TRADE FEDERATION

NUMBER 7 IN OUTER RIM

NUMBER 7 IN AUREBESH

LANGUAGE	A	B	C	D	E	F	G	H	I	J	K	L	M	N	O	P	Q	R	S	T	U	V	W	X	Y	Z
AUREBESH																										
LETTER NAME	*Aurek*	*Besh*	*Cresh*	*Dora*	*Esk*	*Forn*	*Grek*	*Herf*	*Isk*	*Jenth*	*Krill*	*Leth*	*Mern*	*Nern*	*Osk*	*Peth*	*Qek*	*Resh*	*Senth*	*Trill*	*Usk*	*Vew*	*Wesk*	*Xesh*	*Yirt*	*Zerek*
FUTHORK																										
GEONOSIAN																										
MANDO'A																										
TRADE FEDERATION																										
OUTER RIM																										

FORMAL AND INFORMAL SCRIPTS

Futhark is the ancient script of Naboo, used by royalty and the aristocracy. It continues to be used in formal applications, especially by the Naboo government, and the military to identify spacecraft. However, Futhork script is a later development, with more distinct-looking letters. The common Naboo population use it for informal, day-to-day communications.

FUTHARK SCRIPT

FUTHORK SCRIPT

KEY

HELLO

GOODBYE

SORRY

THANK YOU

YES

NO

ROUGH LANGUAGE

RANDOM PHRASES

" Ret'urcye mhi "
MANDO'A

" Sleemo! "
"Slime ball!"
HUTTESE

" Nee choo! "
"Die!"
HUTTESE

" Togo Togu! "
"Hands off!"
JAWAESE

" Den "
EWOKESE

" Keezx "
BOCCE

" Karabast! "
An expression of disgust
LASAT

" Nokeezx "
BOCCE

" H'chu apenkee "
HUTTESE

" Ibana "
JAWAESE

" Labu labu? "
"How much?"
EWOKESE

" Wwwah Rrroooaaah Wha? "
"Want to play holochess?"
SHYRIIWOOK

" Vor Entye "
MANDO'A

" Grua thun "
AQUALISH

" Aargh "
TUSKEN

" Yuow "
SHYRIIWOOK

" Muawa "
SHYRIIWOOK

" N'eparavu takisit "
MANDO'A

" Wah-Wah. Wrry-wrry-nahwikoo! "
"Let's get outta here!"
DROID BINARY

" Wachamio! "
"Let's go!"
TWI'LEKI

" M'um m'aloo "
JAWAESE

" Taa baa "
JAWAESE

" Su cuy'gar "
MANDO'A

" Chak "
EWOKESE

" Zanki "
BOCCE

" Wee now kong bantha poodoo! "
"Now you're bantha fodder!"
HUTTESE

" Mee Jewz Ku "
HUTTESE

" L'a heeting "
NEIMOIDIAN

125

SCIENCE AND TECHNOLOGY

Science fuels all of the technology used across the galaxy, from the grandest Star Destroyers to the simplest comlink tools. The wonders of galactic technology have produced powerful weapons, cutting-edge equipment and life-saving medical facilities, as well as innumerable droids: an essential part of galactic life. The skills of a droid are as valuable as they are varied – Chopper can pilot the *Phantom* shuttle, while C-3PO can interpret millions of languages!

HURID-327 DROID

THE FORCE

The Force is an invisible energy that flows through all living things. Those that are sensitive to it can harness its power to perform incredible feats. The Force has two sides – the light and the dark – and Force-sensitives normally follow one path or the other. However, different cultures draw on the Force in different ways, and some even blend both sides together.

FORCE POWERS

LIGHT ALIGNED

The light side of the Force is selfless, seeking to protect others and maintain peace. Yoda learns from the spirit of Qui-Gon Jinn that it is possible for a Jedi's essence to survive beyond death if they complete a secret course of training.

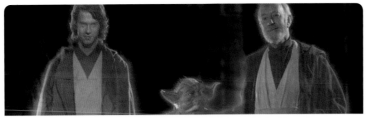

THE FORCE GHOSTS OF ANAKIN SKYWALKER, YODA AND OBI-WAN KENOBI (LEFT TO RIGHT)

DARK ALIGNED

The dark side is fuelled by selfishness. Its users are driven by fear, anger and hatred. These emotions show themselves in the desire to control others and the lust for ever more power. These abilities result in much suffering for their victims.

FORCE CHOKE USED BY ANAKIN SKYWALKER ON PADMÉ AMIDALA

FORCE LIGHTNING USED BY DARTH SIDIOUS ON MACE WINDU

MIND PROBE USED BY KYLO REN ON POE DAMERON

NEUTRAL

Some Force abilities are common to both dark and light side users. Whether they are considered neutral abilities, a blend of dark and light, or the domain of one side or the other, may all depend upon a certain point of view.

BEAST CONTROL USED BY ANAKIN SKYWALKER ON A REEK

FORCE JUMP USED BY YODA IN THE SENATE BUILDING ON CORUSCANT

MIND TRICK USED BY OBI-WAN KENOBI ON ELAN SLEAZEBAGGANO

FORCE ORB USED BY ANAKIN SKYWALKER ON PADMÉ AMIDALA

TELEKENESIS USED BY YODA ON GEONOSIS

FORCE USERS

NEUTRAL

Force-sensitivity can be shown from an early age, and younglings, such as Zinn Toa, are not naturally aligned either to the dark or the light sides. Not all Force users follow one aspect of the Force or the other. Some, like the Father and Bendu, seek a balance between them.

THE FATHER

WEE DUNN

ROO-ROO PAGE

FORCE PRIESTESSES

ZINN TOA

PYPEY

ALORA

BENDU

IGHT ALIGNED

ot all light side users are
edi. Ahsoka Tano leaves the
rder, though she remains
iendly with the Jedi. The
agoyans use the Force for
editation rather than
ghting, and actually shun
e Jedi. Orphne does not
rectly use the Force, but her
agical powers stem from it.

REY

AHSOKA TANO

ORPHNE

MAZ KANATA

DAGOYAN MYSTIC

THE DAUGHTER

DARK ALIGNED

There are dark side Force-
sensitives that are not Sith.
The Imperial Inquisitors hunt
down Jedi and other Force
users on behalf of their Sith
masters. Maul used to be a
Sith apprentice, but he now
follows his own path.

ASAJJ VENTRESS

NIGHTSISTERS

SAVAGE OPRESS

SUPREME LEADER SNOKE

FRANGAWL CULT

THE SON

MAUL

KYLO REN

FIFTH BROTHER

GRAND INQUISITOR

SEVENTH SISTER

EIGHTH BROTHER

INQUISITORS

129

CLONING

The Republic's clone army is commissioned by Sifo-Dyas, a rogue Jedi Master who foresees the need for an army to fight an impending galactic war. Count Dooku has Sifo-Dyas killed, however, and the Sith secretly manipulate the project to sabotage the Jedi Order.

Republic clone troopers are based on a single template: the infamous bounty hunter Jango Fett. On the planet Kamino, clone embryos are mass-produced in the Egg Lab, overseen by Chief Scientist Ko Sai. Their genetic code is altered to dramatically accelerate their growth rate.

OBI-WAN TOURS THE CLONE EGG LAB

TEACHING

Clone children are educated in classrooms packed with hundreds of students, though much of their instruction comes through individual viewscreens. Their accelerated growth means less time for study – so the focus is on military instruction and battle tactics rather than traditional academics.

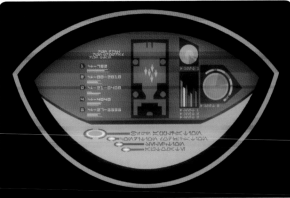

CLONE CLASSROOM VIEWSCREEN

CLONE CHILDREN IN CLASSROOM

TRAINING

The first batches of clones are trained personally by Jango Fett. After his death, the clones are instead trained with the aid of the Arconan bounty hunter, El-Les, and the Siniteen bounty hunter, Bric. They train in simulated battles using holograms and modified battle droids.

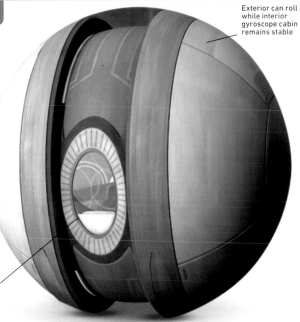

Exterior can roll while interior gyroscope cabin remains stable

Pressurised for space and deep sea travel

Viewport

FLIGHT POD (USED FOR CLONE PILOT TRAINING)

DOMINO SQUAD TRAINING IN WAR GAMES

YOUNG CLONE TROOPERS RECEIVE EQUIPMENT

MEDICAL INTERVENTION

A secret bio chip in the brain of every clone modifies their behaviour to control any counterproductive aggressive tendencies, and enhance their obedience to authority. This inhibitor chip also programs the clones to involuntarily obey Palpatine's Order 66, and destroy their Jedi generals.

CLONE BIO CHIP

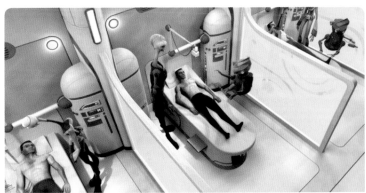

CLONE CADETS IN THE MEDICAL FACILITY

CYBORGS

Cyborgs are living beings that enhance their bodies with machine parts. Such alterations are more profound than just artificial limbs. They change a being's physiology and brain functions in fundamental ways. The process is so invasive that it is usually irreversible.

SENTIENT

Some cyborgs receive their alterations voluntarily. Tseebo's cyborg tech headgear allows him to interface with computers. B'omarr monks reduce themselves to floating brains to eliminate the distractions of the outside world, while Junkers on Lotho Minor use spare parts to build new bodies for themselves. Vader's alterations, however, are a matter of survival after receiving life-threatening injuries on Mustafar.

B'OMARR MONK

NON-SENTIENT

Unfortunately for them, non-sentient creatures have no say in their alterations, which are made to improve their performance in service of their masters. Hydroid Medusas are armoured, electrified jellyfish developed by the Karkarodons. Luggabeats are work animals found on frontier worlds.

HYDROID MEDUSA

Salvaged speeder bike saddle

LOTHO MINOR JUNKER

LOBOT

TSEEBO

DARTH VADER

Purified air and water recycling tanks

Armoured fetlock

LUGGABEAST

GENERAL GRIEVOUS

IN-DEPTH ANALYSIS

General Grievous is re-built as a cyborg to maximise his fighting abilities. He is sensitive about his upgrades, insisting to his droid EV-A4-D that they are "improvements". Little of his original body remains, apart from his eyes, portions of his brain, lungs and heart. Alterations to his brain help him cope with his new mechanical anatomy.

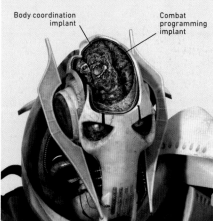

Body coordination implant

Combat programming implant

GRIEVOUS'S BRAIN

SPACE TECHNOLOGY

Over millennia, civilisations have developed all manner of equipment to make space travel not only possible but commonplace. Without it, every planet in the galaxy would be isolated – there would be no Republic or Empire, only primitive societies trapped on their own homeworlds.

PROPULSION

HYPERDRIVES

Starships travel between the stars at faster-than-light speeds with the aid of hyperdrives. Ships with hyperdrives move through an alternate dimension known as hyperspace, taking just hours to cover distances that would otherwise take thousands of years. Jumps must be made on pre-plotted courses to avoid dangerous objects, like stars and planets.

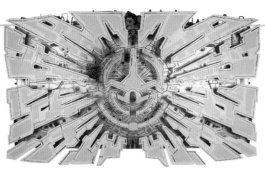

T-14 HYPERDRIVE GENERATOR, NABOO ROYAL STARSHIP

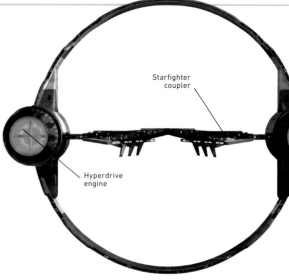

Starfighter coupler

Hyperdrive engine

EXTERNAL HYPERDRIVE BOOSTER RING, OBI-WAN KENOBI'S STARFIGHTER

REACTOR CORES

Space stations, battleships and other large facilities generate their power inside reactor cores. Fusion reactors that use hypermatter fuel are common, but other types include chemical and fission reactors. These devices are sensitive to imbalances and react extremely violently to outside interference.

BREAKING DOWN

When Queen Amidala and her entourage escape the invasion of Naboo, her starship's T-14 hyperdrive malfunctions and they must land on Tatooine to make repairs. A Toydarian junk dealer in Mos Espa called Watto just happens to sell the same model in his shop.

TRACKING THE BOUNTY HUNTER

Jedi starfighters are small and light to make them highly manoeuvrable in combat. They are designed for short-range missions, so lack an inbuilt hyperdrive. The starfighters use a detachable hyperdrive booster ring to travel long distances. Obi-Wan utilises one to track Jango Fett across the galaxy.

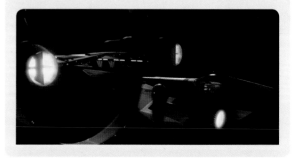

REACTOR CORE, DEATH STAR II

THE *MILLENNIUM FALCON* IN HYPERSPACE

SUBLIGHT DRIVES

Sublight engines propel starships at less than the speed of light. They can be quite fast nonetheless, allowing a ship to clear planetary atmospheres and gravity in a matter of minutes. The most common type is the ion engine, which uses ionised particles to propel a craft. Starfighters use small, powerful engines, while capital ships have vast engines the size of entire buildings.

GEMON-4 ION ENGINES, *IMPERIAL*-CLASS STAR DESTROYER

NUBIAN CREVELD-4 RADIAL ION DRIVES, *INVISIBLE HAND*

NOVALDEX J-77 "EVENT HORIZON" ENGINES, A-WING STARFIGHTER

M8.0 STARDRIVE ENGINES, MON CALAMARI STAR CRUISER

GALAXY-15 ION ENGINES, *REDEMPTION* MEDICAL FRIGATE

GRAVITY TECHNOLOGY

TRACTOR BEAMS

Tractor beams are force fields used to envelope an object or ship and pull them along. They may safely guide a starship into a landing bay, move cargo around, tow heavy objects or even be used to capture enemy ships.

MILLENNIUM FALCON CAUGHT IN THE *ERAVANA*'S TRACTOR BEAM

TRACTOR BEAM REACTOR CORE, FIRST DEATH STAR

REPULSORS

Repulsorlift engines allow a speeder, ship or other machine to defy a planet's gravity and hover above its surface or even fly high in the atmosphere. They do this by pushing against (repulsing) the planet's gravity. Retro-repulsors can also be used to quickly stop a fast-moving vehicle.

CROSS-SECTION OF REPULSORLIFTS INSIDE REY'S JUNKER SPEEDER

SHIELDS

DEFLECTOR SHIELDS

Deflector shields are energy fields that protect starships, buildings, armies and other objects. They may be generated from the actual object that they envelop, or projected from a remote location, such as the shield generator on the Forest Moon that protects the second Death Star.

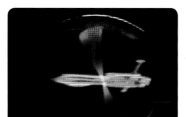

DEFLECTOR SHIELD SURROUNDING *INVISIBLE HAND*

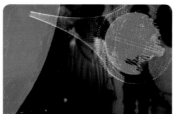

DEATH STAR II SHIELD PROJECTED FROM FOREST MOON

MAGNETIC SHIELDS

Magnetic shields are employed at the mouths of hangar bays in large starships. They allow blast doors to remain open and smaller ships to come and go, while retaining the pressurised atmosphere within the bays.

MAGNETIC SHIELD, *INVISIBLE HAND* DOCKING BAY

LIFE-SUPPORT

SPACE SUITS

Space suits allow organic beings to move freely in space, whether fighting in combat or making external repairs to starships. Many types of suits are available to fit the anatomy, pressure and oxygen requirements of various species.

Life-support regulation tank

Oxygen-filled transparent helmet

Pressurised, airtight suit

Magnetic boots

ANAKIN SKYWALKER IN JEDI SPACE SUIT

GOING OUTSIDE

Anakin Skywalker allows himself to be taken captive aboard a *Munificent*-class frigate by Count Dooku. Wearing a space suit, Obi-Wan Kenobi then manages to infiltrate the ship from outside. They hope to capture Dooku, but he escapes to Vanqor aboard a *Sheathipede*-class shuttle.

NAVIGATION

MAPS

The galaxy is an immense place and accurate maps are vital when hyperspace jumps are required. Maps may be projected onto screens or rendered as three-dimensional interactive holographic projections. When Luke Skywalker goes into hiding, he gives Lor San Tekka a map fragment showing his destination.

HOLOGRAPHIC MAP PROJECTED BY R2-D2

CHILDREN OF THE FORCE

Darth Sidious hires Cad Bane to steal a Jedi holocron containing the locations of Force-sensitive children. Bane is then ordered to kidnap them and bring them to Mustafar. When Anakin Skywalker studies the map in Bane's ship logs, he discovers the bounty hunter's sinister mission.

CAMERA DROIDS

Nobody can be everywhere at once – unless they are a conduit worm – but camera droids allow their operators to have eyes and ears in virtually any location. Most are able to fly using repulsorlifts, and then transmit their sensor data back to a computer controller.

ENTERTAINMENT

Hologlide J57 camera droids hover above podraces, following the exciting action from every angle, and transmit the race back to the audience. Their vantage from the sky protects them from Jawas and other scavengers – but they remain target practice for Tusken Raiders!

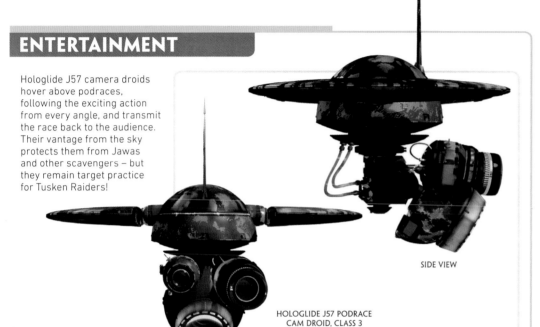

SIDE VIEW

HOLOGLIDE J57 PODRACE
CAM DROID, CLASS 3

RECORD-KEEPING

Senate droids hover in Congress meetings to record the speeches, debates and votes of each senator. These recordings are not immune to meddling however. Corrupt individuals have been known to delete or change the official records.

Motion-sensing
telephoto lens

Holoprojector

Wide angle lens

SENATE HOVERCAM DROID, CLASS 3

SECURITY

Security droids help keep a watchful eye in every corner of First Order bases, Jabba the Hutt's palace and the Coruscant underworld. Their job is not to intercept people, but to screen visitors and passers-by, and report back to their masters.

FIRST ORDER PATROL
DROID, CLASS 4

JABBA'S TT-8L/Y7
GATEKEEPER DROID,
CLASS 4

POLICE CAM DROID, CLASS 4

SECURITY MONITOR DROID, CLASS 4

FIRST ORDER SENTRY DROID, CLASS 4

PYING AND SURVEILLANCE

ark forces such as the Sith,
e Empire and the Separatists
eploy spy droids to gather intel
n the Jedi, or the rebels and
eir allies. Most droids are fitted
ly with recorders and sensors,
ut viper probes and ID9 seekers
ave weapons, too.

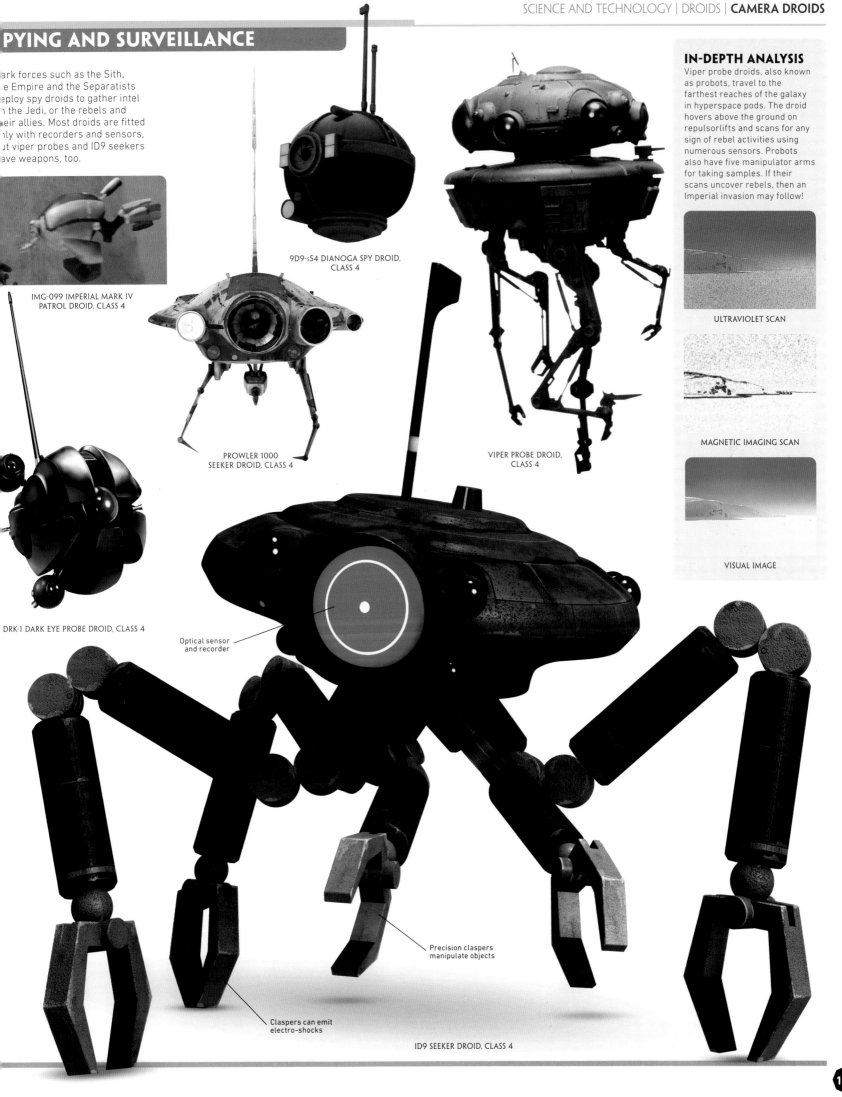

IMG-099 IMPERIAL MARK IV
PATROL DROID, CLASS 4

9D9-s54 DIANOGA SPY DROID,
CLASS 4

PROWLER 1000
SEEKER DROID, CLASS 4

VIPER PROBE DROID,
CLASS 4

DRK-1 DARK EYE PROBE DROID, CLASS 4

Optical sensor
and recorder

Precision claspers
manipulate objects

Claspers can emit
electro-shocks

ID9 SEEKER DROID, CLASS 4

IN-DEPTH ANALYSIS

Viper probe droids, also known
as probots, travel to the
farthest reaches of the galaxy
in hyperspace pods. The droid
hovers above the ground on
repulsorlifts and scans for any
sign of rebel activities using
numerous sensors. Probots
also have five manipulator arms
for taking samples. If their
scans uncover rebels, then an
Imperial invasion may follow!

ULTRAVIOLET SCAN

MAGNETIC IMAGING SCAN

VISUAL IMAGE

LABOUR DROIDS

Labour droids are simplified for very specific tasks, from hard work in hazardous environments, to keeping entire facilities running efficiently. These indispensible droids are not deep thinkers or great at conversation. Some don't even have autonomous brains – they may be controlled by a central computer instead.

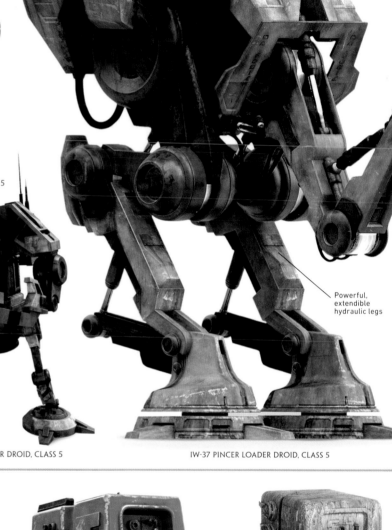

Rechargeable battery module

Heat radiation vents

Blast-resistant durasteel armour plating

Powerful, extendible hydraulic legs

WORKER DROIDS

HEAVY LIFTING

Militaries and factories use powerful worker droids to move weighty and often dangerous cargo between ships and loading bays. These droids have simple operating systems and are built to withstand falling cargo, or even minor explosions.

HOVER LOADER DROID, CLASS 5

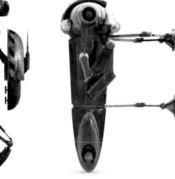

WINDOW INSTALLER DROID, CLASS 5

HURID-327 DROID, CLASS 5

B-U4D "BURFORD" LOADING DROID, CLASS 5

ORDNANCE LIFTER DROID, CLASS 5

IW-37 PINCER LOADER DROID, CLASS 5

POWER PROVIDERS

These mobile fusion generators walk around flight hangars and settlements, where they dutifully recharge machines, ships and other droids. Sometimes the rebels have creative uses for them, too: a GNK droid named EG-86 once served them as a secret courier.

EGL-21 "AMPS" POWER DROID, CLASS 2

PLNK-SERIES POWER DROID, CLASS 2

4B-EG-6 GNK-SERIES POWER DROID, CLASS 2

GNK POWER DROID, CLASS 2

EPAIR AND MAINTENANCE

achines require regular upkeep, but droids
an save their masters time by doing this
ankless job. Treadwells keep moisture
rms operational, pit droids and Otoga-222s
epair podracers, while "Geetaw" (GTAW-74)
erves Jakku's scrap collectors.

GTAW-74 WELDER DROID,
CLASS 2

PK-SERIES WORKER DROID,
CLASS 5

OTOGA-222
MAINTENANCE DROID,
CLASS 5

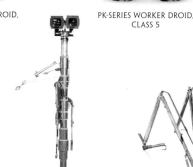

WED-15 TREADWELL DROID,
CLASS 2

FIRST ORDER MSE-SERIES
MOUSE DROID, CLASS 5

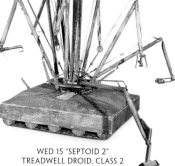

WED 15 "SEPTOID 2"
TREADWELL DROID, CLASS 2

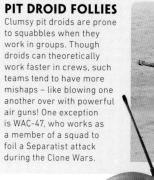

PIT DROID FOLLIES

Clumsy pit droids are prone
to squabbles when they
work in groups. Though
droids can theoretically
work faster in crews, such
teams tend to have more
mishaps – like blowing one
another over with powerful
air guns! One exception
is WAC-47, who works as
a member of a squad to
foil a Separatist attack
during the Clone Wars.

Helmet plate
protects against
falling parts

Monocular photoreceptor
with micro focus

Magnetic
clamp
precision
graspers

Knee joint
can bend
forwards and
backwards

DUM-SERIES
PIT DROID,
CLASS 2

DROID SAFEKEEPING

It's a bad idea to leave pit droids running
around with idle time. Tapping their "nose"
causes them to shut down into a compact
form for easy storage. Pressing the nose
again causes them to unfold and perform
a quick diagnostic check, before they
resume their duties.

MINING DROIDS

hese droids harvest valuable
esources from the environment.
ustafar droids are protected from
oiling lava with carbonite-alloy
rmour and energy shields. Mine
yer droids have protective shells
r accidental detonations. Sifter
roids, however, have no need for
uch shielding as they work in
eace in the sun, processing
and for valuable pieces of junk.

R-H029 SIFTER DROID, CLASS 5

DLC-13 PANNING
DROID, CLASS 5

SN-1F4 MINIATURE SIFTER DROID,
CLASS 5

ELECTROREFINING
DROID, CLASS 5

ORE EXTRACTION DROID, CLASS 5

LIN DEMOLITION AUTONOMOUS MINE LAYER
DROID, CLASS 5

LIN-V8K MINING DROID, CLASS 5

137

SERVICE DROIDS

Without service droids, the lives of many galactic beings would be far more tiresome. The earliest versions performed simple tasks, such as vacuuming and harvesting. Advances in robotics and artificial intelligence have allowed development of service droids capable of a wide array of tasks.

FOUR UNUSUAL DROID JOBS

Most droids fulfil their intended purpose, but some end up serving their masters in the most unusual and unexpected ways!

1 BULLY
A reprogrammed supervisor droid, vicious EV-9D9 oversees the pool of droids that serve crime lord Jabba the Hutt.

2 SPY
Servant droid GA-97 is assigned to work in Maz Kanata's castle and reports unusual activity to the Resistance, such as the arrival of BB-8.

3 SCIENTIFIC ASSISTANT
LEP-86C8, another servant droid, assists mad scientist Doctor Nuvo Vindi – and even helps to create the dangerous Blue Shadow Virus.

4 PERSONAL PILOT
Instead of flying commuters around metropolises, Count Dooku's FA-4 droid has the privilege of piloting his rare solar sailer starship.

CLEANERS

From scrap in a junk dealer's yard to the floors of spaceports, surfaces need to be continuously cleaned. Coruscant's Galactic City and Hosnian Prime's Republic City gleam from the tireless efforts of window cleaner droids that scour their sweeping skyscrapers.

CLE-004 WINDOW
CLEANER DROID, CLASS 5

PERSONAL USE

Resourceful individuals customise ordinary public assistance droids to suit specialised needs. Rebel teams update droids to conceal weapons, work as spies or assist starfighter squadrons.

PUBLIC ASSISTANCE

Tasks that sentient beings find undesirable or dangerous can be taken over by droids. Sometimes their work benefits everyone, such as skills like firefighting. Luxury droids, however, who often work as chauffeurs and nannies, can only be afforded by wealthy individuals.

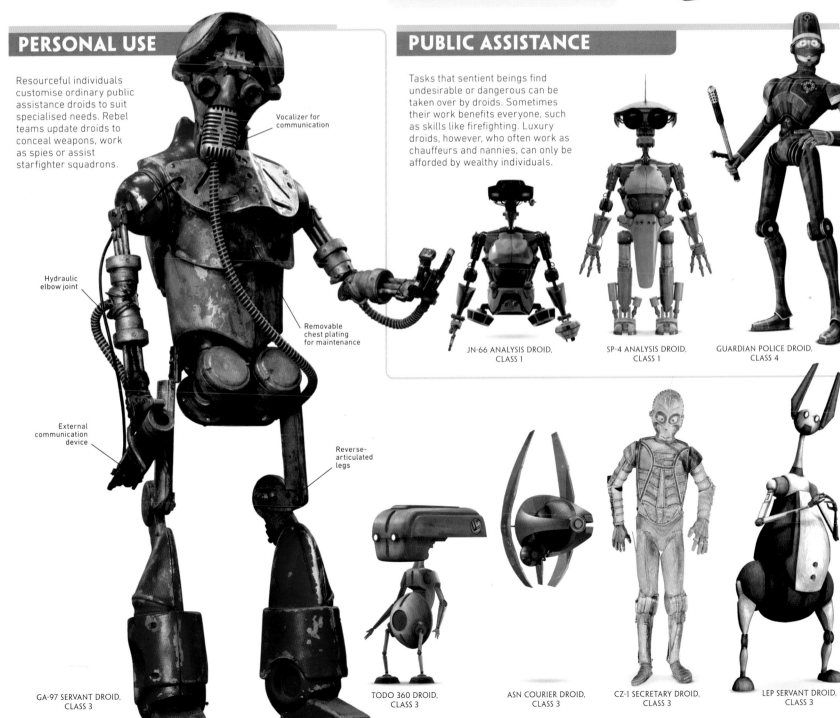

Vocalizer for communication

Hydraulic elbow joint

Removable chest plating for maintenance

External communication device

Reverse-articulated legs

GA-97 SERVANT DROID, CLASS 3

JN-66 ANALYSIS DROID, CLASS 1

SP-4 ANALYSIS DROID, CLASS 1

GUARDIAN POLICE DROID, CLASS 4

TODO 360 DROID, CLASS 3

ASN COURIER DROID, CLASS 3

CZ-1 SECRETARY DROID, CLASS 3

LEP SERVANT DROID, CLASS 3

TALKING MAGNETITE CLEANER, CLASS 5

HANGAR DECK SCRUBBER DROID,
CLASS 5

UX-53 AUTOPOLISHER MK.II DROID,
CLASS 5

COOK DROID, CLASS 3

FIREFIGHTER DROID,
CLASS 3

FA-5 VALET DROID,
CLASS 3

WA-7 WAITRESS DROID,
CLASS 3

" YOU WANT A CUP OF JAWA JUICE? "
WANDA WA-7 TO OBI-WAN KENOBI

TRAVEL DROIDS

From city streets to galactic space lanes, specialised droids make journeys efficient and worry-free. Equipped with navigation programs, travel droids plot routes and use information from public databases like the HoloNet to avoid traffic or bad weather.

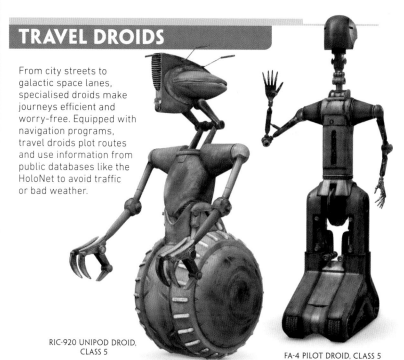

RIC-920 UNIPOD DROID,
CLASS 5

FA-4 PILOT DROID, CLASS 5

EV-9D9 JABBA'S
OVERSEER DROID, CLASS 3

BAKER DROID,
CLASS 3

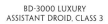

BD-3000 LUXURY
ASSISTANT DROID, CLASS 3

HITCHING A RIDE
Jedi Knight Anakin Skywalker and Senator Padmé Amidala return to Tatooine in search of his mother, Shmi. A RIC-920 working as a rickshaw driver pulls them in a floating, repulsorlift seat to Watto's shop in Mos Espa. The droid's service is the quickest, most comfortable way to travel the hot streets.

PROTOCOL DROIDS

In a galaxy where there are so many different governments and millions of languages being spoken, protocol droids have very important roles. They aid their masters in communication with friends, allies and enemies, attend diplomatic missions and run errands.

COMMAND CENTRE WORKERS

Droids like PZ-4CO and K-3PO work in military command centres for the Resistance on D'Qar and the Rebel Alliance on Hoth. They monitor troop movements, deliver messages personally or operate the loudspeaker announcement systems of the base.

PZ-4CO "PEAZY" COMMS DROID   K-3PO   K-8PO

PERSONAL ASSISTANTS

AGENTS AND EMISSARIES

Personal assistants are handy to have, whether it's R-3PO watching for Imperial spies on Echo Base, an RA-7 working aboard the Death Star or ME-8D9 translating in Maz's castle.

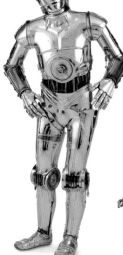

TC-4   RQ PROTOCOL DROID   RA-7 PROTOCOL DROID   ME-8D9 "EMMIE"   TC-14

IN-DEPTH ANALYSIS

C-3PO's visual hardware and software allow him to see much more than the average human. Each of the settings of his Myriad Visual System – MK. 2 provides a unique optical advantage. Human mode gives C-3PO a standard visual reference, while Infra-red mode lets him see at night. Other modes allow him to scan for properties such as gas composition, heat or motion.

HUMAN MODE

NEON MODE

INFRA-RED MODE

C-3PO

For such a dignified droid, C-3PO has humble beginnings. He was built by Anakin Skywalker on Tatooine using second-hand parts. He had many owners from the extended Skywalker family, including Shmi, Padmé Amidala, Luke, Senator Bail Organa and Princess Leia.

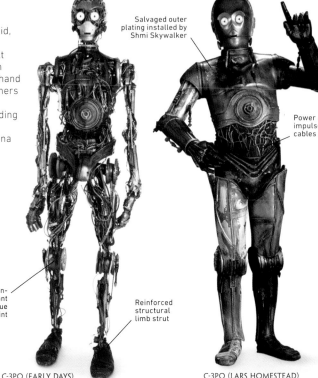

Salvaged outer plating installed by Shmi Skywalker

Power an impulse cables

Corrosion-resistant high-torque knee joint

Reinforced structural limb strut

C-3PO (EARLY DAYS)   C-3PO (LARS HOMESTEAD)

PARE PARTS

etween encounters with
onkey-lizards, Ugnaughts,
eonosian factories and
her mishaps, C-3PO suffers
lot of damage. Fortunately,
otocol droids are easily
paired – though not always
th new components.
me pieces are borrowed
om droids who no longer
ed them.

POWERBUS LINKAGE CABLES

Retainer
Connector

TERTIARY LIMB MOTOR

LOCOMOTORY SYSTEM CONTROLLER

PELVIC SERVOMOTOR

PRIMARY POWER COUPLER

Microwave
emitter/
sensor

Olfactory
sensor

TRANLANG III COMMUNICATION
MODULE

MEMORY SHIELDING RING (INNER SIDE)

MEMORY SHIELDING RING (OUTER SIDE)

SPEECH GENERATOR

> " IT'S AGAINST MY PROGRAMMING
> TO IMPERSONATE A DEITY. "
> **C-3PO**

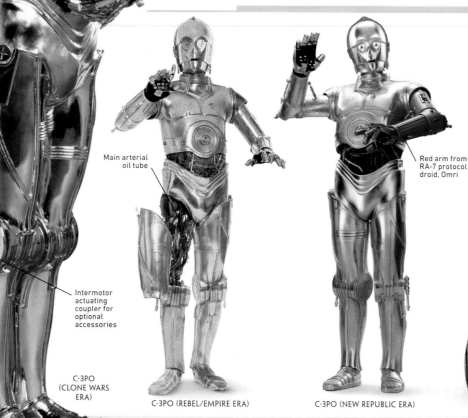

Main arterial
oil tube

Red arm from
RA-7 protocol
droid, Omri

Intermotor
actuating
coupler for
optional
accessories

C-3PO
(CLONE WARS
ERA)

C-3PO (REBEL/EMPIRE ERA)

C-3PO (NEW REPUBLIC ERA)

IN-DEPTH ANALYSIS

The original protocol droid frame that Anakin Skywalker used
to build C-3PO had faulty photoreceptors. He replaces them
with better eyes taken from a hapless old droid in Watto's shop.
When functional, the eyes light up. Unfortunately, C-3PO's
luminous eyes are a tantalising target for Salacious Crumb,
who plucks the droid's right eye out while aboard Jabba's barge.

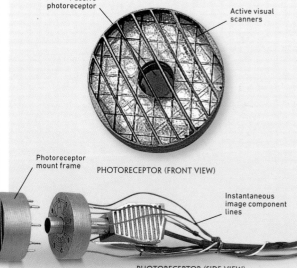

Passive
photoreceptor

Active visual
scanners

Photoreceptor
mount frame

PHOTORECEPTOR (FRONT VIEW)

Instantaneous
image component
lines

PHOTORECEPTOR (SIDE VIEW)

ASTROMECH DROIDS

Whether they are on giant space stations or tiny starships, astromech droids perform a variety of jobs. These versatile class two droids serve both heroes and villains as copilots, navigators, mechanics and more. With a nearly limitless array of tools and attachments, there is almost nothing these little droids can't do.

An evolution of ball-shaped droids used near the end of the Galactic Civil War, the BB Unit is built from the latest and greatest astro-droid technology. Despite their high-tech features, the BB Units play a similar role to older astromechs.

One of six interchangeab tool-bay disks

Internal orbiculate motivator rolls body

BB-8

R-SERIES

DROIDS

One of the most popular models of droid in the galaxy, R-Series astromechs boast a wide variety of finishes and designs. While the dome-shaped head is quite common, some models feature more conical styles or barrel-shaped designs.

Logic function display unit

Dome lifts from standard body

R1-G4

R2-C2 WITH DRINKS TROLLEY

R2-J8

R2-Q5

R2-Y9

R3-T7

R3-S6

R4-I9

R4-G9

R4-P17

R4-P44

R5-D4

M5-BZ

R5-J2

R5-P8

R5-U8

R6-H5

R7-A7

R7-D4

R8-B7

RP-G0

C-SERIES

Although outdated by most standards, the sturdy C-Series astro-droids work as mechanics or copilots on starships both big and small. C-Series droids serve the Republic in Y-wing fighters during the Clone Wars, among other roles.

Replacement leg not factory spec

Durasteel body parts

Sensory impulse cable

CHOPPER
(C1-10P)

STOP THIEF!

Chopper is distracted on a dangerous mission when he spots a match for his leg on a spare parts stall. The Ugnaught vendor sets a high price, so cheeky Chopper pinches the leg and makes a run for it! The astromech droid is delighted by his prize, but he must use all his cunning to escape the Imperials who are on his tail.

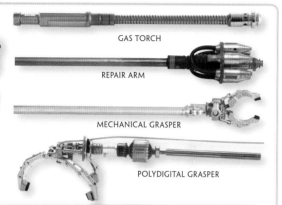

Panels contain variety of tools

Dome spins 360 degrees

Hydraulic arm shaft

R2-D2

R2-D2'S ARMS

Hidden within astromechs' durasteel bodies are gadgets for almost any job. Tools, sockets and replacement parts are standardised to make repairs and replacements easier. R2-D2 contains more than 20 graspers and tool arms.

GAS TORCH

REPAIR ARM

MECHANICAL GRASPER

POLYDIGITAL GRASPER

COMPUTER PROBE ARM

ROCKET BOOSTERS

An astromech's three-wheeled drive system makes it hard to traverse rocky or rough terrain, so some models are equipped with rocket boosters. These short-range rockets allow the droid to fly through the air or navigate in zero gravity environments. When paired with an oil slick, the fiery rockets can even serve as an offensive weapon.

LOGIC DISPLAY ASSEMBLY

MEMORY CHIP

ROCKET THRUSTER

BOOSTER ROCKET ASSEMBLY

MULTI-VISION

Astromech droids navigate through starships and outer space using a full array of sensors and scanners. Astromechs like R2-D2 use multiple environmental sensors to view in many directions at once. In addition to sensing their surroundings, astromechs use sensors to record and replay holographic messages, which they can deliver themselves if the mission requires.

PHOTORECEPTOR

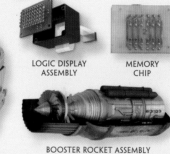

VIEW FROM HOLOGRAPHIC CAMERA

HOLOGRAMS

An astromech can display complex three-dimensional shapes, including images of people, maps and starships. The holograms are projected through a single bulb, housed inside a moving lens unit that displays the image in front of the droid. Holograms can be shown floating in the air or projected onto surfaces.

HOLOGRAM PROJECTOR BULB

HOLOPROJECTOR

DATA PROJECTION MODE

WAR DROIDS

Why fight a war yourself when a droid can do it for you? War droids battle for their masters in small trade disputes, or wars on a galactic scale. Watch out for these class four droids as they trample, roll, fly and blast their way through the battlefront!

IN-DEPTH ANALYSIS
The standard B1 battle droid is designed for one purpose: combat in large numbers. B1s are stripped of complex systems, expensive processors and the capacity for independent action and thought. A single central computer controls this early model.

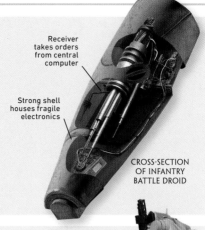

Receiver takes orders from central computer

Strong shell houses fragile electronics

CROSS-SECTION OF INFANTRY BATTLE DROID

BATTLE DROIDS

While the majority of battle droids are basic infantry units, more advanced models serve special roles in the Separatist army. As the Clone Wars rage on, newly designed battle droids are pressed into service against the Republic clone troopers.

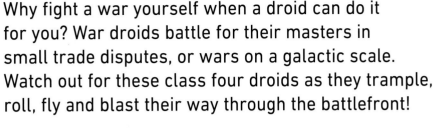

COMMAND OFFICER BATTLE DROID

PILOT BATTLE DROID

SECURITY BATTLE DROID

IN-DEPTH ANALYSIS
For maximum efficiency, the B1 model battle droid folds up to save space. When deployed on the battlefront, they rise from their compact stance. First, arms unbend and legs unfold. The droid straightens out, until finally, the head lifts to attack position, signalling that it is ready for combat.

UNFOLDING BATTLE DROID

INFANTRY BATTLE DROID

COMMANDO DROID

SUPER TACTICAL DROID

SUPER BATTLE DROID

AQUA DROID

T-SERIES TACTICAL DROID

IG-100 MAGNAGUARD

IN-DEPTH ANALYSIS
Designed to mimic a living species – the insect-like Colicoids – droidekas roll into battle in wheel form. As they get near their desired destination, they slow down and angle toward their target. With three legs planted firmly on the ground, they then unfurl into combat stance, taking aim with a pair of twin blasters.

WHEEL FORM

DROIDEKA IN COMBAT STANCE

SHIELDED FORM

1
2
3
4

STAGES OF A DROIDEKA UNFURLING

DROID FIGHTERS

DROID TANKS

When a battle calls for heavier weapons, the Separatists deploy armed and armoured droid tanks for battlefield superiority. Like other battle droids, these hulking machines feature droid brains, allowing them to think on their own.

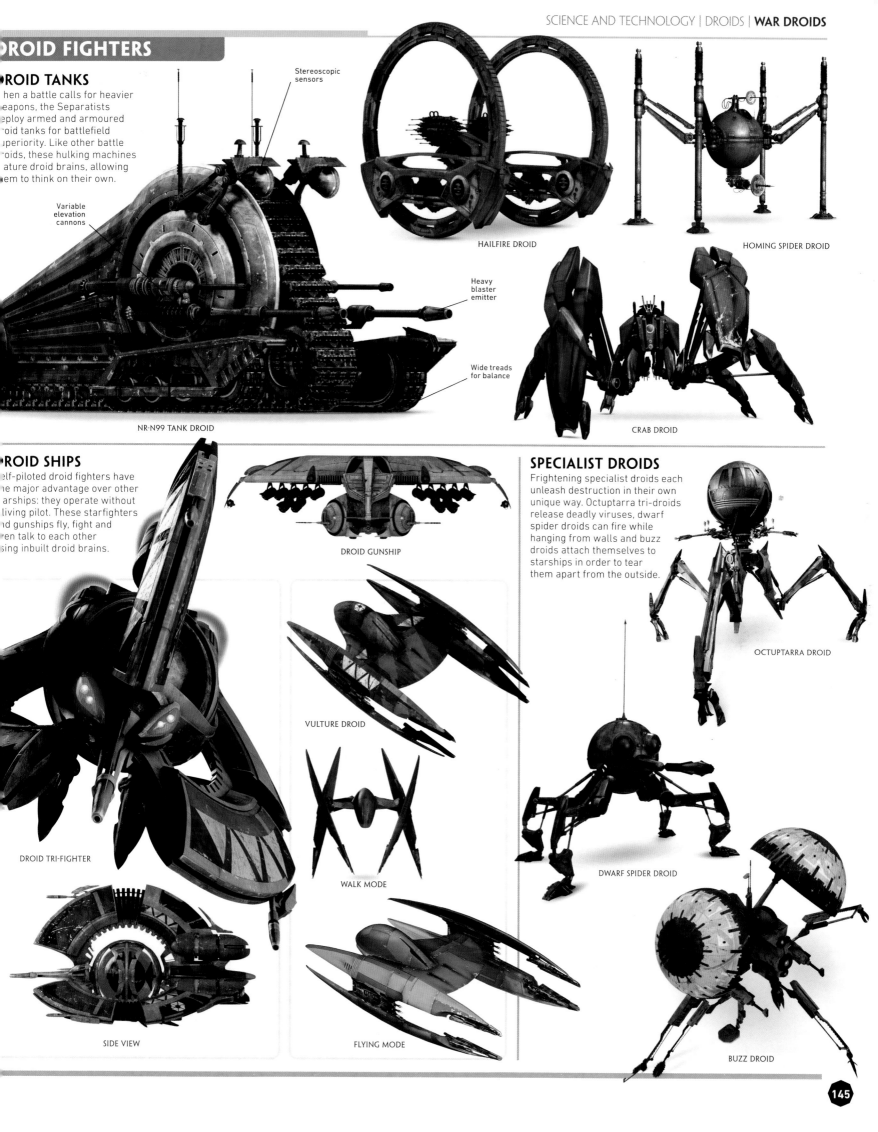

Stereoscopic sensors

Variable elevation cannons

HAILFIRE DROID

HOMING SPIDER DROID

Heavy blaster emitter

Wide treads for balance

NR-N99 TANK DROID

CRAB DROID

DROID SHIPS

Self-piloted droid fighters have one major advantage over other starships: they operate without a living pilot. These starfighters and gunships fly, fight and even talk to each other using inbuilt droid brains.

DROID GUNSHIP

SPECIALIST DROIDS

Frightening specialist droids each unleash destruction in their own unique way. Octuptarra tri-droids release deadly viruses, dwarf spider droids can fire while hanging from walls and buzz droids attach themselves to starships in order to tear them apart from the outside.

OCTUPTARRA DROID

VULTURE DROID

DROID TRI-FIGHTER

WALK MODE

DWARF SPIDER DROID

SIDE VIEW

FLYING MODE

BUZZ DROID

INTERROGATION AND SECURITY DROIDS

Cold, calculating and programmed for pain, these droids make perfect guards, assassins and interrogators. Though they often lack personality, class four droids more than make up for it in ruthless efficiency, doing their dirty work with little concern for the victims.

INTERROGATION AND PUNISHMENT

Knowledge is power, so powerful organisations need ways to extract information from their captives. Merciless interrogator droids are programmed with an uncaring personality and have a variety of techniques to make their victims talk. However, the droid 8D8 doesn't need to ask any questions – his job is to dole out punishments to misbehaving droids.

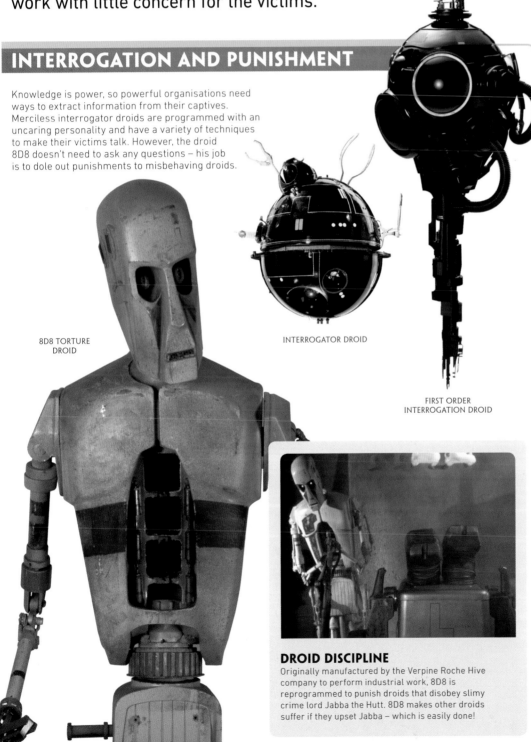

8D8 TORTURE DROID

INTERROGATOR DROID

FIRST ORDER INTERROGATION DROID

DROID DISCIPLINE
Originally manufactured by the Verpine Roche Hive company to perform industrial work, 8D8 is reprogrammed to punish droids that disobey slimy crime lord Jabba the Hutt. 8D8 makes other droids suffer if they upset Jabba – which is easily done!

Droids make capable thugs, bounty hunters and assassins with the right equipment and programming. Models like the IG-RM act as enforcers for criminals, while others like 4-LOM and IG-88 work independently. Total reformatting, such as the work done by rebels on K-2SO, is possible.

IG-88 ASSASSIN DROID

4-LOM BOUNTY HUNTER

ASN-121 ASSASSIN DROID

IG-RM THUG DROIDS

K-2SO IMPERIAL SECURITY DROID

MEDICAL DROIDS

Whether their patient has lost an arm in a lightsaber duel, fallen into a river of lava or been attacked by a wampa, medical droids patch up people who fall into harm's way. These dedicated class one droids do their often thankless duties in medical facilities across the galaxy.

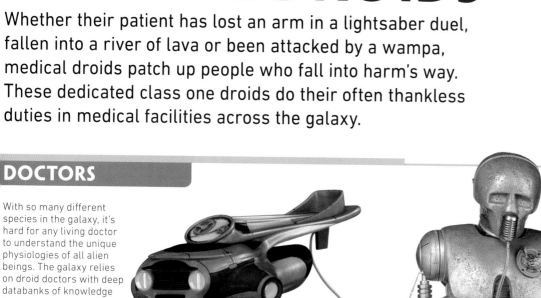

Implant installation data bank

Dual bone retractor arms

Stable tri-leg design

DOCTORS

With so many different species in the galaxy, it's hard for any living doctor to understand the unique physiologies of all alien beings. The galaxy relies on droid doctors with deep databanks of knowledge to properly diagnose and treat ailments.

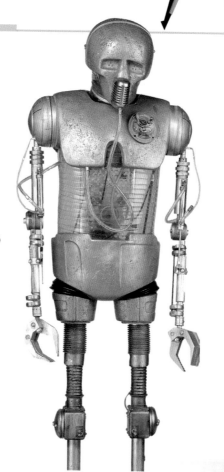

GH-7 MEDICAL DROID

2-1B SURGICAL DROID

DD-13 TRIPEDAL MEDICAL DROID

MEDICAL ASSISTANTS

The FX-series medical assistant droids help doctors with an expansive set of tools. While they lack the personality of other medical droids, they boast a range of inbuilt medical devices that can treat a wide array of ailments.

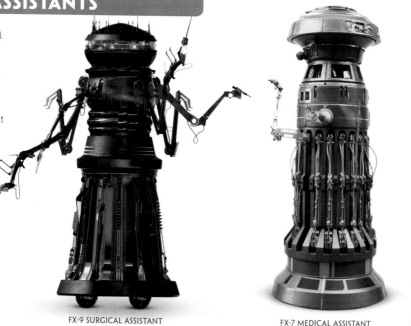

FX-9 SURGICAL ASSISTANT

FX-7 MEDICAL ASSISTANT

MIDWIFE

Midwife droids are caring, soothing models that specialise in delivering babies for a variety of species. This midwife droid is equipped with thermal cushions and paddle appendages that warm and cradle a newborn baby.

MIDWIFE DROID

COMMUNICATIONS TECHNOLOGY

Communication is vital to any endeavour – civilian or military. Vessels need to be located and tracked. Captains direct their crews throughout their ships and request berthing rights from ports of call. A Jedi Knight must report to the Council and request guidance during missions.

COMLINKS

Comlinks are commonly used devices across the galaxy. Typically handheld, they contain microphones and receivers. Due to their popularity, comlinks are easy targets for criminals and spies looking to steal information. For that reason, they are sometimes encrypted.

IN-EAR COMLINK

DARTH MAUL'S WRIST LINK

HEADSET COMLINK

NABOO COMLINK HOLDER

COMLINK

NABOO COMLINK

UNKAR PLUTT'S COMLINK

CLOUD CITY COMLINK

STORMTROOPER'S COMLINK

JEDI COMLINKS

Jedi are tasked with missions that have galactic-level importance. Their comlinks are state-of-the-art, with extended range, variable frequencies and encryption coding. In addition to sending and receiving voice communication, Jedi comlinks can transmit large data packets back to the Council.

OBI-WAN KENOBI'S FIRST COMLINK

OBI-WAN KENOBI'S SECOND COMLINK

SECURITY-ENHANCED COMLINK

YARAEL POOF'S COMLINK

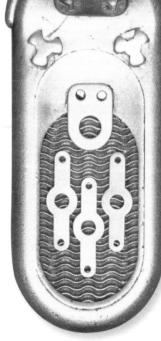

QUI-GON JINN'S COMLINK

TRACKING DEVICES

Tracking devices are used to keep tabs on people and vessels that do not want to be found. They are usually considered the tools of criminal operators and bounty hunters, but government spies are also known to deploy them.

SIGNALLING UNIT

ION LIMPET HOMING BEACON

SITH TRACER BEACON

TRACER BEACON

SUMMONING DEVICES

Summoning requires a calling device and a receiver. Droids fitted with restraining bolts can be summoned by Jawas who use droid callers. Darth Sidious chooses to give his minions summoning chips so he can send for them whenever he desires.

Micro-screen

PAIR OF DARTH SIDIOUS'S SUMMONING CHIPS

Antenna

JAWA DROID CALLER

HOLOPROJECTORS

Holoprojectors transmit and receive holograms: three-dimensional images formed by the interference of beams from a light source. Creating the images requires significant computing resources, restricting their use mostly to businesses, government agents and the wealthy. Transmitters are mainly used for broadcasting audio, but they can also transmit holograms.

HOLOPROJECTOR

HOLOPROJECTOR

HOLOPROJECTOR

RATH RECORDER

HOLOGRAM WATCH

JEDI COUNCIL HOLOPROJECTOR

DESK-MOUNTED HOLOPROJECTOR

Aerial

Audio waveform display

BUSINESS DEAL

In search of new hyperdrive components for Queen Amidala's royal starship, Qui-Gon Jinn uses a holoprojector to display the ship's make – a J-type 327 Nubian – while Anakin Skywalker watches. Anakin's slave owner Watto informs the Jedi he has a T-14 hyperdrive generator, but that it will be costly.

Transceiver
Holographic imager
HOLOPROJECTOR

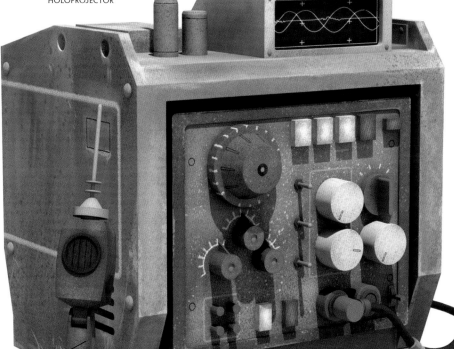
Wireless handset
TRANSMITTER

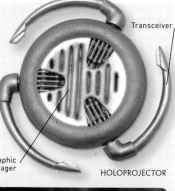

INFORMATION

The galaxy relies on computing technology to obtain and process enormous volumes of data every millisecond. Computers calculate dangerous hyperspace navigation routes. They enable scientific advances in search of a better future, and store records that chronicle knowledge gleaned from the past.

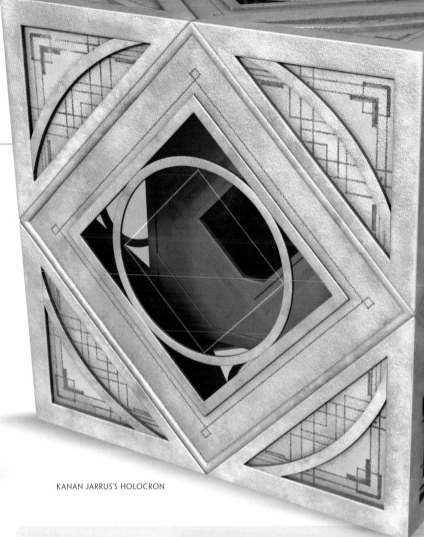

Holocron contains swordfight lessons from Anakin Skywalker

Projection portal

KANAN JARRUS'S HOLOCRON

DATA STORAGE

The Jedi and Sith have curated enormous amounts of information about the galaxy and the Force. Holocrons store this valuable data in holographic form. Allies of both sides assist in gathering stolen, lost or secret information, using simpler devices to keep it safe. Lor San Tekka keeps a close eye on his old device – it contains part of a map to show Luke Skywalker's location.

LOR SAN TEKKA'S DATA STORAGE UNIT

SITH HOLOCRON

GREAT HOLOCRON

JEDI HOLOCRON

SENSITIVE INFORMATION

Bounty hunter Cad Bane needs a Jedi to use the Force to open a holocron. This will allow him to retrieve the location of every Force-sensitive child throughout the galaxy! Anakin Skywalker reluctantly performs the task after his Jedi apprentice Ahsoka Tano is captured by Bane.

DATA RECORDING

Before any piece of data can be preserved, it must be recorded. All manner of data recording is possible, from voice and sound, to images and video. Recording devices have keypads and displays to assist in capturing and deciphering data.

RECORD PAD

MUSTAFAR READOUT

RESISTANCE STATUS PAD

End caps
in locked
position

DATAPADS

Datapads are portable computers, usually handheld, that allow individuals to access and interpret information. They are commonplace across the galaxy. Junk dealers use them to keep track of inventory, and bounty hunters analyse data on their next targets.

JANGO FETT'S DATAPAD

WATTO'S DATAPAD

JEDI TEMPLE ARCHIVE COMPUTER

CRACKING THE CASE

After Republic forces are ambushed on Christophsis, R2-D2 assists Commander Cody and Captain Rex in identifying a traitor. The astromech droid transmits his findings to a datapad held by Rex, showing wavelengths and frequencies. This information provides clues to uncover the clone spy.

VIEWSCREENS

Viewscreens receive and display information. At podraces, fans who want to watch the live broadcast will hold them. A Jedi testing a potential Force user will watch images from a screen and observe if the candidate can decipher their thoughts.

Oversize screen for multiple views

VIEWPAD

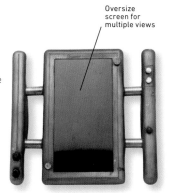

HANDHELD VIEWSCREEN FOR PODRACE

HANDHELD VIEWSCREEN FOR PODRACE

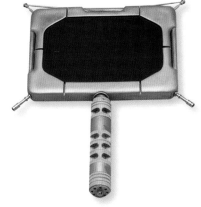

VIEWSCREEN

OBI-WAN KENOBI'S VIEWSCREEN

SCANNERS

A scanner examines objects, interprets information and presents the findings to the owner. Uses can range from simple jobs, such as reading security cards, to more complex tasks, such as a life-form scanner utilised by military units.

SONIC IMAGE SCANNER

OBI-WAN KENOBI'S SCANNER

SCANNER

REBEL SENSOR PACK

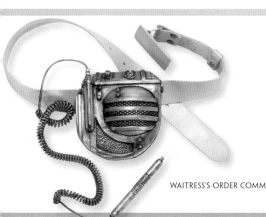

WAITRESS'S ORDER COMM

GYRDA KEYPAD

ELECTRICIAN'S DIAGNOSTIC SCREEN

DIAGNOSTIC SCREEN

HEALTH AND SAFETY

In a galaxy at war, medical supplies are in high demand, but often scarce. Technology helps cope with many hazards and problems – from pests that ravage underworld slums, to harsh planet environments faced by colonising settlers.

MEDICINE

MEDICAL EQUIPMENT

Medical facilities are best on Core Worlds like Coruscant, but outposts such as Kaliidah Shoals and Polis Massa provide excellent care. Severely injured patients are bathed in life-saving bacta chemicals for rapid healing. Jedi blood sample test kits are used to count a person's levels of midi-chlorians – life-forms that allow beings to feel the Force – and thus discover their Force potential.

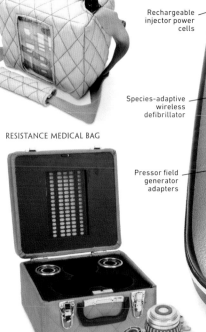

RESISTANCE MEDICAL BAG

BACTA TANK

EXTERIOR AND INTERIOR OF JEDI BLOOD TEST KIT

DOCTOR KALONIA'S FIELD MEDICAL KIT

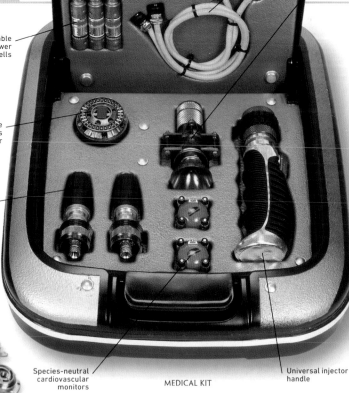

Filtration transpirators promote clear airways

Resuscitation ventilator aid breathing

Injectable vials of bacta, adrenaline, anaesthetics and antibiotics

Oxygen tubes with adapter heads

Universal injector head adapter

Rechargeable injector power cells

Species-adaptive wireless defibrillator

Pressor field generator adapters

Species-neutral cardiovascular monitors

MEDICAL KIT

Universal injector handle

MEDICAL AIDS

The galaxy is dangerous and injuries are common. As a result, technology has developed to assist all kinds of impairments. Hoverchairs float above the ground on repulsorlifts for patients unable to walk. Prosthetic mechanical arms are protected by autoseal gloves.

CLIEGG LARS'S HOVERCHAIR

ANAKIN SKYWALKER'S AUTOSEAL GLOVE

ALIEN MEDICS

Kallidahin exobiologists aid Padmé Amidala when she gives birth. Though they save her infants, they can't save her. These peaceful scientists are usually found searching rocky planetoid Polis Massa for ancient biological samples to clone, using Kaminoan technology.

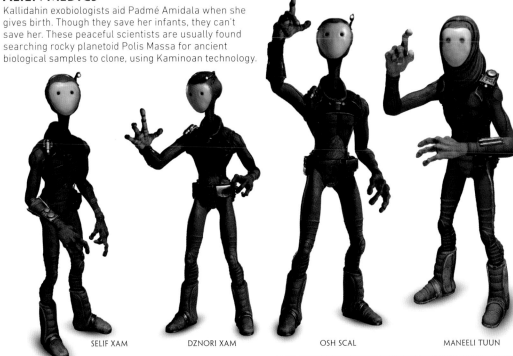

SELIF XAM   DZNORI XAM   OSH SCAL   MANEELI TUUN

BIO-EQUIPMENT

Some controversial devices are used to control patients. Kaminoans wield serum guns and brainwave probes to manipulate clone development. Lobot's cybernetic brain implant allows him to access computer systems, though he struggles with it for control of his mind!

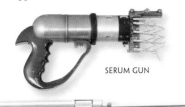

SERUM GUN

BRAINWAVE PROBE

LOBOT'S CYBERNETIC IMPLANT

ANAKIN SKYWALKER'S MECHNO-HAND

Electrostatic fingertip provides limited feeling

Mechanical thumb has greater range of motion than a flesh thumb

Armoured shielding bulks gloves and protects internal mechanics

Electrostatic wires act as nerves

Alloy ligaments allow arm to twist

Internal rechargeable battery module

ANAKIN SKYWALKER'S CYBORG ARM

LIFE-SUPPORT

A life-support device can help its wearer survive in polluted or unnatural settings, such as atmospheric conditions that differ from their homeworld. In contrast, Vader's belt controls his life-support suit, allowing him to survive his terrible injuries.

PLO KOON'S METAL MASK

AIR FILTER

PLO KLOON'S GOGGLES

MAGNETIC FIELD CONDENSER

SURVIVAL OXYGEN

DARTH VADER'S SYSTEMS STATUS BELT

MOST SERIOUS LIGHTSABER INJURIES

Lightsabers are dangerous weapons! These fighters suffer terrible injuries in lightsaber duels. Most of them require serious medical attention and prosthetics afterwards.

○ **DARTH VADER**
Vader loses all his limbs and is burnt so badly he requires a life-support suit!

○ **DARTH MAUL**
Maul is cut in half by Obi-Wan Kenobi, but constructs a cyborg spider body out of garbage.

○ **KANAN JARRUS**
Kanan loses his sight in a duel with Maul. Afterwards he uses the Force to "see".

○ **FINN**
Kylo Ren severely injures Finn's back, leaving him clinging to life by a thread.

○ **LUKE SKYWALKER**
Skywalker loses his right hand in a fierce duel with Vader and receives a mechanical replacement.

ENVIRONMENTAL HEALTH

CLIMATE CONTROL

Technology makes life in hostile climates more bearable. Coolers aid in hot desert climates, while braziers keep homes warm on breezy nights. Sandstats clean up the dust and sand after wind storms, and fog scopes clear up air pollution.

SLAVE QUARTERS BRAZIER   COOLING UNIT   PAIR OF BACKPACK COOLERS

FOG SCOPE

SANDSTAT

PEST CONTROL

Traders and travellers inadvertently transport pests across the galaxy. Exterminators on Coruscant carry equipment to dispatch duracrete slugs, stone mites, snot-hoppers and wasp-worms. Conduit purgers help eradicate obnoxious conduit worms.

CONDUIT PURGER

EXTERMINATOR BACKPACK

EQUIPMENT

The many cultures across the galaxy have produced machines and tools to aid them in virtually any activity. Some are manufactured by droids in factories, using raw materials. Other more basic tools are hand-made by people, using spare parts.

Copper wire coils

One of four demagnetising units

Rack for micro-tools

Mountable base plate

TOOL DEMAGNETISER

AEROMAGNIFIER

TOOLS

TOOL BOX ESSENTIALS

Tools are vital in a galaxy that relies on machines. Chewbacca keeps a collection of tools in his pouch, always ready for the *Millennium Falcon*'s next mechanical problem. On the planet Jakku, Rey has a kit to clean her salvaged ship parts.

CHEWBACCA'S SPACECRAFT REPAIR TOOLS

FUSION CUTTER HEAD

PAIR OF PROBES

BOBA FETT'S JETPACK ADJUSTMENT TOOL

"WESSEX-HEAD" BIT-DRIVER

CHISEL HEAD HAMMER

REY'S SALVAGE CLEANING KIT

REY'S SALVAGE TRAY

CARBON CHISEL

"BLISSEX-HEAD" BIT-DRIVER

CHEWBACCA'S TOOL KIT

CONCEALMENT

When stealth and deception are required, the right device can change one's appearance. Hologram disguise emitters project a "shadow hologram" matrix around the user. It covers users like a holographic cloak with the identity of another person.

HOLOGRAM DISGUISE EMITTER

ART

Sabine Wren's airbrushes are ideal for graffiti art, defacing Imperial propaganda, leaving symbolic messages or drawing her signature rebel starbird. The airbrush dials allow her to change paint colours, pressure and the nozzle focus.

PAIR OF AIRBRUSHES

INTERROGATION

First Order interrogations are a nasty business! Much like the interrogation chairs of the Empire's Inquisitors, Kylo Ren's version is designed to confine prisoners and inflict great pain.

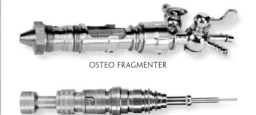

OSTEO FRAGMENTER

NEURAL DRILL

TENDON CHARGER

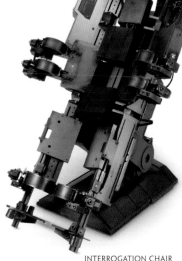

INTERROGATION CHAIR

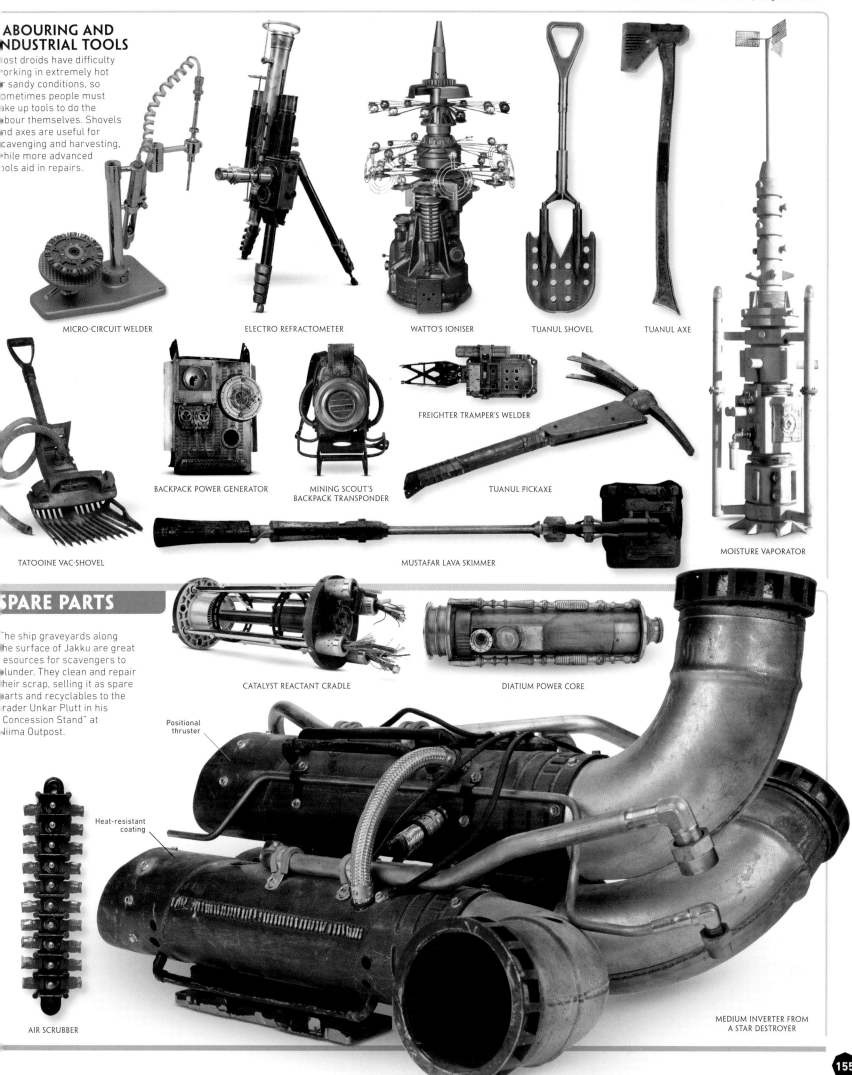

ABOURING AND NDUSTRIAL TOOLS

ost droids have difficulty
orking in extremely hot
r sandy conditions, so
ometimes people must
ake up tools to do the
bour themselves. Shovels
nd axes are useful for
cavenging and harvesting,
hile more advanced
ools aid in repairs.

MICRO-CIRCUIT WELDER

ELECTRO REFRACTOMETER

WATTO'S IONISER

TUANUL SHOVEL

TUANUL AXE

BACKPACK POWER GENERATOR

MINING SCOUT'S
BACKPACK TRANSPONDER

FREIGHTER TRAMPER'S WELDER

TUANUL PICKAXE

MOISTURE VAPORATOR

TATOOINE VAC-SHOVEL

MUSTAFAR LAVA SKIMMER

SPARE PARTS

he ship graveyards along
he surface of Jakku are great
esources for scavengers to
lunder. They clean and repair
heir scrap, selling it as spare
arts and recyclables to the
rader Unkar Plutt in his
Concession Stand" at
iima Outpost.

CATALYST REACTANT CRADLE

DIATIUM POWER CORE

Positional
thruster

Heat-resistant
coating

AIR SCRUBBER

MEDIUM INVERTER FROM
A STAR DESTROYER

FIELD GEAR

From farmboys to stormtroopers, and bounty hunters to Jedi, everyone needs handy tools to use on the go. The gear employed varies based on each user's specific needs and helps them accomplish tasks – whether their goal is to breathe underwater or to sneak into high-security areas.

SECURITY

Pilots position sensor markers around a new planetary base, to create an invisible threshold and detect any incomers or vehicles. On the other hand, spies and bounty hunters often thwart security devices, using tools such as false eyes and lock breakers to gain entry to secured buildings or containers.

FALSE EYE
FALSE TOUCH
BOBA'S ANTI-SECURITY BLADES

FIELD SECURITY OVERLOADER
SENSOR MARKER
LOCK BREAKER

UTILITY BELTS

Field gear is often carried on a sturdy utility belt, keeping it within easy reach of the wearer. Different types of gear can be placed in pouches attached to the belt or clipped on directly using a fastener.

UTILITY POUCHES

LUKE SKYWALKER'S BELT POUCH

JANGO FETT'S UTILITY BELT

OBI-WAN'S UTILITY BELT

BREATHERS

Breathable atmospheres and natural environments vary greatly from planet to planet. However, they pose no problem for an individual with an A99 aquata breather. Standard field gear for Jedi, the compact device operates underwater, in toxic air and in a vacuum.

A99 AQUATA BREATHER

BREATHER POUCH
REBREATHER

UNDERWATER ESCAPE

After barely surviving an assassination attempt on Naboo, Qui-Gon Jinn and Obi-Wan Kenobi befriend the Gungan Jar Jar Binks. He offers to take the Jedi to Otoh Gunga. The A99 aquata breather allows Obi-Wan to swim down to the underwater city.

PADMÉ AMIDALA'S BELT

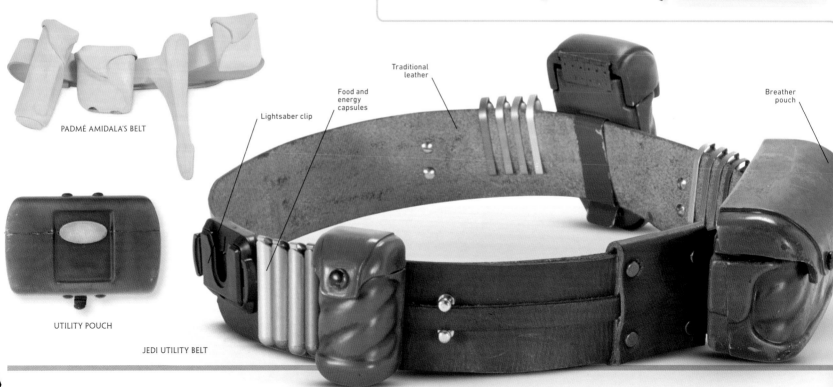

Traditional leather

Food and energy capsules

Lightsaber clip

Breather pouch

UTILITY POUCH

JEDI UTILITY BELT

RANSPORTATION

RAPPLING HOOKS

appling hooks embed into
surface or wrap around a
otrusion, providing a fixed
int to enable swinging or
ppelling. Naboo Guards
e ascension guns to deploy
appling hooks. Clone
oopers attach separate
appling hook launchers
their DC-15 blaster rifles.

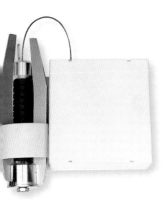

STORMTROOPER GRAPPLING HOOK

GRAPPLING
HOOK

GRAPPLING HOOK
AND CABLE

CABLE
RETRIEVER

UTILITY POUCH WITH
GRAPPLING HOOK AND LINE

ETPACKS

ommonly associated with
andalorians, jetpacks allow
eir users to swiftly move
bout in combat zones, providing
tactical advantage. Some
tpacks are equipped with a
p-loaded missile. However,
ey do have vulnerabilities, as
harp blows can send the wearer
lasting off uncontrollably.

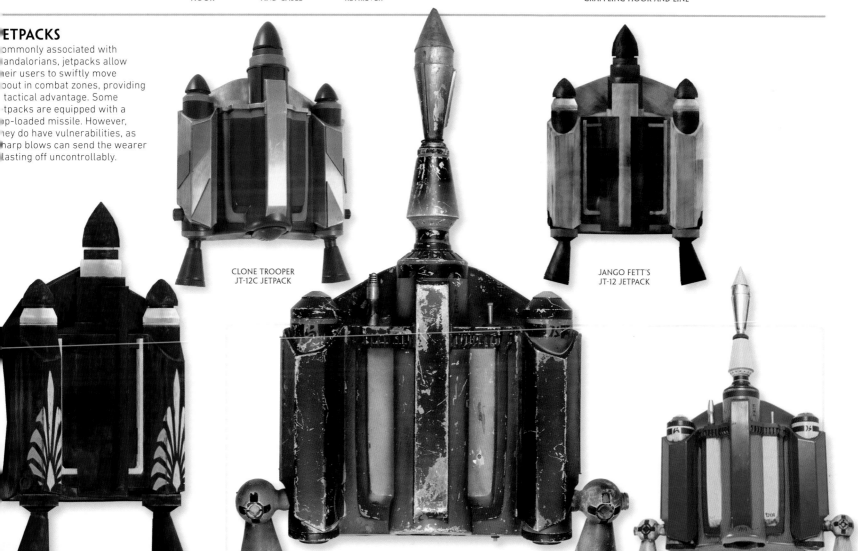

CLONE TROOPER
JT-12C JETPACK

JANGO FETT'S
JT-12 JETPACK

OBI-WAN KENOBI'S
JT-12 EVA JETPACK

BOBA FETT'S MODIFIED Z-6 JETPACK

JANGO FETT'S Z-6 JETPACK

BINOCULARS

Magnifying devices like monoculars, binoculars and quadnoculars are used far and wide across the galaxy. These vision-enhancing devices have many uses, from bird watchers spotting their favourite convor, to farmers guarding crops and soldiers scouting ahead for trouble.

MONOCULARS AND TELESCOPES

Monoculars and telescopes increase the apparent size of distant objects, producing 2-D images. A telescope has better range, capable of viewing objects in space. A monocular is lighter, simpler and commonly used at sporting events like podracing.

MACROTELESCOPE

PODRACING FAN'S MONOCULAR

MACROBINOCULARS

Unlike a monocular or telescope, macrobinoculars produce a three-dimensional image. The Heads Up Display, known as HUD, will identify limited data such as range and zoom. Macrobinoculars are common among farmers, hunters and less advanced militaries.

PODRACING FAN'S MACROBINOCULARS

REPUBLIC MACROBINOCULARS

JEDI FIELD BINOCULARS

Dial to adjust focus

Eyepiece

Oil magnifier lens

Hand grip

200

0 . 525 . 550

0015+

·20447

VIEW FROM LUKE SKYWALKER'S MACROBINOCULARS

EZRA BRIDGER'S MACROBINOCULARS

FARSEEIN
(GUNGAN BINOCULARS)

JEDI MACROBINOCULARS

WHAT'S HIDING OUT THERE?

Many dangers lurk beyond the Lars family's moisture farm homestead on Tatooine. Luke Skywalker scans the horizon at the perimeter of the homestead. He hopes to spot the missing R2-D2, the droid his uncle recently acquired, who has fled in search of General Obi-Wan Kenobi.

CLONE POLARISED MACROBINOCULARS

BATTLE DROID OFFICER MACROBINOCULARS

QUADNOCULARS

The two pairs of telescopes that make up quadnoculars allow them to automatically track objects at a distance. Quadnocs, as they are called by soldiers, were first developed for field use by the Empire. They are now basic kit for First Order and Resistance fighters.

NEURO-SAAV TE4.4 FIELD QUADNOCULARS

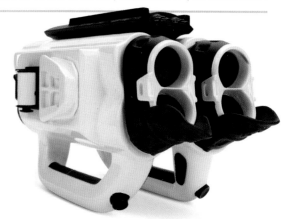

STORMTROOPER QUADNOCULARS

ELECTROBINOCULARS

Electrobinoculars have inbuilt zoom capability and a wider depth of field than macrobinoculars. They can also automatically enhance objects for advanced reconnaissance. Adjustable radiation settings and night-vision make electrobinoculars a favourite among smugglers, bounty hunters and the military.

PAIR OF PODRACING FAN ELECTROBINOCULARS

RESISTANCE GROUND CREW ELECTROBINOCULARS

IMPERIAL ELECTROBINOCULARS

DARTH MAUL'S ELECTROBINOCULARS

IN-DEPTH ANALYSIS

On the vast desert plains of Tatooine, Sith apprentice Darth Maul hunts for the missing Queen Amidala and her Jedi guardians. As the sun sets, his electrobinoculars' computer employs sensors beyond visible light to search for his prey across the horizon. Once he narrows down their location, the Sith plans to attack Qui-Gon Jinn and Obi-Wan Kenobi.

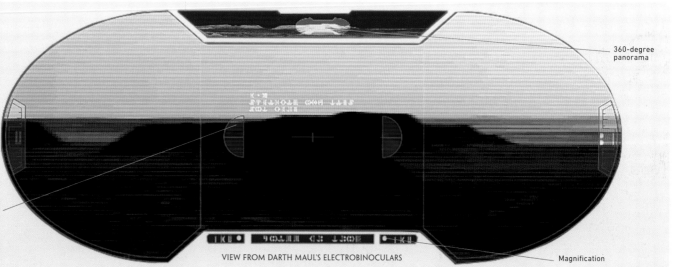

360-degree panorama

Alarm for visualised targets

VIEW FROM DARTH MAUL'S ELECTROBINOCULARS

Magnification

STATIONARY WEAPONS

The huge beasts of the battlefield, stationary weapons like artillery, cannons and turbolasers dish out damage from a fixed point. Though they cannot move, they more than make up for their lack of mobility with raw destructive power.

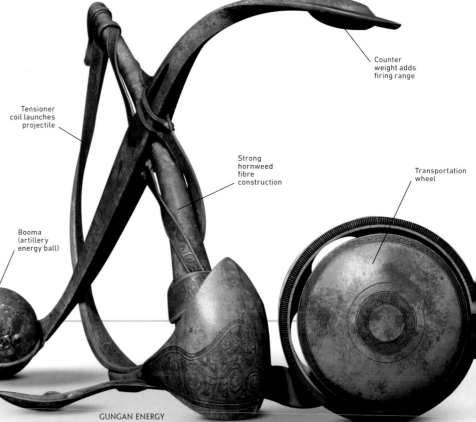

Counter weight adds firing range

Tensioner coil launches projectile

Strong hornweed fibre construction

Transportation wheel

Booma (artillery energy ball)

GUNGAN ENERGY CATAPULT

GROUND WEAPONS

Often used in defensive situations, ground weapons provide heavy hitting power for ground troops. The Rebel Alliance uses 1.4 FD P-Tower and DF.9 anti-infantry batteries with limited success at the battle of Hoth, where Imperial AT-AT walkers tear through the rebel lines.

GEONOSIAN SONIC CANNON

Cannon only fires when legs are in stationary position

IN-DEPTH ANALYSIS

The 1.4 FD P-Tower can operate in extreme temperatures ranging from -73°C (-100°F) to 49°C (120°F). The Rebel Alliance stations these towers on the frigid ice planet Hoth as a last defence against ground assaults. Though they are cheap to produce, their lack of mobility makes them easy targets for AT-AT walkers.

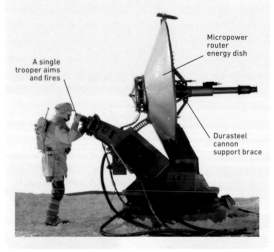

Micropower router energy dish

A single trooper aims and fires

Durasteel cannon support brace

SELF-PROPELLED HEAVY ARTILLERY TURBOLASER (SPHA-T)

1.4 FD P-TOWER USED ON HOTH

E-WEB REPEATING BLASTER

V-150 PLANET DEFENDER

DF.9 ANTI-INFANTRY BATTERY

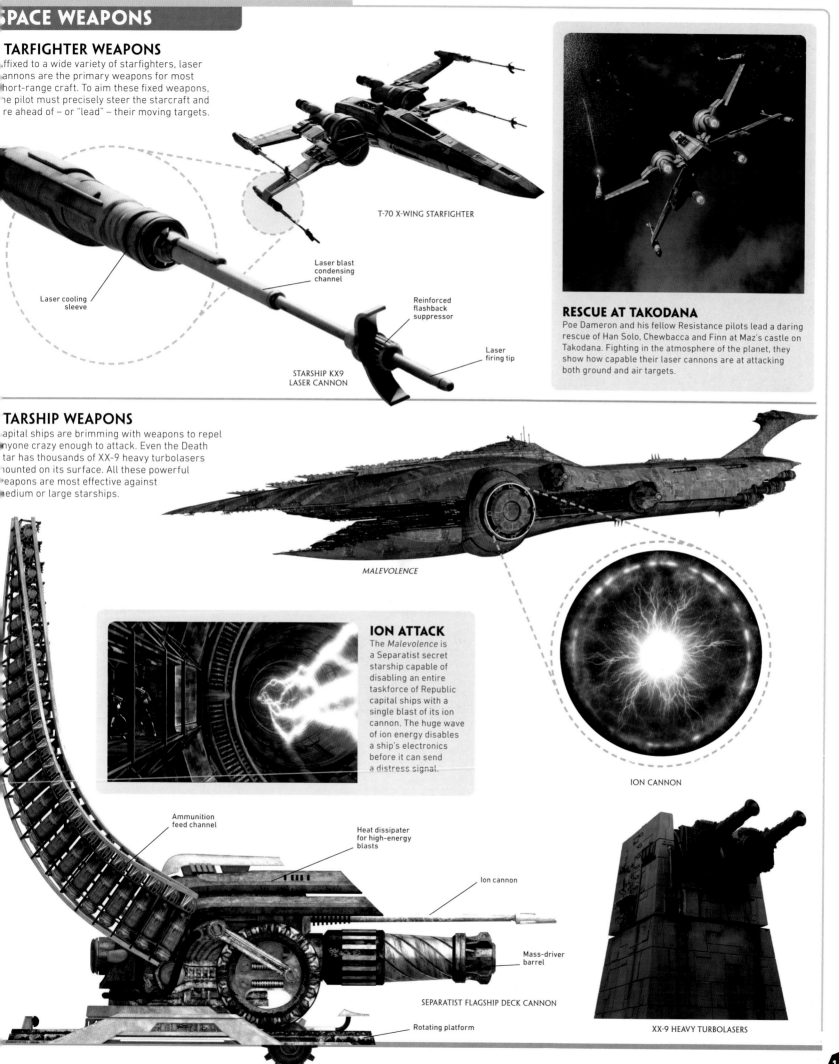

SPACE WEAPONS

STARFIGHTER WEAPONS

Affixed to a wide variety of starfighters, laser cannons are the primary weapons for most short-range craft. To aim these fixed weapons, the pilot must precisely steer the starcraft and fire ahead of – or "lead" – their moving targets.

Laser cooling sleeve

Laser blast condensing channel

Reinforced flashback suppressor

Laser firing tip

T-70 X-WING STARFIGHTER

STARSHIP KX9 LASER CANNON

RESCUE AT TAKODANA

Poe Dameron and his fellow Resistance pilots lead a daring rescue of Han Solo, Chewbacca and Finn at Maz's castle on Takodana. Fighting in the atmosphere of the planet, they show how capable their laser cannons are at attacking both ground and air targets.

STARSHIP WEAPONS

Capital ships are brimming with weapons to repel anyone crazy enough to attack. Even the Death Star has thousands of XX-9 heavy turbolasers mounted on its surface. All these powerful weapons are most effective against medium or large starships.

MALEVOLENCE

ION ATTACK

The *Malevolence* is a Separatist secret starship capable of disabling an entire taskforce of Republic capital ships with a single blast of its ion cannon. The huge wave of ion energy disables a ship's electronics before it can send a distress signal.

ION CANNON

Ammunition feed channel

Heat dissipater for high-energy blasts

Ion cannon

Mass-driver barrel

SEPARATIST FLAGSHIP DECK CANNON

Rotating platform

XX-9 HEAVY TURBOLASERS

BLASTERS: THE GOOD

Though peaceful negotiation is preferred, heroes must sometimes fight in the name of freedom and justice. In the right hands, a trusty blaster can mean the difference between good prevailing over evil, or even determine the fate of the galaxy.

The DC-17 pistol is the standard sidearm of the Republic's clone troopers. It is a favourite of clone Captain Rex, who wields a pair of them throughout the Clone Wars. The Republic has long fought beside the Wookiees of Kashyyyk. Their blasters use durable components, and are the traditional copper colour used in all Wookiee technology.

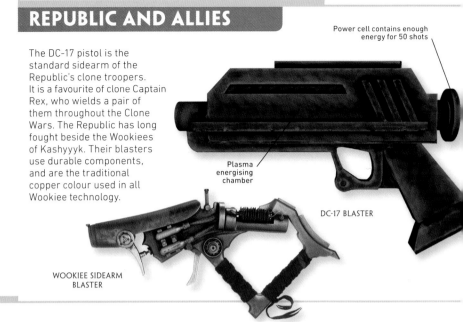

Power cell contains enough energy for 50 shots

Plasma energising chamber

DC-17 BLASTER

WOOKIEE SIDEARM BLASTER

REBELS

ARMS OF THE ALLIANCE AND RESISTANCE

Unlike the Imperials, who use standard-issue weapons, many rebels supply their own blasters. Sabine Wren carries rapid-fire Mandalorian pistols manufactured on the moon of Concordia. Like her armour, each features a custom paint scheme. The Resistance must rely on New Republic surplus, meaning its troops are often outgunned by the First Order.

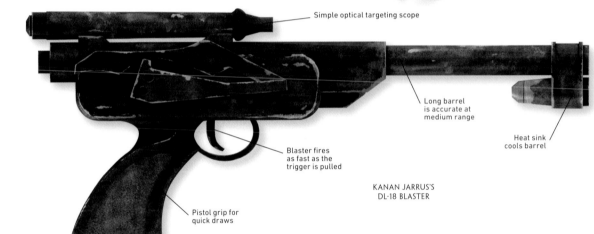

Simple optical targeting scope

Long barrel is accurate at medium range

Heat sink cools barrel

Blaster fires as fast as the trigger is pulled

Pistol grip for quick draws

KANAN JARRUS'S DL-18 BLASTER

REBEL DL-21 BLASTER

REY'S NN-14 BLASTER

HERA SYNDULLA'S BLURRG-1120 HOLDOUT BLASTER

GENERAL LEIA ORGANA'S EIRRISS RYLOTH DEFENSE TECH GLIE-44 BLASTER

SABINE WREN'S BLUE WESTAR-35 BLASTER

SABINE WREN'S YELLOW WESTAR-35 BLASTER

SMUGGLER SIDEARMS

Han Solo has owned a long series of BlasTech DL-44 blasters, which he never ceases to customise and modify. These hard-hitting weapons are powerful enough to blast through stormtrooper armour in one shot. Han always keeps spare blasters onboard his ship, the *Millennium Falcon*.

HAN SOLO'S DL-44 FROM TATOOINE

HAN SOLO'S DL-44 FROM TAKODANA

HAN SOLO'S DL-44 FROM ENDOR

ROYALTY

NABOO

Though they are a peaceful people, the Naboo maintain a small security force to protect their planet in times of trouble. Naboo soldiers are equipped with hand-crafted weapons of the highest quality – all made from local Naboo materials and finished to exquisite standards.

Accurised barrel

Dart launcher for grappling cable

Perlote wood fittings, made from native Naboo trees

CAPTAIN PANAKA'S BLASTER

Long range targeting scope

Heavy blaster barrel

Carrying sling for long guard duties

CR-2 HEAVY BLASTER

S-5 BLASTER

CAPTAIN TYPHO'S BLASTER

ALDERAAN

Fitting for the wealthy ruler of Alderaan, Bail Organa's silver sidearm is one of the most luxurious blasters anywhere in the galaxy. As an outspoken opponent of the Clone Wars, Organa must be ready to defend himself and his allies.

ALDERAAN KUEGET LN-21 BLASTER

BAIL ORGANA'S TARGET BLASTER

ELG-3A DIPLOMAT'S BLASTER

PERSONAL DEFENCE

Citizens living in lawless parts of the galaxy can't rely on security forces for protection, so they must defend themselves. Unable to afford the latest technology, some cobble together homemade blasters from speeder parts, vaporator scrap and other junk.

Scatter barrel best at short ranges

Built from spare parts of other blasters

Rechargeable energy cells

CORUSCANT UNDERWORLD BLASTER

MAZ KANATA'S BLASTER

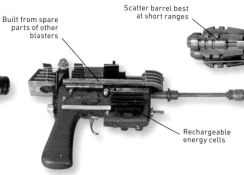

HOMEMADE SETTLER BLASTER

SCATTER BLASTER

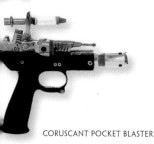

CORUSCANT POCKET BLASTER

BLASTER WITH FOREGRIP

CORUSCANT BLASTER WITH SCOPE

DASHA PROMENTI'S JAKKU BLASTER

BLASTERS: THE BAD

They've served bounty hunters, soldiers, pirates, thugs and more. Some of these powerful little weapons are as infamous as the beings that carry them. Whatever you do, don't cross their owners or you might find yourself at the wrong end of one of these blasters!

IMPERIAL

Imperial forces have a large selection of blasters available to keep their hold over the galaxy. Scout troopers carry an EC-17 hold-out blaster that fits neatly inside a boot holster. Stormtroopers and officers alike might carry the SE-14C, known for its poor recoil but a high rate of fire.

MERR-SONN POWER 5 BLASTER

SE-14C BLASTER

SCOUT TROOPER EC-17 BLASTER

FIRST ORDER

Thanks to a secret partnership between renowned manufacturers Merr-Sonn and BlasTech, the First Order's armouries are filled with the latest and greatest small arms. The joint venture leads to innovative features like a vibrating pulser ammunition indicator.

FIRST ORDER OFFICER BLASTER

SONN-BLAS SE44C BLASTER PISTOL

SEPARATISTS

General Grievous will go to any length and use any weapon to win in battle. Aside from a growing collection of stolen lightsabers, the cyborg general also uses a custom DT-57 blaster that he nicknames "Annihilator".

BLASTECH CUSTOM DT-57 "ANNIHILATOR"

HEAVILY MODIFIED

Some of these weapons have been altered so much that using them in combat is considered inhumane. A Trandoshan doubler or tripler added to the barrel of a blaster or a standard pistol creates a devastating hand cannon, banned by the Convention of Civilized Systems.

REFURBISHED DH-17 BLASTER

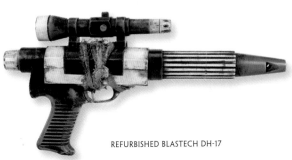

REFURBISHED BLASTECH DH-17

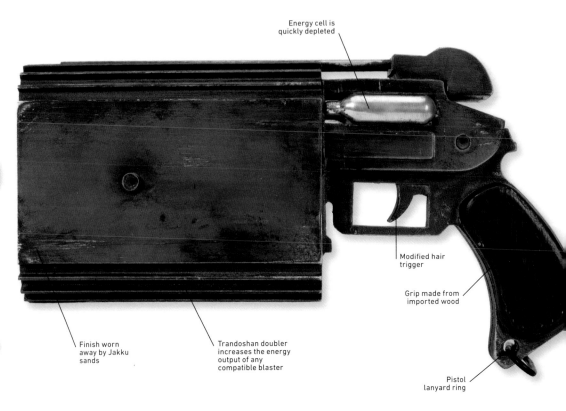

Energy cell is quickly depleted

Modified hair trigger

Grip made from imported wood

Finish worn away by Jakku sands

Trandoshan doubler increases the energy output of any compatible blaster

Pistol lanyard ring

TRANDOSHAN DOUBLER ON TARGET BLASTER

PIRATES AND THUGS

A pirate's life is full of adventure, profit and plunder at the expense of others. Pirates' blasters – smuggled or stolen – play an important role in convincing hapless beings to part with their valuables.

PRU SWEEVANT'S BLASTER

SNUB-BLASTER

SHORT-RANGE ASSASSIN'S BLASTER

MODIFIED DL-21

SKIFF GUARD'S MODIFIED DL-18 BLASTER

HITMAN'S DH-23 BLASTER

Long distance sight adapter

Standard short-range sight

Sight folds down

Cooling vents

Barrel shroud receiver

Blast emitter

Pressure-sensitive trigger

Grip weighted for perfect balance

ALTERNATE SIDE VIEW

REAR VIEW

CIKATRO VIZAGO'S "VILMARH'S REVENGE" BLASTER

BOUNTY HUNTERS

The best weapons can be found with these hired hands. Jango Fett's WESTAR-34 pistols are custom made to the specifications of the bounty hunter himself. He requested a special heat-resistant dallorian alloy for rapid fire shooting and hollow handles for a quick draw.

ZAM WESELL'S KYD-21 BLASTER

Vents prevent overheating in hot climates

Slender grip for easy concealment

Power setting dial

WESTAR-34 BLASTER

AURRA SING'S MODIFIED DX-13 BLASTER

434 DEATHHAMMER

RIFLES

Rifles offer heavier firepower, greater range and more accuracy than a blaster pistol. In the hands of a skilled shot, a rifle can be used for sport or for combat. In the hands of a soldier, a rifle can help start and end wars on a galactic scale!

GUARDS

These rifles are built as much for ceremony as they are built for fighting. No expense is spared when building a guard's rifle; a guard's gear and weapon are a symbol of the rank and power of the beings that they protect.

TOYDARIAN ROYAL GUARD BLASTER RIFLE

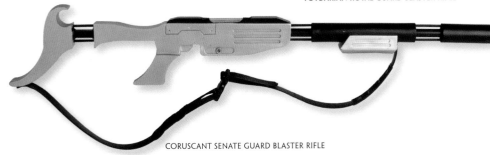

CORUSCANT SENATE GUARD BLASTER RIFLE

GENERAL USE

A trusty rifle is not only a weapon; it is a tool for survival. The Tusken Raider's slug thrower is used for hunting, self-defence and raiding settlements. Without it, Sand People could not survive on Tatooine.

MUSTAFARIAN BLASTER RIFLE

TUSKEN RAIDER RIFLE

LASER RIFLE

TATOOINE THUNDERBLASTER RIFLE

ILCO MUNICA'S BLASTER RIFLE/CLUB

Barrel replaced for close range

Stock wrapped to reduce recoil

Wrappings for camouflage

"JAKKU NIGHT SPECIAL" BLASTER RIFLE

CRIMINALS

Bounty hunters, pirates and gangsters live and die by the blaster rifle. Big game hunter Grummgar and bounty hunter Zam Wesell use long-barrelled rifles to strike their targets at incredibly long range. Their prey might never even hear the shot!

ZAM WESELL'S PROJECTILE RIFLE

GRUMMGAR'S HUNTING RIFLE

CAPTAIN ITHANO'S BLASTER RIFLE

LI-THRULL'S BOILER RIFLE

BOBA FETT'S EE-3 BLASTER CARBINE

TASU LEECH'S "HUTTSPLITTER" BLASTER RIFLE

RAZOO QIN-FEE'S "WASP" BLASTER RIFLE

JAWA IONISATION BLASTER

SARCO PLANK'S BLASTER RIFLE

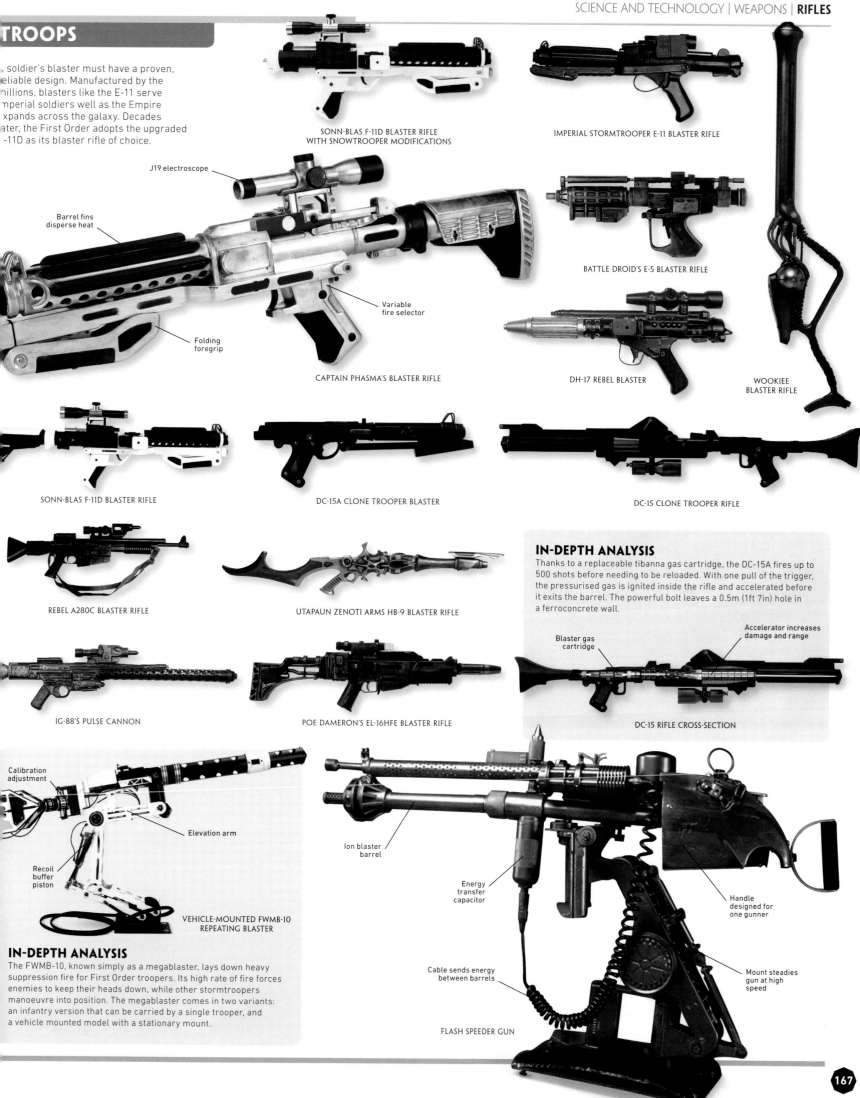

TROOPS

soldier's blaster must have a proven,
reliable design. Manufactured by the
millions, blasters like the E-11 serve
Imperial soldiers well as the Empire
expands across the galaxy. Decades
later, the First Order adopts the upgraded
-11D as its blaster rifle of choice.

SONN-BLAS F-11D BLASTER RIFLE
WITH SNOWTROOPER MODIFICATIONS

IMPERIAL STORMTROOPER E-11 BLASTER RIFLE

J19 electroscope

Barrel fins
disperse heat

Variable
fire selector

Folding
foregrip

CAPTAIN PHASMA'S BLASTER RIFLE

BATTLE DROID'S E-5 BLASTER RIFLE

DH-17 REBEL BLASTER

WOOKIEE
BLASTER RIFLE

SONN-BLAS F-11D BLASTER RIFLE

DC-15A CLONE TROOPER BLASTER

DC-15 CLONE TROOPER RIFLE

REBEL A280C BLASTER RIFLE

UTAPAUN ZENOTI ARMS HB-9 BLASTER RIFLE

IN-DEPTH ANALYSIS

Thanks to a replaceable tibanna gas cartridge, the DC-15A fires up to
500 shots before needing to be reloaded. With one pull of the trigger,
the pressurised gas is ignited inside the rifle and accelerated before
it exits the barrel. The powerful bolt leaves a 0.5m (1ft 7in) hole in
a ferroconcrete wall.

Blaster gas
cartridge

Accelerator increases
damage and range

IG-88'S PULSE CANNON

POE DAMERON'S EL-16HFE BLASTER RIFLE

DC-15 RIFLE CROSS-SECTION

Calibration
adjustment

Elevation arm

Recoil
buffer
piston

VEHICLE-MOUNTED FWMB-10
REPEATING BLASTER

Ion blaster
barrel

Energy
transfer
capacitor

Handle
designed for
one gunner

IN-DEPTH ANALYSIS

The FWMB-10, known simply as a megablaster, lays down heavy
suppression fire for First Order troopers. Its high rate of fire forces
enemies to keep their heads down, while other stormtroopers
manoeuvre into position. The megablaster comes in two variants:
an infantry version that can be carried by a single trooper, and
a vehicle mounted model with a stationary mount.

Cable sends energy
between barrels

Mount steadies
gun at high
speed

FLASH SPEEDER GUN

UNUSUAL WEAPONS AND POISONS

There are many ways to take down an opponent, and different cultures build their own peculiar weapons. Wookiees, Gungans, Geonosians, Dathomirians, Twi'leks and Trandoshans all face violent conflicts with unique technology. Some devices are defensive or offensive, but others are downright sinister!

SONIC WEAPONS

Bounty hunters often employ unusual devices like sonic weapons to incapacitate their prey. Geonosians are best known for perfecting this technology by harnessing sound energy inside a plasma containment charge. They fire this energy with super-destructive sonic blasters and canons.

BOWCASTER

CROSS-SECTIO

RANGED WEAPONS

BOWCASTERS

Wookiees are famous for their traditional, hand-crafted bowcasters. A pair of ball-shaped alternating magnetic polarizers energise a blast bolt called a quarrel, which fires from the barrel. Even though they require a Wookiee's strength to fire well, Han Solo enjoys borrowing Chewbacca's bowcaster!

Targeting macroscope

Conduction chamber

Skeletal stalk and butt

Woven Kashyyyk-vine shoulder strap

Negative-default alternating magnetic polarizer

CHEWBACCA'S NEW BOWCASTER

CHIRRUT ÎMWE'S LIGHTBOW

STUN GUNS

Cheap, low-powered weapons are common among thugs, petty criminals or even everyday folks just trying to protect themselves. They do little good in a serious firefight with armoured stormtroopers. Ion stunners fire an electromagnetic pulse of ionised particles, most effective when used on droids.

TATOOINE SETTLER'S STUN GUN

STUN GUN

ION STUNNER

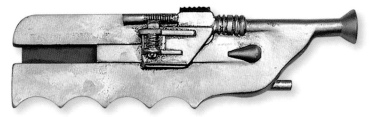

GEONOSIAN SONIC BLASTER

BOBA FETT'S SONIC BEAM WEAPON

POISONS

On Tatooine, Jabba's head of staff, Bib Fortuna, keeps a supply of deadly poisons for wicked purposes. Though the most difficult to obtain, krayt venom is the least toxic. It aids the dragon as an acid in pre-digestion of its meals.

DRIED KRAYT DRAGON VENOM

POWDERED ROCK WART VENOM

CRYSTALLISED CHALL

WEIRD AND SPECIALITY

Unusual situations require speciality weapons, while some cultures simply develop technology in different directions. Gungan atlatls and slings throw "boomas", or plasma energy balls. Sadistic assassin droids wield discrete dart guns armed with toxins. The First Order uses flamethrowers.

CHEWBACCA'S CLONE WARS BOWCASTER

IG-88'S NEEDLE DART GUN

GUNGAN SLING

GUNGAN ATLATL

Barrel

FIRST ORDER D-93 INCINERATOR FLAMETHROWER

BAZE MALBUS'S MWC-35C REPEATING CANNON

IG-88'S TRION GAS DISPENSER

ENERGY-MATTER WEAPONS

Some weapons harness energy, causing it to behave like matter. Ezra's slingshot electro-line is pulled back to generate low-voltage charges. A Trandoshan net gun fires a wide energy net. The net stuns victims on contact, before it disintegrates.

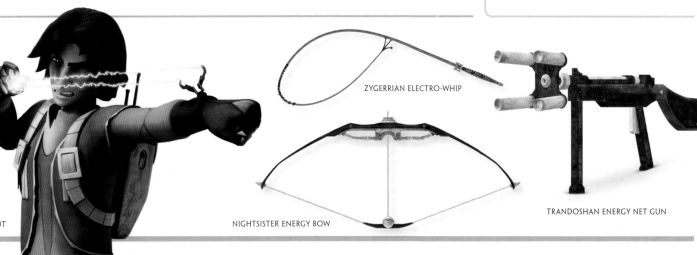

EZRA BRIDGER'S SLINGSHOT

ZYGERRIAN ELECTRO-WHIP

NIGHTSISTER ENERGY BOW

TRANDOSHAN ENERGY NET GUN

169

PROJECTILES AND SHIELDS

In galactic warfare, there is a constant tug of war between technology designed to protect a fighter and weapons designed to destroy. The finest example of this struggle can be found in shield technology and projectiles. Weapons designers are always looking for a way to shift the balance in their favour.

EXPLOSIVES

Handheld explosives hold a large amount of destructive power in a small package. While some are triggered remotely, many have a timed fuse. The wielder has just moments to throw the explosive or risk blowing themselves up.

STORMTROOPER THERMAL DETONATOR

MULTI-DETONATOR

HAN SOLO'S DETONATOR

THERMAL DETONATOR

EMP PULSE GRENADE

PYRO DENTON EXPLOSIVE

NABOO DETONATOR

IG-88'S CONCUSSION DISC

GUNGAN ENERGY BALL

BAG OF PYRO DENTON EXPLOSIVES

SHOCKING WEAPONS

Gungan energy balls, known to the Gungans themselves as "boomas", come in multiple sizes, from smaller handheld types, to huge artillery rounds strong enough to disable an armoured tank. The largest types must be carried in wagons by beasts of burden and then loaded into giant catapults. The balls contain plasma energy and cause electric shocks when they explode on contact.

AMMUNITION

DARTS

Small projectiles like darts are part of some bounty hunters' arsenals. While less common than blasters, darts provide a quick, quiet way to take down a target. These solid projectiles can often penetrate energy shields when blasters can't.

BOBA FETT'S KNEE PAD ROCKET DARTS

GRAPPLING HOOK DART

SABERDART

QUARRELS

Metal quarrels are projectiles that are enveloped by plasma energy as they launch from a bowcaster. The magnetic field created by this cycle boosts the quarrel to high speeds. Some quarrels can knock a fully armoured soldier off their feet!

QUARREL (BOWCASTER)

MISSILES

Missiles are typically launched from starships. They carry a destructive payload that gives even the smallest starfighter a boost in firepower that laser cannons can't deliver. Unlike other missiles however, the discord missile carries buzz droids, rather than explosives.

DISCORD MISSILE

MG7 PROTON TORPEDO

BANDOLIERS

Bandoliers are essential gear when carrying solid projectiles like quarrels or flares. Wookiee warriors fashion leather bandoliers that give them quick access to a variety of bowcaster ammunition, gas cartridges and other supplies.

AMMO HALTER

CHEWBACCA'S BANDOLIER AND CARRY-POUCH

RESISTANCE BANDOLIER AND SIGNAL FLARES

SHIELDS

The Gungan Grand Army employs massive energy shield bubbles that encapsulate their troops on the battlefield. Pairs of fambaa shields form one enormous defensive bubble that can withstand attack from blaster cannons, though slow-moving enemies can sneak into the shield perimeter.

COCKPIT AT THE FRONT OF GUNGAN SHIELD GENERATOR

SHIELD SYSTEM

Giant fambaa swamp lizards carry Gungan shield generators and projectors into battle. A single Gungan warrior controls the shield from inside a protective cockpit attached to the generator. If the generator is damaged or the fambaas move out of alignment, the entire shield system fails.

SHIELD PROJECTOR DRUM CARRIED BY FAMBAA

FIRST ORDER STORMTROOPER SHIELD

PLANETARY SHIELD GENERATOR

CLONE SENATE RIOT SHIELD

WOOKIEE KLORRI-CLAN BATTLE SHIELD

GUNGAN ENERGY SHIELD

SHIELD HELD BY GUNGAN WARRIOR

WOOKIEE WAR SHIELD

MANDALORIAN SHIELD

MELEE WEAPONS

From small skirmishes to enormous campaigns, battles are not fought merely with blasters: hand-to-hand melee weapons play a large part, too. Warriors choose weapons to enhance their fighting techniques and suit their physical characteristics, whether they have brute strength or Jedi-like reflexes.

BRUTE STRENGTH

BLADES

Blades often double as tools. A Jakku scavenger's knife can slice through a snare, while an Ewok's hunting knife can stab prey. Not all simple weapons are primitive – Twi'leks, for instance, craft elegant daggers.

TUSKEN RAIDER BLOODLETTING BLADE

GAMORREAN GUARD AXE

EWOK HUNTING KNIFE

TWI'LEK DAGGER

REY'S KNIFE

BOBA FETT'S SURVIVAL KNIFE

IG-88'S BLADE EXTENSION SET

STAFFS AND PIKES

Not all species have embraced technological advances, and their weapons reflect the simplicity of their lifestyle. Long poles like gaderffi sticks and quarterstaffs can double as walking aides. A two-handed grip makes these weapons ready for attack.

TUSKEN RAIDER IN FIGHTING STANCE WITH GADERFFI STICK

REY'S QUARTERSTAFF

TUSKEN RAIDER GADERFFI STICK

CLUBS AND MACES

These heavy weapons are used for battering and bludgeoning. In the jungles of the planet Endor, Ewoks pack-hunt with clubs. This technique also proves effective against stormtroopers, who aren't prepared for the unique battle tactics of a primitive society.

EWOK FIGHTING CLUB

TUANUL MACES

CHARGED WEAPONS

STAFFS AND PIKES

Charging a pike or staff with energy increases its lethal effect in combat. Pikes are used primarily for collective defence in coordination with other soldiers, whereas staffs can be very effective for attack when wielded by individuals with martial arts training.

IN-DEPTH ANALYSIS

Very few weapons are able to match a lightsaber. During the Clone Wars, however, General Grievous's MagnaGuards fight Jedi in single combat using energised electrostaffs that can withstand lightsaber blades. The deadly tips will stop a heart with a well-placed blow.

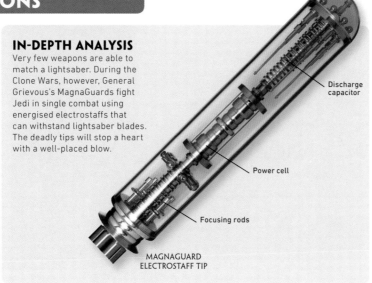

Discharge capacitor

Power cell

Focusing rods

MAGNAGUARD ELECTROSTAFF TIP

BATON

Energised batons are carried by First Order stormtrooper units assigned to subdue riots. The baton can be used to shock the opponent or to pummel a combative foe. Troopers armed with these weapons must train to avoid inflicting harm upon themselves.

Collapsible conductor contact vanes

Energised staff core

Magnatomic adhesion grip

Z6 RIOT CONTROL BATON

BO-RIFLES

Used almost exclusively by the Lasan Honor Guard, the bo-rifle fuses the functionality of an electrostaff with the range of a blaster rifle. In the extended position, the tips are electrified for close-quarters combat. In the retracted position, the rifle is effective at long distances in skilled hands. Agent Kallus's bo-rifle is a trophy taken from an Honor Guard during battle.

IMPERIAL AGENT KALLUS'S BO-RIFLE

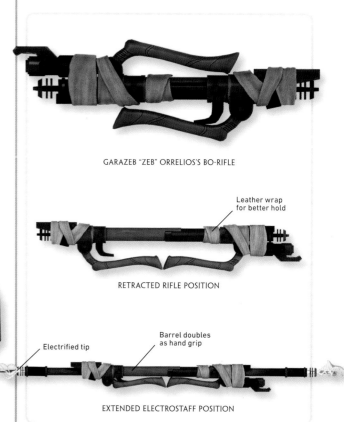

GARAZEB "ZEB" ORRELIOS'S BO-RIFLE

Leather wrap for better hold

RETRACTED RIFLE POSITION

Electrified tip

Barrel doubles as hand grip

EXTENDED ELECTROSTAFF POSITION

IMPERIAL GUARD FORCE PIKE | GENERAL GRIEVOUS'S ENERGY STAFF | VIBRO-AXE POLEARM | GUNGAN CESTA | GUNGAN ELECTROPOLE | ELECTROSTAFF | GEONOSIAN STATIC PIKE | IONISATION SPEAR

LIGHTSABERS

A close quarters weapon most commonly associated with the Jedi and Sith, the lightsaber is an elegant energy weapon with the power to slice through almost anything and deflect blaster bolts. It is one of the most rare and mysterious weapons in the galaxy.

> " THE LIGHTSABER IS THE JEDI'S ONLY TRUE ALLY. "
> **HUYANG, ARCHITECT AND LIGHTSABER DESIGNER**

CONSTRUCTION

KYBER CRYSTALS

At the core of a lightsaber sits a kyber crystal. Before crystals bond with a Force-sensitive, they are clear. They take on a colour when they come in contact with someone who "awakens" them. Lightsabers are constructed around the kyber crystal.

BLUE KYBER CRYSTAL

RED KYBER CRYSTAL

LIGHTSABER ENERGY CORE

Enhances grip

Blade length adjust

Kyber crystal

POMMEL CAP

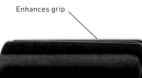

HAND GRIP

CONTROLS

IN COMBAT

TRAINING

Jedi younglings train from a young age in the art of lightsaber combat. Their early training focuses on defence. Younglings spend hours honing their ability to block blaster bolts with their eyes covered.

TRAINING LIGHTSABER

LUKE'S TRAINING

Luke Skywalker practises with a training remote onboard the *Millennium Falcon* under the guidance of Master Obi-Wan Kenobi. Though it is one of the first times he has used his father's lightsaber, Luke proves himself to be a fast learner.

YODA'S YOUNGLINGS

Master Yoda teaches some of the youngest students in the Jedi Temple on Coruscant. As one of the Order's finest lightsaber duellists, he has much to teach these students about the ways of the lightsaber and the Force.

STANCES

Members of the Jedi Order practise seven distinct forms of lightsaber combat. Each form has its own style and is suited to certain types of conflict. All Jedi have a favourite, but the truly skilled master all seven forms.

TRAINING REMOTE

YOUNGLING IN TRAINING

FORM I

OTHER MECHANICS

Most lightsabers share a similar basic design. Darth Maul's lightsaber not only has double blades, but double of almost every internal part. This allows one blade to continue to function even if the second blade is damaged.

DARTH MAUL'S DOUBLE-BLADED LIGHTSABER

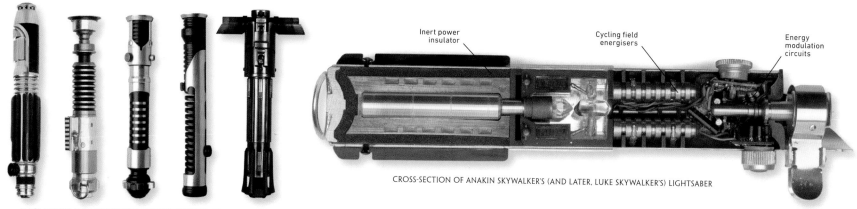

MACE WINDU, LUKE SKYWALKER, OBI-WAN KENOBI, QUI-GON JINN
AND KYLO REN'S LIGHTSABERS

Inert power insulator

Cycling field energisers

Energy modulation circuits

CROSS-SECTION OF ANAKIN SKYWALKER'S (AND LATER, LUKE SKYWALKER'S) LIGHTSABER

MAIN HILT

FOCUSING LENS

BLADE EMITTER

LIGHTSABER FORMS

- **FORM I: SHII-CHO**
  The basic moves, as drilled by trainees.

- **FORM II: MAKASHI**
  Promotes precision and discipline over strength or power. Often used in duels.

- **FORM III: SORESU**
  The most defensive form. Includes using the lightsaber as a shield against blaster fire.

- **FORM IV: ATARU**
  Uses acrobatic jumps, twirls and twists to drive power into bold attacks.

- **FORM V: SHIEN/DJEM SO**
  The two versions developed as a more aggressive version of defensive Form III.

- **FORM VI: NIMAN**
  Focuses on balance and harmony rather than brute force.

- **FORM VII: JUYO/VAAPAD**
  A bold style that taps into emotions, but which can open a Jedi up to the dark side.

Calm, meditative expression

Strong, horizontal position

Weapon pulled back for cutting sweep

FORM II   FORM III   FORM IV   FORM V   FORM VI   FORM VII

CONVENTIONAL LIGHTSABERS

Every lightsaber is a unique reflection of its owner. The Force itself guides their creation and design. The colour of the blade is determined by a kyber crystal. These are clear Force-attuned crystals, which take on a colour when "awakened" by a Force-sensitive. A crystal, lightsaber and owner share a deep bond.

JEDI

VIOLET BLADE

Most Jedi lightsabers are blue or green, but rarely a Jedi discovers that their crystal is violet in colour. Jedi like Mace Windu and the Rodian Huulik use rare violet lightsabers in the final days of the Old Republic.

MACE WINDU'S LIGHTSABER

MACE WINDU IN FORM VII STANCE

LIGHTNING DEFENCE

A skilled lightsaber wielder can block Force lightning using their lightsaber's energy blade. In his fight with Darth Sidious at the end of the Clone Wars, Mace Windu uses his lightsaber to save himself from the life-draining effects of the Sith's Force lightning.

BLUE BLADE

Blue-bladed lightsabers have served countless Jedi over the millennia. Obi-Wan Kenobi has had three: the first is destroyed by Darth Maul and the second is lost on Geonosis, but the third serves him throughout the Clone Wars, and in his final duel with Darth Vader.

OBI-WAN KENOBI'S LIGHTSABER

KI-ADI-MUNDI LIGHTSABER

OBI-WAN KENOBI'S LIGHTSABER

PLO KOON'S LIGHTSABER

ADI GALLIA'S LIGHTSABER

KANAN JARRUS'S LIGHTSABER

ANAKIN SKYWALKER'S LIGHTSABER

ANAKIN SKYWALKER'S LIGHTSABER

GREEN BLADE

Luke Skywalker's first lightsaber is handed down from his father, Anakin. When that lightsaber is lost in his duel with Vader at Cloud City, Luke must construct a new one. His own lightsaber has a vibrant green blade, like the lightsabers used by Qui-Gon Jinn and others.

QUI-GON JINN'S
LIGHTSABER

EETH KOTH'S
LIGHTSABER

BULTAR SWAN'S
LIGHTSABER

SAESEE TIIN'S
LIGHTSABER

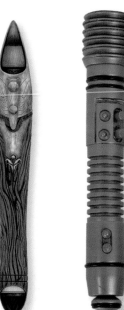

GUNGI'S
LIGHTSABER

KIT FISTO'S
LIGHTSABER

Energy blade
emitter

Ridged handgrip

Activation
switch

Power cell
housing

LUKE SKYWALKER'S
SECOND LIGHTSABER

SITH

As fiery and menacing as their owners, Sith lightsaber blades are red in colour. Their handles can appear elegant, like Sidious's, or functional, like Vader's. However they look, in the hands of a Sith, a lightsaber is always a weapon of evil.

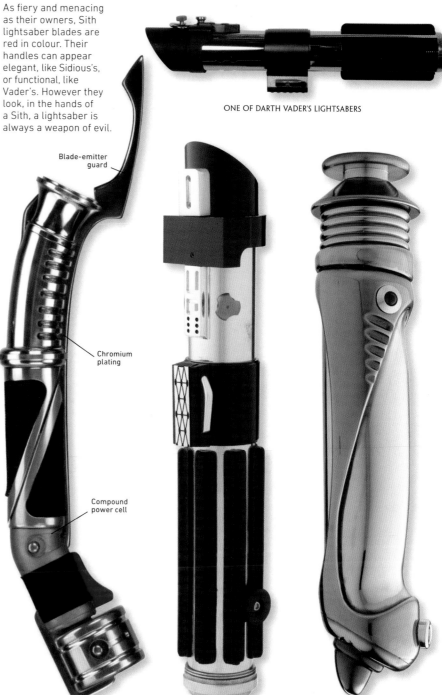

ONE OF DARTH VADER'S LIGHTSABERS

Blade-emitter
guard

Chromium
plating

Compound
power cell

DARTH TYRANUS'S
LIGHTSABER

DARTH VADER'S FIRST
RED LIGHTSABER

ONE OF DARTH
SIDIOUS'S LIGHTSABERS

A TRAITOR'S LIGHTSABER

Count Dooku honed his lightsaber technique as a Jedi Knight. He is a refined duellist who favours speed, skill and fluid moves instead of raw power. His curved lightsaber hilt is perfect for this fighting style. Dooku teaches this technique to his apprentice, Asajj Ventress, though her skills are not as elegant as Dooku's.

UNORTHODOX LIGHTSABERS

Building a custom lightsaber is a rite of passage for Force users. Lightsabers come in many forms to suit individual fighting styles. They may be crafted with unusual materials from their maker's culture, or conform to the style of the order to which they belong.

SINGLE-BLADED

CANE

Tera Sinube's cane lightsaber helps balance the elderly Jedi while walking. Darth Maul's cane lightsaber, however, is used for deception. He employs the cane as a prop, pretending to be a harmless old man in order to gain Ezra Bridger's confidence.

TERA SINUBE WIELDING HIS LIGHTSABER

DARTH MAUL WITH HIS CANE LIGHTSABER

TERA SINUBE'S LIGHTSABER

TERA SINUBE'S CANE

BLASTER

With guidance from Master Yoda, Ezra finds a kyber crystal in a Jedi temple on Lothal. He constructs an unconventional lightsaber-blaster using parts donated by the *Ghost* crew. After Vader destroys the lightsaber, Ezra constructs a more traditional replacement.

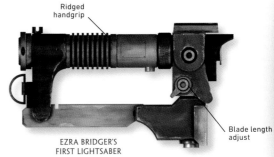

Ridged handgrip

Blade length adjust

EZRA BRIDGER'S FIRST LIGHTSABER

SHOTO

Shotos are mini lightsabers used by diminutive Jedi such as Master Yoda. Some Jedi, including Ahsoka Tano, also use them in combination with larger lightsabers – akin to fighting with both a sword and dagger.

YODA'S LIGHTSABER

DARKSABER

Pre Vizsla, leader of the Mandalorian Death Watch faction, acquires the black-bladed Darksaber weapon and it becomes the symbol of his power. Darth Maul takes it from Vizsla during a duel. He then takes it back to his home on Dathomir, where Sabine Wren later finds it.

DARKSABER

CROSSGUARD

Kylo Ren creates his lightsaber using a design that is thousands of years old, originally used during the Great Scourge of Malachor. The secondary side blades act as vents for the lightsaber's main blade. Kylo's crude weapon uses a cracked kyber crystal, giving its blades a ragged, unstable appearance.

ANCIENT CROSSGUARD LIGHTSABER

KYLO REN'S LIGHTSABER

ANCIENT ARTEFACT

Ezra discovers an ancient crossguard lightsaber on Malachor. It appears to be a relic from a battle between Jedi and Sith, and the green blade suggests it belonged to a light side user. Unfortunately, its diatium power core is almost drained.

DOUBLE-BLADED

STATIC EMITTERS

Savage Opress wields a lightsaber with blade-like emitter shrouds, similar in design to those of Count Dooku, but which also recall the axe blades of the pike that Opress once carried. Jedi Temple Guards protect the temple with yellow-bladed double-lightsaber pikes.

SAVAGE OPRESS'S LIGHTSABER

JEDI TEMPLE GUARD LIGHTSABER PIKE

DUAL WIELDING

SEPARATE LIGHTSABERS

Some Jedi are trained to fight with multiple lightsabers at once. Pong Krell's four-armed Besalisk anatomy makes him uniquely suited for wielding two double-bladed lightsabers. Ahsoka Tano constructs new white-bladed sabers when she leaves the Jedi Order, to signify her independence.

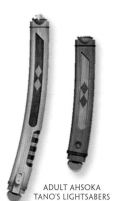

ADULT AHSOKA TANO'S LIGHTSABERS

PONG KRELL WITH HIS TWO DOUBLE-BLADED LIGHTSABERS

MOBILE EMITTERS

The Empire's Inquisitors use lightsabers that function in several modes. These include a single blade mode and a spinning double-bladed mode. The inbuilt repulsor assembly in the hilt can be used to helicopter the wielder short distances.

FATAL FLAW

The Grand Inquisitor's overconfidence blinds him to a flaw in his otherwise intimidating lightsaber. The swirling blades may be deadly, but the interior of the rotation disc is vulnerable. Kanan inserts two lightsabers and slices outwards, causing the Inquisitor's weapon to fly apart.

1

2

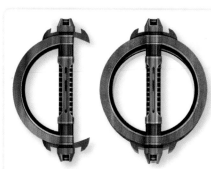

CRESCENT MODE   DISC MODE

INQUISITOR'S LIGHTSABER

TWO BECOME ONE

Asajj Ventress is trained by Count Dooku to fight in two modes: with two separate lightsabers, or with both combined into a double-bladed saberstaff. After she is betrayed by Dooku and becomes a bounty hunter, Asajj loses her lightsabers to Barriss Offee.

ONE OF ASAJJ VENTRESS'S CURVED LIGHTSABERS

ASAJJ VENTRESS WITH HER SEPARATED CURVED LIGHTSABERS

SABERSTAFF MODE

ASAJJ VENTRESS WIELDING HER SABERSTAFF

SUPERWEAPONS

When Emperor Palpatine orders the construction of the Death Star superweapons, he is following an ancient tradition of the Sith. Long ago, legend says the Sith created superweapons powered by immense kyber crystals. Supreme Leader Snoke's ambition goes beyond even Palpatine's when he converts a planet into a weapon of even greater magnitude.

FATEFUL PLANS

Early designs for the Death Star can be traced to engineers on Geonosis. Count Dooku carries these off-world to Darth Sidious as the Clone Wars begin. Many years later, Jyn Erso and Cassian Andor lead a group of rebels to steal the plans from the Empire.

DEATH STAR AND DEATH STAR II

The Death Star and its successor are gigantic mobile space stations armed with superlasers capable of destroying entire planets. The overconfidence of Grand Moff Tarkin leads to the destruction of the first Death Star by the Rebellion, while the arrogance of the Emperor himself results in the obliteration of the second.

> " THE POWER THAT WE ARE DEALING WITH HERE IS IMMEASURABLE. "
> **DIRECTOR ORSON KRENNIC**

DEATH STAR

IN-DEPTH ANALYSIS

As a fully-functional battle station, the Death Star has all the facilities and resources required to support a longer-term crew, including a command centre for overseeing operations, suites for senior officer conferences, prison blocks for holding captured rebels or evicted populations, hangars for ship maintenance and waste compactors for refuse disposal. Its huge garrison and fleets of starfighters allow it to wage war across the galaxy.

CONFERENCE ROOM

HANGAR

PRISON CELL

COMMAND CENTRE

WASTE COMPACTOR

STARKILLER BASE

Starkiller Base is a mysterious planet, formerly mined for kyber crystals. It is converted into a colossal superweapon by the First Order. The weapon drains the energy from a nearby star, then uses it to fire a beam capable of destroying whole star systems – even ones on the other side of the galaxy.

STARKILLER BASE

END OF THE REPUBLIC

General Hux orders Starkiller Base to fire on the New Republic's capital world, Hosnian Prime. After the Hosnian system is obliterated, the Resistance is forced to reveal itself and provide the First Order with its next target: the planet D'Qar. Hux is unaware that his base has been infiltrated, however, and he also underestimates Poe Dameron's X-wing squadrons.

DEATH STAR II

IN-DEPTH ANALYSIS

In an attempt to improve upon the design of the original, the second Death Star is more highly weaponised, with the fatal design flaws removed. The three-minute superlaser recharge time is a big improvement over the previous Death Star's 24 hours, and the superlaser's targeting systems have been improved, allowing it to target even relatively small starships. The Emperor oversees it all from his throne room, perched at the top of a 100-story spire on the second Death Star's north pole.

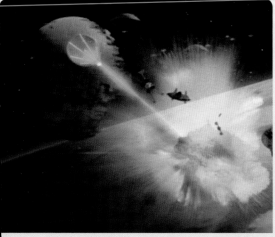

EMPEROR'S SPIRE

MALACHOR SUPERWEAPON

In ancient times, the Sith and the Jedi battle at the site of a Sith temple on the planet Malachor. Neither side wins the fight – both are destroyed in the struggle. At the dark heart of the temple is an ancient Sith superweapon, powered by a giant kyber crystal and capable of horrific destruction.

EZRA'S FOLLY

Darth Maul manipulates Ezra Bridger into helping him gain access to the ancient Sith temple on Malachor. Maul desires the Sith holocron at the temple core. When Ezra accesses the holocron, which is animated by the personality of a mysterious female Sith Lord, he unintentionally activates the superweapon.

DEATH STAR II DESTROYS A MON CALAMARI STAR CRUISER

MALACHOR SUPERWEAPON

WARSHIPS

From devastating destroyers to sophisticated stealth ships, warships come in a variety of shapes and sizes. Some are small and speedy, while others transport thousands of troops. No matter how they were designed, they all have one thing in common: they are ready for war!

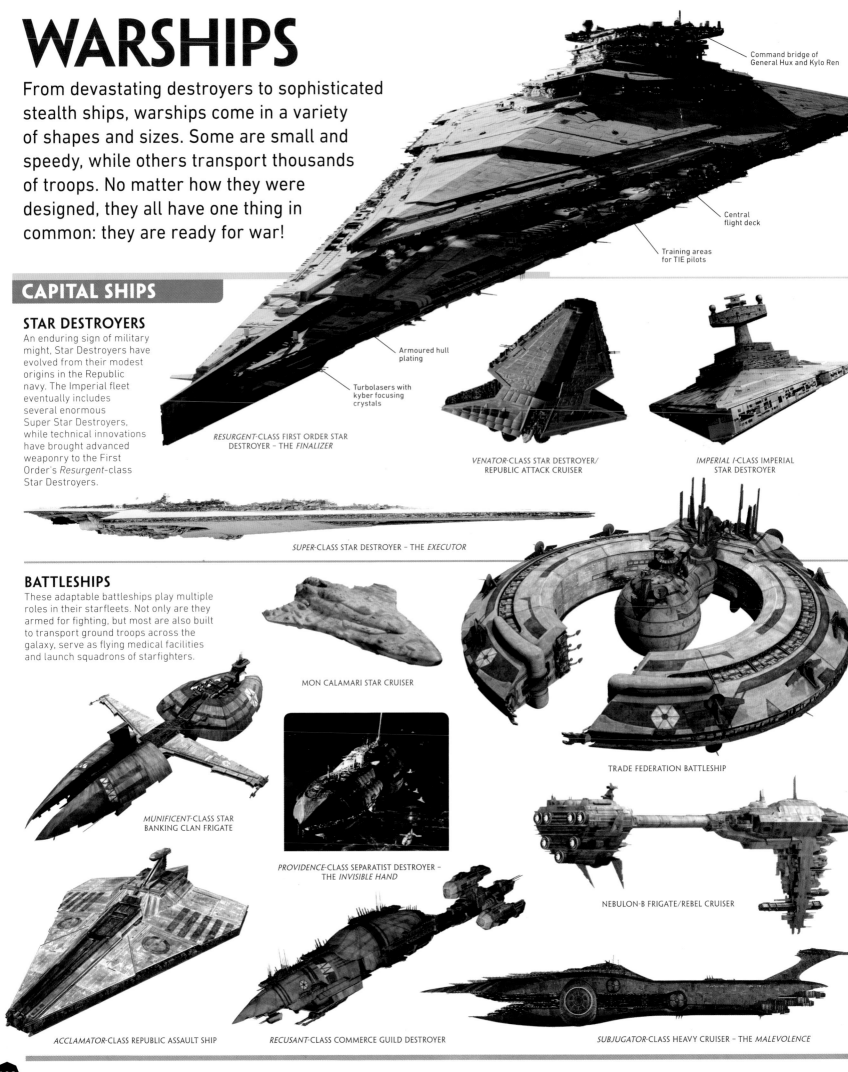

Command bridge of General Hux and Kylo Ren

Central flight deck

Training areas for TIE pilots

CAPITAL SHIPS

STAR DESTROYERS

An enduring sign of military might, Star Destroyers have evolved from their modest origins in the Republic navy. The Imperial fleet eventually includes several enormous Super Star Destroyers, while technical innovations have brought advanced weaponry to the First Order's *Resurgent*-class Star Destroyers.

Armoured hull plating

Turbolasers with kyber focusing crystals

RESURGENT-CLASS FIRST ORDER STAR DESTROYER – THE *FINALIZER*

VENATOR-CLASS STAR DESTROYER/ REPUBLIC ATTACK CRUISER

IMPERIAL I-CLASS IMPERIAL STAR DESTROYER

SUPER-CLASS STAR DESTROYER – THE *EXECUTOR*

BATTLESHIPS

These adaptable battleships play multiple roles in their starfleets. Not only are they armed for fighting, but most are also built to transport ground troops across the galaxy, serve as flying medical facilities and launch squadrons of starfighters.

MON CALAMARI STAR CRUISER

TRADE FEDERATION BATTLESHIP

MUNIFICENT-CLASS STAR BANKING CLAN FRIGATE

PROVIDENCE-CLASS SEPARATIST DESTROYER – THE *INVISIBLE HAND*

NEBULON-B FRIGATE/REBEL CRUISER

ACCLAMATOR-CLASS REPUBLIC ASSAULT SHIP

RECUSANT-CLASS COMMERCE GUILD DESTROYER

SUBJUGATOR-CLASS HEAVY CRUISER – THE *MALEVOLENCE*

ROOP TRANSPORTATION SHIPS

hile capital ships
arry ground troops
rough space, it falls
other transportation
ehicles to deliver those
oldiers to the battlefront
nd into combat. These
mple craft usually hold
quads of troopers and are
ghtly armed compared to
her types of warships.

C-9979 LANDING CRAFT

NU-CLASS ATTACK SHUTTLE

AT-TE CARRIER

REPUBLIC LAAT/I
REPULSOR GUNSHIP

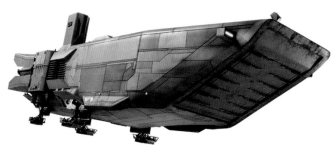

RESISTANCE TRANSPORT

ATMOSPHERIC ASSAULT LANDER

ATTACK SHIPS

irates, bounty hunters
nd sneaking Separatists
ke the fighting power that
ttack craft bring and the
inimum crew they require to
perate at peak performance.
nlike most spacecraft, the
rident Drill can even attack
hile underwater!

SS-54 ASSAULT SHIP – THE *HALO*

PATROL SHIPS

These patrol craft represent some of
the galaxy's finest naval technology.
One of the Republic's best-kept secrets
is their stealth ship, an experimental
corvette. The ship uses rare stygium
crystals to power a cloaking device
that renders the ship virtually invisible
to the naked eye.

WOOKIEE AUZITUCK
ANTI-SLAVER GUNSHIP

FLARESTAR-CLASS
ATTACK SHUTTLE

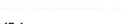

REPUBLIC STEALTH SHIP

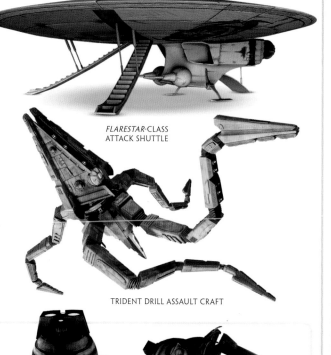

TRIDENT DRILL ASSAULT CRAFT

DROCH-CLASS BOARDING SHIP

EXTENDED PINCER
VIEW

SLAVE I

A *Firespray*-31-class patrol and
attack craft, *Slave I* is the infamous
ship of bounty hunter Jango Fett
and later his son, Boba. The younger
Fett is taught to use the ship's
multitude of weapons – including
torpedoes and seismic charges –
by his father.

Advanced sensors
readouts display data

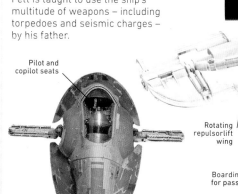

Pilot and
copilot seats

Rotating
repulsorlift
wing

Boarding ramp
for passengers

Hull repainted by
Hondo Ohnaka

JANGO FETT'S *SLAVE I*

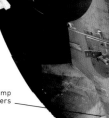

360 degree
twin blaster
cannons

BOBA FETT'S MODIFIED *SLAVE I*

SPACE TRAVEL

Interplanetary space travel is regulated with chartered space lanes, allowing travellers to traverse the galaxy with ease. The hyperdrive propulsion system enables some starships to move between star systems in an instant.

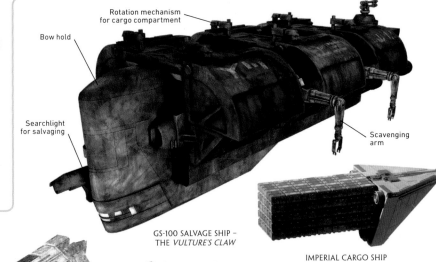

Rotation mechanism for cargo compartment

Bow hold

Searchlight for salvaging

Scavenging arm

GS-100 SALVAGE SHIP – THE *VULTURE'S CLAW*

IMPERIAL CARGO SHIP

FREIGHTERS

CARGO FREIGHTERS

Cargo freighters haul all manner of goods between star systems. These ships must be highly dependable, so captains keep their vessels well maintained and prepared to ward off space pirates.

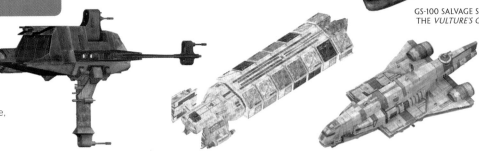

G9 RIGGER FREIGHTER – THE *TWILIGHT*

TRANDOSHAN PRISONER SHIP

IMPERIAL *GOZANTI*-CLASS CRUISER

TRADE FEDERATION *LUCREHULK*-CLASS SHIP

SMUGGLERS' SHIPS

Not all cargo moving about the galaxy is legal. Smugglers can make hefty profits by sneaking contraband goods past customs inspectors for shadowy crime lords. Losing a load can spell trouble, though – so captains regularly upgrade their ships for speed and fire power.

MODIFIED CORELLIAN YT-1300 TRANSPORT – THE *MILLENNIUM FALCON*

Floodlight

Dorsal laser cannon

Main engine

Nose turret gunner station

Boarding ramp

MODIFIED VCX-100 LIGHT FREIGHTER – THE *GHOST*

Scorch mark earned in battle

Container transport grid

ERAVANA BULK FREIGHTER

MODIFIED C-ROC *GOZANTI*-CLASS CRUISER – THE *BROKEN HORN*

PASSENGER TRANSPORTS

Beings need to move around the galaxy for a variety of reasons: tourism, relocation and business, to name a few. Passenger transports offer varying levels of comfort, from cramped quarters to luxurious suites.

AA-9 CORUSCANT FREIGHTER

STAR COMMUTER 2000 SHUTTLE

INSIDE VIEW

REBEL GALLOFREE YARDS GR-75 TRANSPORT

DIPLOMATIC SHIPS

Diplomatic ships cover great distances, carrying diplomats and their staff. Some contain conference facilities for hosting negotiations. Most have defences like reinforced shields and enhanced speed for escape, in the event diplomatic talks fail.

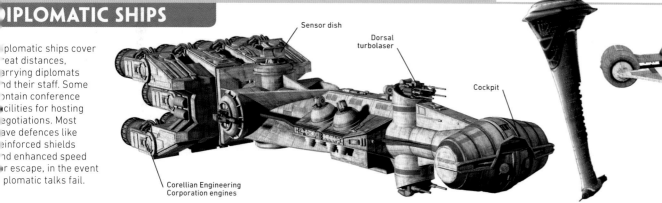

Sensor dish

Dorsal turbolaser

Cockpit

Corellian Engineering Corporation engines

CR90 CORELLIAN CORVETTE – THE *TANTIVE IV*

CUSTOM LUXURY SPACELINER – THE *CORONET*

REPUBLIC CRUISER

SMALL SPACECRAFT

PERSONAL CRUISERS

High-level government officials and wealthy individuals take advantage of vessels at their personal disposal. These ships are tailored to their specific needs and allow them to bypass the restrictive time schedules of commercial charters.

J-TYPE 327 NUBIAN ROYAL STARSHIP

J-TYPE NABOO STAR SKIFF

J-TYPE DIPLOMATIC BARGE

H-TYPE NUBIAN YACHT

Sail compartment

COUNT DOOKU'S SOLAR SAILER

RAINHAWK-CLASS TRANSPORT – THE *FALFA*

SOLAR SAILS UNFURLED

As leader of the Confederacy of Independent Systems, Count Dooku must be able to move about the galaxy swiftly. His solar sailer yacht reflects his noble status with its stylish lines and unique propulsion system. The enormous solar sails unfurl to harness streams of interstellar energy.

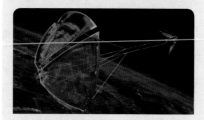

SHUTTLES

Shuttles deliver personnel between a base ship and a destination, such as another ship in space or a planet's surface. Military shuttles like troop transports or boarding craft have specific fleet functions. Some shuttles are specially designed for high-ranking dignitaries.

NEIMOIDIAN SHEATHIPEDE SHUTTLE

CHANCELLOR PALPATINE'S SHUTTLE

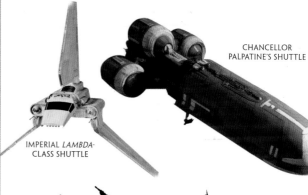

IMPERIAL *LAMBDA*-CLASS SHUTTLE

Static discharge vane

Warning light

Long-range sensor arrays

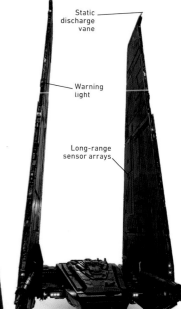

ORSON KRENNIC'S *DELTA*-CLASS SHUTTLE

KYLO REN'S *UPSILON*-CLASS SHUTTLE

ESCAPE AIDES

Space travel is a dangerous endeavour. In the event of an emergency, ejector seats and escape pods allow crew and passengers to evacuate. Some escape pods are capable of landing; others must be rescued by starships.

TANTIVE IV ESCAPE POD

CONFEDERACY ESCAPE POD

YODA'S E3 ESCAPE POD

TIE FIGHTER EJECTOR SEAT

STARFIGHTERS

Streaking through both air and space with brave star pilots at their helm, tiny starfighters have the ability to turn farmboys into heroes and bring empires crashing down. From the sleek Naboo starfighter to the rugged Y-wing, these starfighters all pack a punch.

IN-DEPTH ANALYSIS
Some craft, like the Delta-7B *Aethersprite*-class light interceptor used by the Jedi Order, don't have an internal hyperdrive unit. To travel long distances in hyperspace, it relies on an external hyperdrive booster ring that can be detached when not in use.

Syliure hyperdrive booster ring

REPUBLIC ERA

REPUBLIC
The often graceful and always capable starfighters of the Republic serve throughout the Clone Wars. Even noble Jedi Knights fly a variety of starfighters as they try to restore peace to the crumbling republic.

Z-95 STARFIGHTER

AGGRESSIVE RECONNAISSANCE
ARC-170 STARFIGHTER

ETA-2 *ACTIS*-CLASS
INTERCEPTOR

DELTA-7B
AETHERSPRITE-CLASS
JEDI STARFIGHTER

NABOO N-1 STARFIGHTER

V-19 TORRENT STARFIGHTER

ALPHA-3 *NIMBUS*-CLASS
V-WING STARFIGHTER

DELTA-7 *AETHERSPRITE*-CLASS
JEDI STARFIGHTER

SEPARATIST
While much of the Separatist starfighter fleet is made up of droid starfighters, piloted ships also serve their cause. Chief of these is General Grievous's own starfighter, a customised Belbullab-22, *Soulless One*, which serves him in battles over Bothawui, Utapau and more.

NANTEX-CLASS GEONOSIAN STARFIGHTER

UMBARAN STARFIGHTER

GENERAL GRIEVOUS'S BELBULLAB-22 STARFIGHTER
– THE *SOULLESS ONE*

ASAJJ VENTRESS'S *GINIVEX*-CLASS
FANBLADE STARFIGHTER

SITH
The Sith infiltrator *Scimitar* serves Darth Maul and his master Darth Sidious for decades. The ship's cloaking device is a technological masterpiece, turning the vessel completely invisible whenever a situation calls for it – the perfect shuttle for secretive Sith.

SITH INFILTRATOR – THE *SCIMITAR*

BOUNTY HUNTERS
Cad Bane's reputation as a fearsome bounty hunter is built upon his use of technology like the *Xanadu Blood*. This modified *Rogue*-class starfighter boasts elite weapons and a cloaking device. It is given to Bane as payment from Darth Sidious himself.

CAD BANE'S *ROGUE*-CLASS STARFIGHTER – THE *XANADU BLOOD*

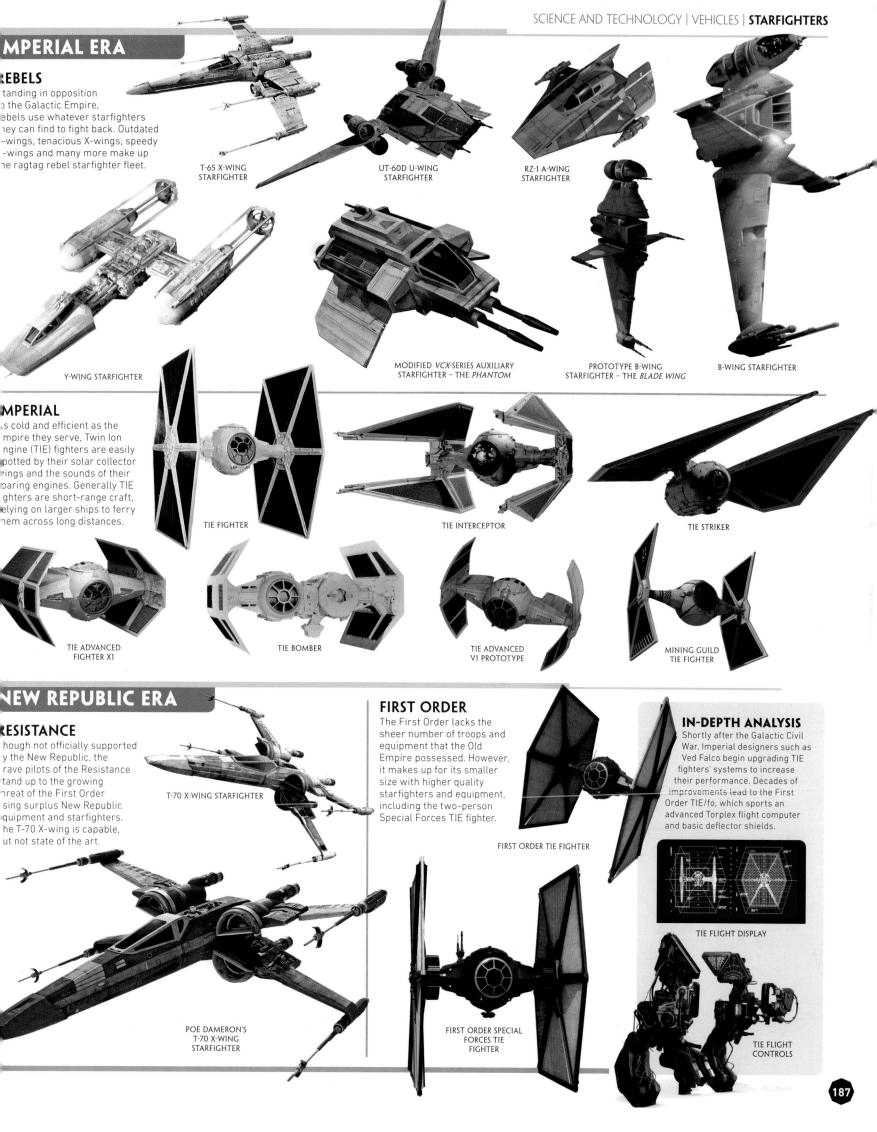

IMPERIAL ERA

REBELS

Standing in opposition to the Galactic Empire, rebels use whatever starfighters they can find to fight back. Outdated Y-wings, tenacious X-wings, speedy A-wings and many more make up the ragtag rebel starfighter fleet.

T-65 X-WING STARFIGHTER

UT-60D U-WING STARFIGHTER

RZ-1 A-WING STARFIGHTER

Y-WING STARFIGHTER

MODIFIED *VCX*-SERIES AUXILIARY STARFIGHTER – THE *PHANTOM*

PROTOTYPE B-WING STARFIGHTER – THE *BLADE WING*

B-WING STARFIGHTER

IMPERIAL

As cold and efficient as the Empire they serve, Twin Ion Engine (TIE) fighters are easily spotted by their solar collector wings and the sounds of their roaring engines. Generally TIE fighters are short-range craft, relying on larger ships to ferry them across long distances.

TIE FIGHTER

TIE INTERCEPTOR

TIE STRIKER

TIE ADVANCED FIGHTER X1

TIE BOMBER

TIE ADVANCED V1 PROTOTYPE

MINING GUILD TIE FIGHTER

NEW REPUBLIC ERA

RESISTANCE

Although not officially supported by the New Republic, the brave pilots of the Resistance stand up to the growing threat of the First Order using surplus New Republic equipment and starfighters. The T-70 X-wing is capable, but not state of the art.

T-70 X-WING STARFIGHTER

POE DAMERON'S T-70 X-WING STARFIGHTER

FIRST ORDER

The First Order lacks the sheer number of troops and equipment that the Old Empire possessed. However, it makes up for its smaller size with higher quality starfighters and equipment, including the two-person Special Forces TIE fighter.

FIRST ORDER TIE FIGHTER

FIRST ORDER SPECIAL FORCES TIE FIGHTER

IN-DEPTH ANALYSIS

Shortly after the Galactic Civil War, Imperial designers such as Ved Falco begin upgrading TIE fighters' systems to increase their performance. Decades of improvements lead to the First Order TIE/fo, which sports an advanced Torplex flight computer and basic deflector shields.

TIE FLIGHT DISPLAY

TIE FLIGHT CONTROLS

AIR VEHICLES

Zooming through air is faster and more efficient than travelling along the ground. Repulsorlifts allow speeders to hover above the surface. Jet engines provide maximum speed, while auxiliary thrusters alter direction. But the similarities end here – air vehicles are just as diverse as the environments they fly in.

SWAMP VEHICLES

Swamp speeders must be fast but easily manoeuvrable to avoid wetland hazards at the water's surface, like fallen trees, rocks and dragonsnakes. On Nal Hutta, the Hutts ride flat *Pongeeta*-class speeders. Clone troopers pilot Infantry Support Platforms (ISPs).

CLONE SWAMP SPEEDER ISP

HUTT SWAM SPEEDER

SPEEDERS

MULTI-TERRAIN VEHICLES

Some missions require travel off the beaten path. Trandoshans travel the lagoons and tropical jungles of Wasskah, Kashyyyk and Felucia, hunting for prey. On Naboo, speeders whiz through forests and rolling grasslands. Ubrikkian speeders fly over rugged mountains and treacherous terrains on Dathomir.

LUKE SKYWALKER'S T-16 SKYHOPPER

Headlights shine in normal, ultraviolet and infrared light

JEDI PRAXIS Mk. I TURBO SPEEDER

V-35 COURIER LANDSPEEDER

REY'S SPEEDER

Front mesh protects driver

JAKKU RAIDER SPEEDER

LUKE SKYWALKER'S X-34 LANDSPEEDER

Winches haul trophies and nets carrying prisoners

TRANDOSHAN MSP80 PTEROPTER HOVER POD

IN-DEPTH ANALYSIS

Luke Skywalker fixes up his old landspeeder so he can visit Tosche Station and race around the desert with his friends. The speeder fits one driver and passenger, with rear magnetic clamps to haul droids and other metal cargo.

Magnetic clamps hidden under outer hull

Fuel lines to starboard jet engine

Heat sink

REAR VIEW

NIGHTSISTER UBRIKKIAN SPEEDER

NABOO SECURITY SPEEDER

RESISTANCE BASE SPEEDER

PADMÉ AMIDALA'S RIAN-327 AIRSPEEDER

CITY VEHICLES

Travel is both vertical and horizontal in cities like Coruscant, Bespin and Mandalore! Speeders carry passengers from skyscrapers among the clouds, down to the murky underworld below. Drivers must be quick thinkers in heavy traffic, and unafraid of heights – but accidents do happen!

BAIL ORGANA'S CUSTOM XJ-2 AIRSPEEDER

CORUSCANT AIR TAXI

MANDALORIAN POLICE SPEEDER

CORUSCANT FIRE SUPPRESSION SHIP

XJ-6 CORUSCANT AIRSPEEDER

UTAPAU SCOOPER SKIMMER

ZAM WESELL'S KORO-2 ALL-ENVIRONMENT AIRSPEEDER

STORM IV TWIN POD CLOUD CAR

CORUSCANT POLICE SPEEDER

RGC-16 AIRSPEEDER

SNOW VEHICLES

Snowspeeders face the biting cold and strong winds of worlds like Hoth, Orto Plutonia and Starkiller Base. Republic Freeco bikes and Rebel T-47s have enclosed cabins, allowing pilots to go on longer missions. First Order speeders are only useful close to base.

FIRST ORDER SNOWSPEEDER

INCOM T-47 AIRSPEEDER

FREECO BIKE

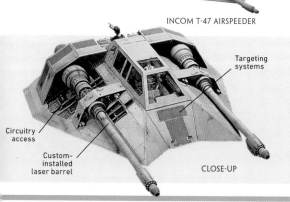

Targeting systems

Circuitry access

Custom-installed laser barrel

CLOSE-UP

IN-DEPTH ANALYSIS

T-47 airspeeders aren't actually designed for Hoth's icy weather! Their rear radiator fins have been insulated by rebel technicians to keep the engines from seizing up in the freezing air. Laser cannons were also added to convert the craft from civilian to military use.

SPEEDER BIKES

Speeder bikes sacrifice unnecessary systems for greater speed or agility. Jedi jumpspeeders can be folded up for easy portability. Police droids fly military-grade BARC (Biker Advanced Recon Commando) speeders, which navigate heavy traffic at all altitudes. Maul's *Bloodfin* has no weapons – he prefers to use his lightsaber instead.

SABINE WREN'S JUMP SPEEDER

OWEN LARS'S ZEPHYR-G SWOOP BIKE

POLICE BARC SPEEDER BIKE

GEONOSIAN FLITKNOT SPEEDER BIKE

DARTH MAUL'S MODIFIED RAZALON FC-20 SPEEDER BIKE – THE *BLOODFIN*

SCOUT TROOPER'S 74-Z SPEEDER BIKE

BARC SPEEDER

EZRA BRIDGER'S CUSTOMISED 614-AvA SPEEDER BIKE

STARHAWK SPEEDER BIKE

STAP (SINGLE TROOPER AERIAL PLATFORM)

KANAN JARRUS'S SPEEDER BIKE

SURFACE AND SEA VEHICLES

On primitive worlds where technology and energy are limited, travel via surface and sea is a necessity. Other cultures live in environments where repulsorlift technology is impractical, while some simply utilise surface vehicles for leisure. In warfare though, these vehicles can actually offer tactical advantages.

SEA VEHICLES

Aquatic species often build cities and even wage war beneath the sea. Though some may be adept swimmers, vehicles can still make travel on or under the water faster, more comfortable and more efficient. Heavily-armed transports can of course help win battles too.

TRIDENT DRILL ASSAULT CRAFT

SURFACE VEHICLES

WHEELS AND TREADS
Some vehicles move along the ground using mechanical wheels and treads. The ride is bumpier but requires less energy use than repulsorlift engines. Such vehicles are also typically more durable than their repulsor-powered counterparts. Jawa sandcrawlers and General Grievous's TSMEU-6 wheel bike are both repurposed mining vehicles.

JAWA SANDCRAWLER

REPUBLIC HAVw A6 JUGGERNAUT

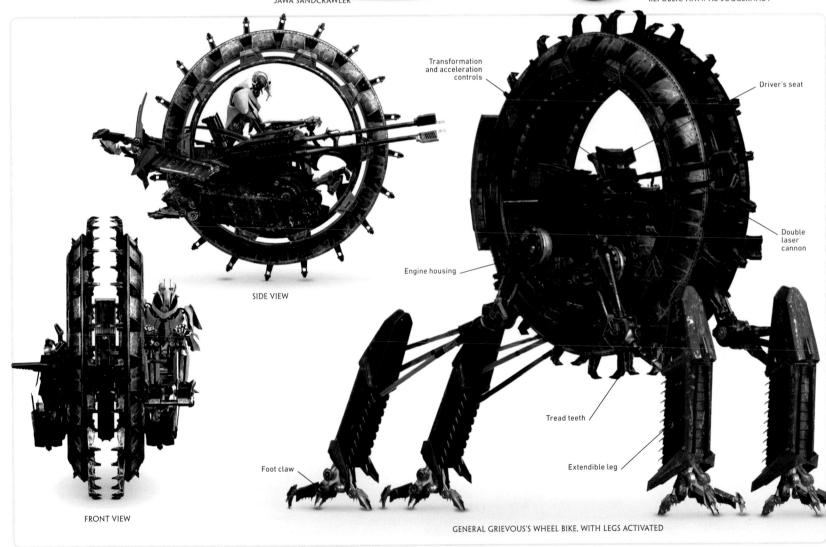

SIDE VIEW

FRONT VIEW

Transformation and acceleration controls

Driver's seat

Double laser cannon

Engine housing

Tread teeth

Foot claw

Extendible leg

GENERAL GRIEVOUS'S WHEEL BIKE, WITH LEGS ACTIVATED

" MASTER, WHAT'S A BONGO? "
OBI-WAN
" A TRANSPORT, I HOPE. "
QUI-GON

GUNGAN BONGO SUBMARINE

NABOO LAKE COUNTRY
GONDOLA SPEEDER

QUARREN UTS
(UNDERWATER TURBO
SLED) PIKE

WOOKIEE CATAMARAN

REPUBLIC OMS (ONE MAN
SUBMERSIBLE) DEVILFISH

UNDERWATER WAR

The Quarren of Mon Cala
align with the Separatists
against their neighbours, the
Mon Calamari. The Nautolan
Jedi Kit Fisto leads the
Republic defence against the
Separatists. Fisto rides his
OMS Devilfish to defend the
Mon Calamari against
invading aqua droids.

KAMINOAN SUBMARINE

WAGONS AND SLEDS

Sometimes it just makes more sense to move things
the old-fashioned way – with brute force. Gungans use
beasts of burden to haul battle machinery on Naboo.
"Crusher" Roodown drags spare parts across the
Jakku wastes in his sled.

GUNGAN BATTLE WAGON, TOWED BY A FALUMPASET

"CRUSHER" ROODOWN'S SLED

WALKERS

Mighty walkers are armoured cavalry vehicles that cross the battlefield on mechanical legs. Larger models, such as AT-ATs, are armour-plated and boast powerful cannons for ground assaults. Faster and more manoeuvrable bipedal models like AT-RTs can scout the enemy and strike quickly.

IMPERIAL

Intimidating Imperial walkers compromise stability to gain the psychological advantage against under-equipped rebel forces. They can crush uprisings with only the occasional loss of a walker, if a foe manages to get close enough to topple one.

REPUBLIC

Republic walkers favour designs lower to the ground, to allow easy transport and deployment of clone troopers. Models with large numbers of legs are slow and steady, and able to cover most types of terrain. They can stay upright even with two damaged legs.

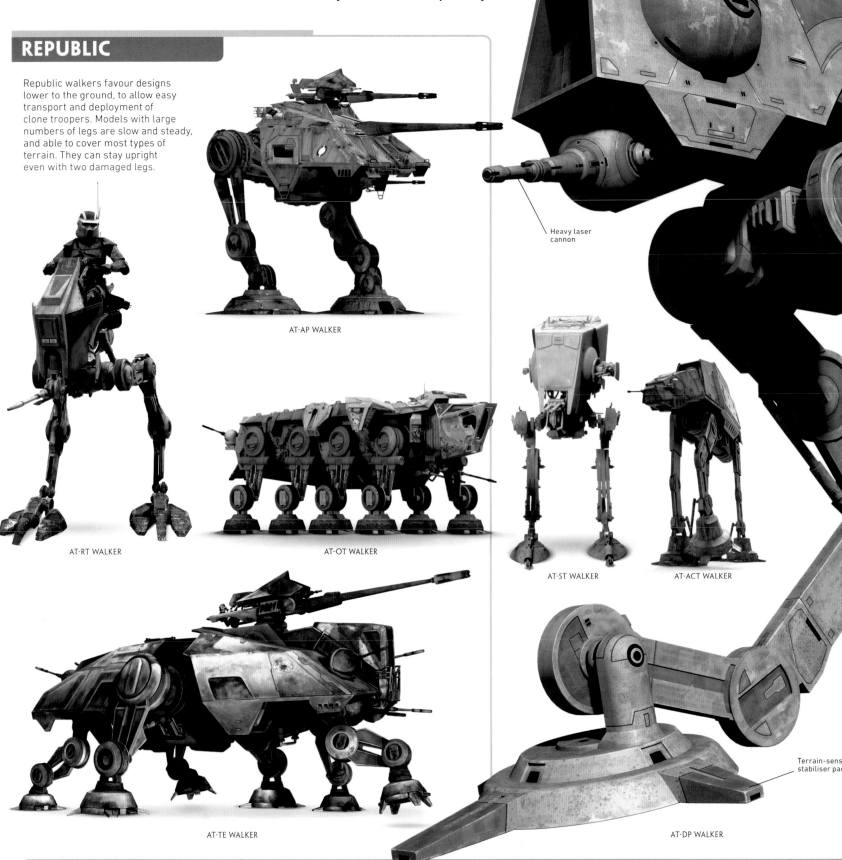

Heavy laser cannon

AT-AP WALKER

AT-RT WALKER

AT-OT WALKER

AT-ST WALKER

AT-ACT WALKER

AT-TE WALKER

Terrain-sensing stabiliser pad

AT-DP WALKER

TANKS

Tanks are capable of extreme mobility thanks to their tracks, or a repulsorlift. Often found charging into front-line combat, tanks carry large cannons mounted on rotating turrets. Sturdy armour protects the crew operating the weapons and the propulsion system inside.

Hydraulic limbs

AT-AT WALKER

IN-DEPTH ANALYSIS

AT-AT drivers require special training to operate the advanced mechanical leg units. Because this training is costly, the drivers are sometimes given an extra layer of protection with life-support suits. The suits are fitted with long-lasting power packs. Targeting sensor controls are designed to be manipulated with a gloved hand.

High-yield battery

Thermally shielded wiring

Energy monitor contact

AT-AT PILOT POWER PACK CONTROL UNIT

System linkage

Echo transmitter

Signal amplifier

Receptor filaments

AT-AT TARGETING SENSOR

REPUBLIC

Tanks plow head-on into locations unsuitable for walkers. Not only does the Grand Army of the Republic use tanks as traditional fighting vehicles, it also develops alternative functions for them, such as draining targets of their energy – or even laying bridges!

UT-AT "TRIDENT"

STUN CANNON TANK

SEPARATIST

The Trade Federation's Armored Assault Tank, or AAT, is a favourite resource of the Confederacy of Independent Systems, devastating everything in its path. However, this experimental super tank is discontinued after significant losses at the Second Battle of Geonosis.

Heavy forward cannon

Armour plating

Reinforced ray shielding

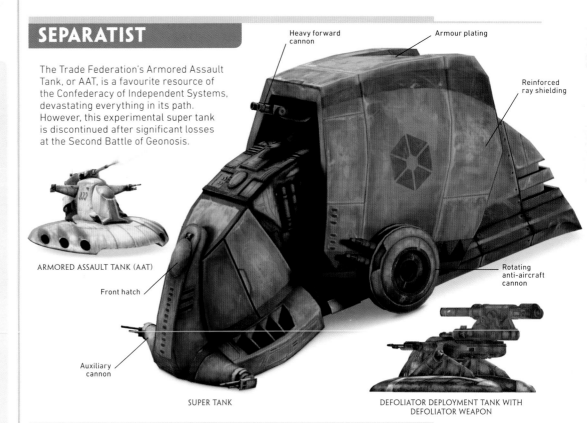

ARMORED ASSAULT TANK (AAT)

Front hatch

Auxiliary cannon

Rotating anti-aircraft cannon

SUPER TANK

DEFOLIATOR DEPLOYMENT TANK WITH DEFOLIATOR WEAPON

IMPERIAL

On worlds occupied by the Empire, heavy ground assault vehicles (GAVs) are deployed to intimidate and maintain military control. These combat assault tanks are also used to transport precious loads of kyber crystals, and are able to manoeuvre in narrow streets on their segmented track treads.

TX-225 "OCCUPIER" COMBAT ASSAULT TANK

INDEX

Page numbers **in bold** refer to main entries.

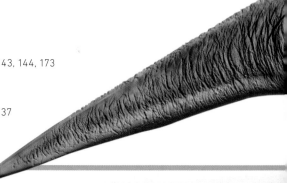

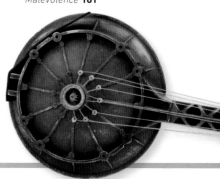

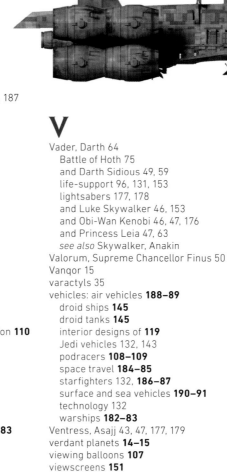

Project Editor Ruth Amos

Project Art Editor Toby Truphet

Senior Editor Elizabeth Dowsett

Designers Rosamund Bird, Mark Richards, Gary Hyde

Additional editing by Matt Jones, Natalie Edwards,
David Fentiman, Emma Grange

Additional design by Abi Wright, Owen Bennett

Pre-production Producer Marc Staples

Senior Producer Mary Slater

Managing Editor Sadie Smith

Managing Art Editor Ron Stobbart

Art Director Lisa Lanzarini

Publisher Julie Ferris

Publishing Director Simon Beecroft

DK would like to thank: Frank Parisi, Leland Chee,
Matt Martin, Pablo Hidalgo and Michael Siglain at Lucasfilm;
Chelsea Alon at Disney Publishing; Dennis Muren and Courtney Miller
at ILM; Jason Fry for his expertise and help on the map of the galaxy
and planet spreads; Lynne Moulding and Chris Gould for design
assistance; Ben Davies, Lauren Nesworthy, Lisa Stock and
Eleanor Rose for editorial assistance; Lindsay Kent for
proofreading; and Vanessa Bird for the index.

First published in Great Britain in 2017 by
Dorling Kindersley Limited
80 Strand, London WC2R 0RL
A Penguin Random House Company

17 18 19 20 21 10 9 8 7 6 5 4 3 2 1
001–300045–Sept/2017

A CIP catalogue record for this book
is available from the British Library.

ISBN 978-0-24128-846-7

Printed and bound in China

A WORLD OF IDEAS:
SEE ALL THERE IS TO KNOW
www.dk.com
www.starwars.com